SECURING LIBRARY TECHNOLOGY

A How-To-Do-It Manual®

PAUL W. EARP

AND

ADAM WRIGHT

HOW-TO-DO-IT MANUALS®

NUMBER 162

NEAL-SCHUMAN PUBLISHERS INC.
New York   London

Published by Neal-Schuman Publishers, Inc.
100 William St., Suite 2004
New York, NY 10038

Printed and bound in the United States of America.

The paper used in this publication meets the minimum requirements of American National Standard for Information Sciences—Permanence of Paper for Printed Library Materials, ANSI Z39.48-1992.

Library of Congress Cataloging-in-Publication Data

Earp, Paul W., 1961-
   Securing library technology : a how-to-do-it manual / Paul W. Earp and Adam Wright.
     p. cm. — (How-to-do-it manuals ; no. 162)
   Includes bibliographical references and index.
   ISBN 978-1-55570-639-5 (alk. paper)
   1. Library information networks—Security measures—Handbooks, manuals, etc. I. Wright, Adam, 1970- II. Title.

Z674.73.E19 2009
005.8—dc22   2008046166

CONTENTS

List of Illustrations ix

Preface xiii

1. Exploring Library Technology 1

Common Technologies in Libraries 1
    Integrated Library Systems 1
    Office Systems. 3
    Public Systems 5
Computer Security and Access. 6
    Basic Security Considerations for
    Desktop/Laptop Computers. 7
    Network Basics 8
Review Questions. 11
Key Points and Conclusion. 12
Readings and Resources. 13

2. Examining Library Security Principles 15

Understanding Library Security 15
Implementing Library Security 16
    Security Principles and Inventory 16
    Security Principles and Policies 17
    Policy Implementation and Enforcement 17
Access-level, Physical-level, and Software-level Security 18
Review Questions. 19
Key Points and Conclusion. 19
Readings and Resources. 20

3. Performing a Technology Inventory 21

Beginning the Inventory: What Should Be Recorded?. 21
    Media Access Control Addresses 22
Compiling a Comprehensive Technology Inventory 23
Review Questions. 29
Key Points and Conclusion. 29
Readings and Resources. 30

4. Creating a Network Security Policy 31

Building a Written Policy for Library Security 31
Classifying Information 32

1. Classification of Information 32
Server Policy. 34
   2. Location and Access. 35
   3. Server Administrators. 37
   4. Backups and Restore 40
   5. Security Patches and Software Upgrades. 43
   6. Authority and Responsibility Delegation. 43
   7. Personnel Additions, Departures, and Terminations 44
Staff Technology Policy: Desktops, Laptops, Printers 47
   8. Technology Security Leader. 48
   9. Appropriate Computer Use 49
   10. Staff Computers 50
   11. Staff Laptops 50
   12. Printers 51
Public Technology Policy: Desktops, Laptops, Printers. 53
   13. Definition of Valid Patron or User 53
   14. Patron Rights 54
   15 Patron Agreement 54
   16. Proper Use of Technology 55
   17. Personally Owned Computers/Laptops/Wireless Products 56
   18. Printing. 56
   19. Sanctions 56
Network Policy: Routers, Firewalls, Switches,
Wireless Access, Monitoring Software/Appliances 57
   20. Network Policy. 62
   21. Network Health Tools. 62
   22. Routers 62
   23. Firewalls 63
   24. Switches 63
   25. Wireless Access 65
   26. Inappropriate Employee or Patron Conduct. 66
   27. Criminal Activity 67
   28. Official Law Enforcement Investigation 67
Review Questions. 70
Key Points and Conclusion. 70

5. Understanding Threats from Hackers and Malcontents **73**
Hackers 101 73
A History of Hacking 74
   1960s: The Dawn of Hackers 74
   1970s: Innovation and Creativity 75
   1980s: Hacker Clubs and Movies 75
   1990s: Raids and Arrests. 76
   Hackers of the Twenty-first Century 77
Hacker Mind-set. 77
Hacker Attack Modes 78

Additional Hacker Methodology   80
Network Infrastructure Vulnerabilities   81
  Hacker Methods and Tools   81
  Wireless Local Area Networks   83
  Operating Systems Hacks   84
  Vulnerabilities of Other Operating Systems   85
  Netware Vulnerabilities   86
  Application Hacks: E-mail,
  Instant Messaging, and Voice-over Internet Protocol   86
  Vulnerabilities of Web Servers   87
Viruses   88
  Virus History   89
  Current Top Virus Threats   90
Spyware   93
  Spyware History   94
  Types of Spyware   94
Review Questions   96
Key Points and Conclusion   96
Readings and Resources   97

**6. Planning for Security Implementation and
   Auditing Weaknesses** **99**
Determining Security Needs   104
  Security Audit: Finding Security Weaknesses   104
Security Audit Tools and Techniques   105
  Port Scanners   105
  Vulnerability Scanners   108
  Application Scanners   109
  Web Application Assessment Proxy   110
  Security Procedure Audit   110
Building a Plan to Implement the Audit   111
Review Questions   113
Key Points and Conclusion   114
Readings and Resources   114

7. Implementing Policies for Secure Public Technology **115**
Background for a Sound Security Foundation   115
  Library Security Profile and Checklist   116
Public Access Computing Policies   117
  Usage Policies   117
  Public Access Security for Patron Laptops   118
Phishing   119
  Link Manipulation   119
  Phone Phishing   119
  Web Site Forgery   119
  Software for Phishing Protection   120

Protecting Patron Privacy with Library Technology 121
    Internet Temporary Files 122
    Browser History 122
    Cookies 122
    Form Memory 122
Public Access Security Solutions 123
    Microsoft Windows SteadyState 123
    Deep Freeze 124
    Thin Clients 126
Review Questions 127
Key Points and Conclusion 127
Readings and Resources 128

8. Developing Security for Library Office Technology 129
Securing Staff Computers: Best Practices 129
    Provide Security Training for Staff 129
    Monitor Computer Abuse by Library Staff 131
    Provide Employee Compliance Checks 132
    Choose Secure Passwords 132
    Emphasize Safe Internet Browsing Habits 133
    Back Up Data 133
    Keep the Computer Up to Date with Patches 134
Antivirus Solutions 135
    Best Practices 135
    Antivirus Software 137
Antispyware Solutions 138
    Best Practices 139
    Antispyware Software 139
Review Questions 141
Key Points and Conclusion 141
Readings and Resources 142

9. Establishing Server Security 143
Understanding Servers and How They Work 143
Web Servers 145
    Securing the Web Server 146
    HTTPS: Secure Web Servers 147
    FTP: File Transfer Protocol 147
    SMTP Service 148
Microsoft Domain Controllers and Active Directory 148
    Domain Controllers 149
    Active Directory 155
    NIS Servers 157
    Conclusions 158
Domain Name System 158

Exchange Server; E-mail/Calendar Servers 159
   Microsoft Exchange Server 160
Terminal Servers 160
Review Questions 164
Key Points and Conclusion 164
Readings and Resources 165

10. Securing the Library Network from External Threats 167
Access to the Internet: A Brief Review 167
Using Firewalls for External Protection 169
   Firewalls and Data Transmission 169
   Ethernet 171
   Specifications for Firewall Location 174
   Obtaining and Configuring the Firewall 174
Local Computer-level Protections from Internet Threats 179
Firewall Software 180
   Windows XP 180
   Linux, Red Hat, and Other Flavors of Operating Systems . . . 186
Review Questions 186
Key Points and Conclusion 187
Readings and Resources 188

11. Securing the Library Network from Internal Threats 189
LAN Design and Configuration 189
Wireless Access Points and Wireless Security 194
   Wired Equivalent Privacy 194
   Using Routers for Internal Protection 195
   Using Firewalls for Internal Protection 197
Public Access Systems: Securing Workstations 198
Protecting the Internal Network from Patron Laptops 199
Securing Staff Systems from Internal Threats 200
   Security Considerations for Staff Laptops 202
Review Questions 203
Key Points and Conclusion 204

Appendix A. Links to State Laws on Cyber or
               Computer Crime 205

Appendix B. Vendor or Software Web Sites 211

Glossary 213

Index 237

About the Authors 245

LIST OF ILLUSTRATIONS

FIGURES

Figure 1-1   Visual Examples of Common Library Technologies . . .   2

Figure 1-2   Visual Examples of Office Systems Technology   4

Figure 1-3   Visual Examples of Computer-specific
Office Systems Technology   5

Figure 1-4   Common Layout for a Public Library Network
Infrastructure with Typical Components Identified
and Labeled.   10

Figure 1-5   A Larger Public Library Layout, with Multiple Switches
in Place to Segment Computers and Their Tasks
or Locations   11

Figure 3-1   Screen Capture Showing How to Obtain the Computer
Network MAC Address through the Windows
Graphical User Interface.   24

Figure 4-1   A Diagram of a Server Room Located One Layer
Away from Public Areas.   36

Figure 4-2   Visual Description of the Common Items
in a Library Network.   59

Figure 4-3   Visual Depiction of Data Being Transmitted
over a Network   60

Figure 4-4   Visual Depiction of Data Being Transmitted
over a Network, with a Network Traffic Monitor.   61

Figure 5-1   Screen Capture of a Command Prompt Showing a
Queried Web Server Response and Version
of the Web Server   83

Figure 6-1   Screen Capture of the Window That Allows Use
of the Command Prompt.   106

Figure 6-2   Screen Capture of the Command Prompt Window.   107

Figure 9-1   Visual of How a Server Handles and Transports Data . .   144

Figure 9-2   The Location of a Terminal Server within a
Library Network   162

Figure 9-3   Using Additional Switches to Segment
Workstations from Computers and Laptops   163

Figure 10-1 Visual of Both Logical and Physical Network
Designs for a Library   168

Figure 10-2 Depiction of Data Traveling as Traffic on the Internet . . 170

Figure 10-3 List of Ports Used for Communication
over the Internet or Intranet. 170

Figure 10-4 Screen Capture of the "General" Tab
of Windows Firewall Control Panel 182

Figure 10-5 Screen Capture of the "Exceptions" Tab
of Windows Firewall Control Panel 183

Figure 10-6 Screen Capture of the "Advanced" Tab
of Windows Firewall Control Panel 184

Figure 11-1 A Basic Library Network Design 190

Figure 11-2 A Library Network Design Incorporating Security
by Placing Firewall between Public Stations and
Office/Administrative Network 191

Figure 11-3 A Library Network Using a Router to Separate Public
Stations from the Office and Administration
Network While Keeping All Components behind
a Firewall 192

Figure 11-4 Two or More Ethernet Switches Can Connect
through a Serial Port to Act as a Single Switch 193

Figure 11-5 Multiple Ethernet Switches on a Network That Exceed
the Maximum Number of Hops 193

Figure 11-6 Network Address Translation (NAT) Being Used
within a Library Network 196

Figure 11-7 Firewall Separating the Publicly Accessible Network
from the Staff and Administration Network 197

TABLES

Table 1-1 Library Systems and Related Technology   3

Table 1-2 Three Computer Access Categories   7

Table 9-1 Sample Checklist of Services Commonly Provided
by Servers 146

Table 9-2 How a Domain Uses Workgroups to Segment and Separate
Computers and Users within the Domain. 150

Table 9-3 Example of How to Use Two Domains to Separate
Different Workgroups. 151

Table 9-4 List of the Different Components under the "Computer
Name" Tab of "My Computer" Properties Window. 152

Table 9-5 Examples of Log-on Time Restrictions for Computers
Joined to a Domain and the Users Who Can Log On . . . 154

Table 9-6 Standard Groups and Their Definitions under Windows . 154

Table 9-7   A List of Domain and Global Groups Defined
            by a Domain Controller   155

Table 9-8   Simplified Visual Depiction of Active Directory
            and How It Deals with Users, Computers, and
            All Aspects of Domain Control   156

Table 9-9   Terminal Server Control of Workstations and
            How They Interact   161

Table 10-1 Numerical Value of Hexadecimal Characters.   167

Table 10-2 List of the OSI Model with Simplified Definitions   171

Table 10-3 List of Lower-layer Protocols and Simplified
            Definitions of Each Component.   172

Table 10-4 List of Upper-layer Protocols and Simplified
            Definition of Each Component.   173

Table 10-5 Sample List of Software, Subscriptions, etc.,
            That Require Specific Ports to Function Properly   177

Table 11-1 List of Recommended Restrictions to Be Applied
            to Public Computers.   199

EXHIBITS

Exhibit 3-1   How to Use the Windows Command Prompt
              to Obtain the Computer Network MAC Address   22

Exhibit 3-2   A Walk-through on Obtaining the Computer Network
              MAC Address on a Macintosh OS X Computer   23

Exhibit 3-3   Sample Inventory Sheet: Computers.   25

Exhibit 3-4   Sample Inventory Sheet: Network Computer
              Information   26

Exhibit 3-5   Sample Inventory Sheet: Network Equipment
              Information.   27

Exhibit 4-1   Anytown Public Library Network Security Policy   34

Exhibit 4-2   Anytown Public Library Server Policy   45

Exhibit 4-3   Anytown Public Library Staff Policy   52

Exhibit 4-4   Anytown Public Library Public Access to
              Technology Policy.   58

Exhibit 4-5   Static IP Address Documentation   64

Exhibit 4-6   Static IP Address Request   65

Exhibit 4-7   Anytown Public Library Network Policy   68

Exhibit 6-1   Library Security Checklist.   99

Exhibit 7-1   Sample Security Checklist.   116

Exhibit 8-1   Security Checklist for Library Office Technology   130

PREFACE

Securing Library Technology: A How-To-Do-It Manual is designed to empower maximization of computer network benefits while mitigating the inherent risks by directly and comprehensively addressing the unique issues the library's open environment poses for IT managers. It is intended to help librarians build a foundation to make sound decisions supporting the security of library technology infrastructure and, by extension, of the people who use it. These decisions need not be severe or restrictive; the ideas outlined in this book, along with a bit of planning, some foresight, and a pinch of common sense, will allow protection of a library's network (and its users) without unduly restricting free use.

ORGANIZATION

The opening chapters provide brief introductions to library technology and related security issues. Chapter 1, "Exploring Library Technology," offers a broad overview of library technology, demonstrating the ways various components of a library's computer network interrelate. Chapter 2, "Examining Library Security Principles," provides a brief discussion of the security principles on which the rest of the book is built.

The next two chapters focus on assessing library technology and developing formal policies supporting its maintenance. Chapter 3, "Performing a Technology Inventory," describes the elements of a successful technology inventory and shows how to gather comprehensive information about the hardware and software that make up a library's technology profile. Chapter 4, "Creating a Network Security Policy," involves writing formal policies for governing technology maintenance and use. Taken together, these two chapters are designed to provide a fuller understanding of the library technology environment and to help establish productive guidelines for its use.

Chapter 5, "Understanding Threats from Hackers and Malcontents," addresses specific threats against a library's technology infrastructure. These threats may be aimed specifically at your library, and they may have as their goal a certain dire result (extracting data from workstations, crashing servers, and so on). More common threats are represented by passive, opportunistic attacks, such as spyware unwittingly downloaded while visiting a Web site, which may seriously degrade the network's performance. This chapter describes a wide array of such threats, covers their history, and identifies their features and pathologies.

The next four chapters of *Securing Library Technology* discuss practical approaches to securing the full range of library technologies. Building on the earlier chapters about inventory management and policy writing, Chapter 6, "Planning for Security Implementation and Auditing Weaknesses," provides a framework for implementing a comprehensive security plan. Chapter 7, "Implementing Policies for Secure Public Technology," Chapter 8, "Developing Security for Library Office Technology," and Chapter 9, "Establishing Server Security," discuss what can be done to shore up and defend a library's overall technology network.

The final chapters examine how to defend individual elements of your library's network and how to safeguard the network as a whole. Chapter 10, "Securing the Library Network from External Threats," describes in detail the steps to take to thwart external threats before they enter your library. Chapter 11, "Securing the Library Network from Internal Threats," presents ways to safeguard your network from threats invited, intentionally or otherwise, by staff and patrons.

We, the authors, have used the strategies presented in *Securing Library Technology* during our years managing technology infrastructure in various libraries. We hope our book will give readers the confidence that comes from a comprehensive, well-documented, and time-tested approach to network security.

1 EXPLORING LIBRARY TECHNOLOGY

This chapter briefly explores the composition of a typical library's technological infrastructure, including hardware and software for both public and staff. We then describe the basic features of the computers and networks that combine to form a library's physical technological infrastructure, and of the security policies governing their use. After reading this chapter, you will have a basic understanding of what constitutes a secure network and of the need for supporting policies to better assist the patrons while still protecting technology investments.

COMMON TECHNOLOGIES IN LIBRARIES

Excluding media-service technology, most libraries feature office technology, such as personal computers, printers, multifunction copiers, microfiche machines, and scanners. Public systems include catalog access computers, workstations, equipment (laptops, projectors), and self-checkout units. Network equipment includes cables, routers, etc.; Internet access; servers; and network copies and printers. For visual examples of these technologies, see Figure 1-1.

INTEGRATED LIBRARY SYSTEMS

A library's integrated library system (ILS) is built around a catalog containing descriptions of library holdings and made available to the public via the Web through an online public access catalog (OPAC) application. Almost all current library systems are modular, meaning that the ILS vendor provides a base system containing essential components, onto which specialized modules can be added. Base systems generally include catalog and OPAC functions. Modules can offer basic library services such as circulation capabilities, acquisitions-management functions, and the like. They can also provide advanced services such as electronic resource management, link resolution, federated searching, and other functions that may

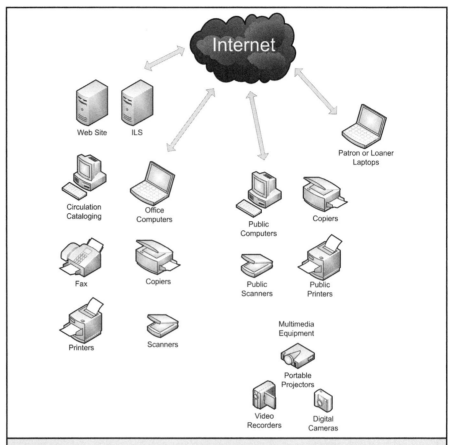

Figure 1-1. Visual Examples of Common Library Technologies

be of significant interest only to a portion of an ILS's overall user base. This allows each ILS vendor to provide the same basic product to various libraries while offering enough flexibility to address the needs and budgetary realities of each customer. (See Table 1-1 for a list of library systems and their related technologies.)

The hardware required for the ILS modules varies depending on the software used. Many ILS vendors provide installation and migration services allowing their products to run on equipment purchased, owned, and maintained by each library. Some provide "turnkey" systems in which a physical server is provided to the library, and all installation and physical maintenance is performed by the ILS vendor. All present-day ILSs can be run, catalog size notwithstanding, from one server. If a library's catalog describes a large collection, more servers may be required, even if only in the interest of providing information quickly and efficiently. Many large library systems maintain several servers that balance the needs of various ILS tasks in order to increase overall performance. In addition, many large

Table 1-1. Library Systems and Related Technology	
Integrated Library System (ILS)	Circulation, OPAC, fiscal/bookkeeping, management, Web interface modules, etc.
Office Systems	Personal computers, printers, multifunction print/fax/copy, laptop computer docking stations, video conferencing equipment/room, copiers, microfiche machines, scanners
Public Systems	Catalog access computers, public workstations, classroom workstations, computer labs, issued equipment (laptops, projectors, book-readers/pads), self-checkout units
Network	Physical infrastructure (cabling, routers, switches, wireless), Internet access (DSL, cable, T-1), domain servers, Web servers, network copiers/printers

systems employ some sort of storage area networks (SANs) to store and manage the data in the ILS. SANs are special networks that connect storage devices, such as tape libraries, to servers. A detailed discussion of SANs lies outside the scope of this book, but several good resources are available should you decide to investigate this approach. In addition to providing ILS software, and sometimes hardware, these companies usually also provide contracted support for their products.

When Web-based access is provided to the ILS, it is best practice to have the Web site served from a computer that is physically separate from the main ILS server. Since the Web is full of not-so-nice hackers who love to compromise computer systems, it is dangerous to use the main ILS server as the Web server. To do so effectively leaves the ILS—which may well include patron records and other potentially compromising information—open to the outside world. Chapter 9 describes in detail how to best secure a Web server for the ILS.

The ILS will require computers for staff to use. Ideally, each staff member will have a dedicated workstation providing access to the ILS, but for some libraries, this represents an untenable expense. At the very least, the library should have one workstation for each of the various major library functions, such as cataloging, circulation, and reference. In addition, there will most likely be at least one computer in the library devoted to public use.

OFFICE SYSTEMS

In this book, we refer to the technology used by library personnel as *office systems*. The computers included in these systems are used by staff to perform everything from catalog maintenance to traditional office suite duties such as word processing and spreadsheet creation. Library staff also use peripherals such as printers, fax machines, copiers, and scanners. Office

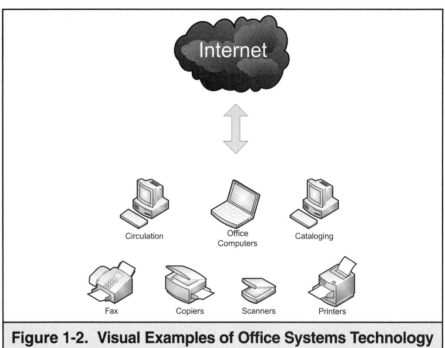

Figure 1-2. Visual Examples of Office Systems Technology

Office computers pose threats if an unattended computer in an open office is being used by a patron, or if seemingly innocuous software downloaded by an office user turns out to be easily compromised by hackers. Disgruntled employees may also use their access to destroy data or otherwise cause problems. Because it occurs behind the library network's firewall protection, malicious activity on office computers provides easy access to servers and other computers within the confines of the network.

systems also include communication devices such as telephones and video conferencing systems (for visual examples, see Figure 1-2).

Office systems have become an integral part of every type of library. These computers and peripherals are important parts of nearly every staff member's daily workflow at most libraries, providing everything from word processing to database maintenance to payroll administration. When it comes to security, however, staff workstations can present huge potential risks: there is typically a better chance of a network or ILS system being breeched from an office computer than from an external entity operating over the Internet when appropriate protections are in place on the library's Internet connection. Chapter 8 discusses office-system security in detail.

Because the security of any office system depends in large part on the use made of office technology, a successful security effort relies on effective written policies governing staff use of office systems. These policies should be arranged in a logical, straightforward way, and should be written in a style that is easy for anyone to understand. Too much technical jargon will reduce a policy's effectiveness among staff members with limited technical backgrounds, and will reduce your library's ability to assign basic systems-related tasks to nonsystems staff (a necessary approach at many libraries). The policies should cover basic computer security measures such as antivirus protection, spyware protection, phishing protection, and firewall protection. Security policies should also be in place on how to best secure other office systems hardware such as printers and fax/copier/printer machines. We discuss how to write these policies in Chapter 4.

PUBLIC SYSTEMS

Public systems technology includes public access workstations and circulated mobile equipment such as laptops and MP3 players. Some larger library systems will also include computer labs and computer classrooms. The same basic peripheral equipment as with office systems is often present in public systems, as shown in Figure 1-3.

Securing public systems technology presents an interesting challenge, as the question must be considered from the perspective of myriad users with different backgrounds and levels of technical aptitude. Library patrons sometimes attempt to personalize public systems technology by changing the wallpaper or screen savers on the public access computers; however, these are prime avenues for viruses, spyware, and other security threats. Administrative settings on public workstations can be

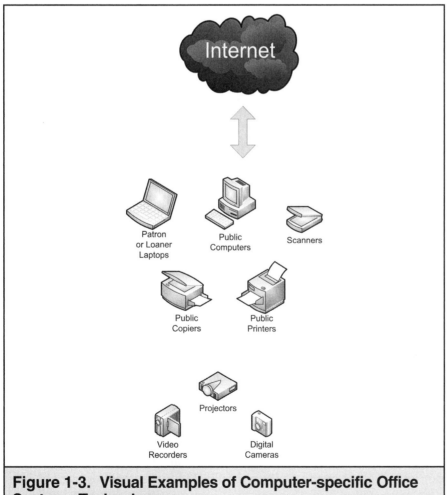

Figure 1-3. Visual Examples of Computer-specific Office Systems Technology

Microsoft uses the settings that are standard in the operating systems to secure the desktop. A program available to quickly define those settings is TweakUI. By doing a search at www.download.com, a very reliable site, with the terms "securing desktop user," you will be able to locate a variety of software in different price ranges, each with a review of the software (when available).

adjusted, and dedicated software applications exist to prevent these modifications.

In addition, operating systems can often be configured to automatically "turn off" certain functionality based on the user's log-in profile. The ability to run programs, for instance, may be granted to the administrator account, whose credentials are shared only with library staff, but denied to the public account, whose credentials are shared freely. Dedicated applications exist that build on this approach and provide more detailed control over system functions. Others allow system administrators to create a perfect image of a given computer's hard drive, including system settings, and revert to that perfect image after each reboot. Other public systems technology can be secured in place as with the office systems technology.

You may have heard of a specific type of hardware known as "data terminals." Companies such as Wyse and Sun offer small data terminals that have no actual computer processor or hard drive. When turned on, they link to a server and present the user a standard operating system screen. Since the screen the public sees reflects a remote instance of the operating system, the user is less readily able to make harmful changes to system settings, let alone to hack or otherwise damage the system. These data terminals can come with attachable or built-in DVD/CD-ROM writers, USB (Universal Serial Bus) access ports, and even floppy disk drives.

With new technology comes new challenges, and these systems—although well protected and designed for public use—are not inexpensive to implement, and would need to be part of a comprehensive growth plan. They have not gained significant popularity in libraries yet, largely because of their initial cost.

For all the benefits of public access to computers in public areas of libraries, just as many possibilities exist for security breaches. Chapter 7 provides a deeper discussion of public library technology security.

COMPUTER SECURITY AND ACCESS

Before moving on to networks, note that desktop and laptop computers, whether used by staff or the public, are not terribly secure straight out of the box. Formal steps must be taken to ensure that any computer is properly secured within a library environment. Toward this end, librarians need a strong foundational understanding of security fundamentals for computers and networks. In many ways, security boils down to providing the right levels of access to the right people for the right purposes. Access to computers (including servers) can be divided into the three categories presented in Table 1-2.

Table 1-2. Three Computer Access Categories	
Physical	Physical access involves the location of the computer, physical access to that location, and the act of directly logging on to the computer locally, through a network controller, or via a biodevice fingerprint reader or USB key.
Network	Network access involves the shared folders or files that a computer or server has for easy access over a network or the Internet. This includes Web sites and Web/Network catalog access. A VPN (virtual private network) would also fall in this category.
Policy	Policy access involves categories of people and functions. This is the library's written and/or practiced policy describing who is authorized to access each computer or technology, and which function is available to different user groups (patron, staff, administrator, and so on).

VPN (virtual private network): A secure connection between two locations, either two computers, a computer and server, or server to server, that offers communication that is protected from access by anyone else through encryption. VPN is often used to allow remote users (librarians working from home or away at conferences, for example) access to materials on a library's internal file server.

BASIC SECURITY CONSIDERATIONS FOR DESKTOP/LAPTOP COMPUTERS

Chapter 2 discusses security principles in detail. To help set that scene, let's run through a few basic features of computer workstations and networks that affect security.

A typical desktop computer will retain settings for all currently installed software (and, in some cases, for software that has nominally been uninstalled). For example, each computer's wallpaper is stored on the computer's hard drive as a specific setting. The choice of screen saver, how soon it starts, and whether it requires a password to bypass, are also stored settings.

Simply uninstalling software does not always remove it. In Windows, many programs save basic settings information to the operating system's registry, a central repository of information fundamental to system performance. Registry entries can sometimes be difficult to completely remove. The drive may have several key files and folders that are stored in a temporary format—files and software (executable files) that are frequently used or accessed to improve performance. These files may address core functions of the computer's operating system, specific programs, or individual files. Under normal conditions, this is not a problem: operating systems (Windows, Mac OS X, Unix, Linux) retain hundreds of stored settings so that when a computer is started at the beginning of the day, it will be the same as it was when it was turned off the day before.

The computer also retains log files, date/time stamps, and, depending on the software, multiple copies of currently opened working documents (word processing files, spreadsheets, and so on). These files are often not erased automatically when their host programs are closed, and with

Products that will reset the computer to an original setting at each reboot are available for use on public systems. Centurion Guard is one such program that we recommend. In a simplified explanation, it creates a "virtual" desktop that is completely and safely erased when the power is turned off. Regardless of changes, downloads, or quantity of temporary files and logs we mention here, each reboot effectively erases it all.

appropriate software and know-how, can be restored to be viewed, even after the original file has been deleted.

Even when putatively erased, files may still exist and be accessible. Deleted files are not immediately physically erased from the hard drive. Instead, descriptive information for the "deleted" file, including its name, location, and physical size, is removed from a table indicating the file's location on the hard drive. The deleted information will survive until the computer physically replaces it with another file (or portion of a file). This allows an opportunity for recovery if work is interrupted (for instance by a catastrophic event such as an operating system crash, or by a more mundane occurrence such as a run-down laptop battery).

Under the default settings of most browsers, Web sites you visit are also stored on the hard drive—every graphic and HTML–encoded page of every Web site visited is stored temporarily. The graphics even include small items such as click-buttons, backgrounds, etc.

There is a reason why these files aren't erased regularly. When you visit a Web site, as mentioned, all of the graphics and text are downloaded and stored in a temporary location called a *cache*. Web browsers look to this cache every time you visit a Web page, hoping to find a locally saved copy of the page and thus speed up the page-loading process and reduce Internet traffic. (The browser first checks to see if any newer files are available than those it has stored, of course.)

Many available software packages clear all Internet history records and cached files, clean up the drive of temporary files, and erase the "hidden-temporary" files stored on a computer. Files may also be flushed (often stored as a cache) with settings and tools included with the operating system being used.

On most computers, then, the amount of stored information reflected by immediately available files and programs is a mere fraction of the total information recorded on the hard drive. The grey areas mentioned previously—system setting and registry files, backup copies, Internet caches—represent a major front in the battle for library technology security.

> Windows provides this basic functionality through "Disk Cleanup." By right-clicking on the icon for the "C:\" drive and selecting "Properties" in the drop-down menu, the "General" tab shows a pie chart of the hard drive's capacity and use. Next to that is the button "Disk Cleanup," which will allow you to erase the temporary files. A third-party vendor that has software to offer a little more flexibility in cleaning these files is Symantec, with their Norton Utilities.

NETWORK BASICS

Before discussing specific network security issues, let's examine the basic elements of a library computer network. This section is intended as a quick summary of network structure; subsequent chapters will discuss security considerations for the network elements outlined here.

The physical infrastructure of your network isn't nearly as complex or unfathomable as you may think. Most libraries connect their local networks via Ethernet. The principle behind Ethernet is fairly simple. Network computers and peripherals are connected via a system of wires, a terminal of which plugs into each device. Each device does nothing more, really, than listen through its wire for traffic; when a given computer is commanded by its user to send out a request for a Web page or a file, it takes its turn and makes the request. The same happens on the other end: the computer receiving the request waits for its turn and then replies through a network of wires with the appropriate information.

It's a bit like driving in traffic. Everybody is required to follow the same rules, and when the roadways are designed for maximum flow and everyone obeys the law, traffic moves smoothly. A library network is like a small town with a connection to an interstate. Some needs may be met by going to town without having to get on the interstate, whereas other items can be found only in larger cities most readily accessible via the highway, so, in some cases, you hop onto the interstate and go to the appropriate city for what you need.

The library's connection to the Internet is made through an *Internet service provider*. Chapter 4 discusses different types of connectivity available to library networks, and then describes a typical network's composition, defining routers, hubs, switches, basic network design, and the cabling that connects everything. For now, let's take a broad look at the components of a basic library computer network.

The original approach to allowing computers to communicate over long distances involved the use of a modem. Technically speaking, a modem is a device that takes digital information and translates it to a sine wave that is placed on an analog carrier, such as a telephone line. The signal travels over copper phone wire to a switching station operated by a telephone company, and is then sent to its destination via phone lines designed originally to transmit signals representing the human voice; the process is reversed by the receiving modem so that the computer can accept analog signals and translate them into digital information.

In plain terms, a modem takes the information provided by a computer, converts it to something the phone company equipment can handle, and sends it out over phone lines. The computer receiving the information in question uses its own modem to convert the analog information back into a digital format that it can understand. A modem translates information for sending and receiving.

As phone companies developed more efficient equipment to handle computer information or data, modems in turn became more efficient. As demand for capacity (bandwidth) grew, phone companies and technology companies developed hardware to bypass modems and streamline the direct communications of computers.

We now have a multitude of ways to network large geographical areas together, called wide area networks (WANs), as well as an array of protocols allowing them to communicate with each other. (For the purpose of this book, this doesn't include remote sites that are connected via the Internet through a virtual private network.) Some of these protocols may be familiar to you: asynchronous transfer mode (ATM), frame relay, integrated services digital network (ISDN), and fiber distributed data interface (FDDI) to name a few. Transmissions between buildings can now be made in a variety of ways: along copper or fiber optic cables, radio signals, or

> **WAN**: A wide area network is defined for the purpose of this book as an organization's physical network that may include several different buildings over a space but geographically local to an area. **ISDN**: A service provided by most phone companies, in which voice (analog) and data (digital) are combined and translated to be transmitted over existing phone lines.

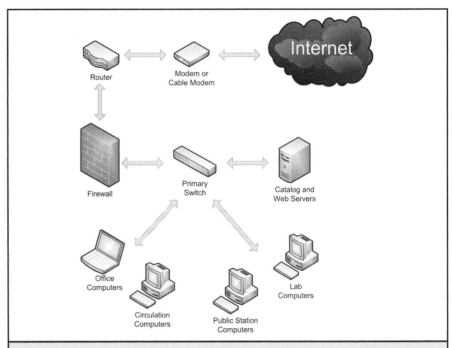

Figure 1-4. Common Layout for a Public Library Network Infrastructure with Typical Components Identified and Labeled

infrared waves. ISDN, among the most popular approaches, is the phone companies' answer to broadband Internet connectivity along coaxial cable lines, and is a considerable step up from a telephone modem. It requires special equipment (an ISDN modem) to function.

Figure 1-4 shows a very basic configuration of a library network, whereas Figure 1-5 shows a larger, more involved configuration. The difference between the two is the quantity of switches and the ways in which they are connected to one another. Keep in mind as you look at this, that the difference between a switch and a hub is the difference between driving on a city street and driving in a demolition derby. A switch has controls that effectively keep traffic moving efficiently; a hub has little or no control on traffic—whoever makes it through in one piece wins.

Under this basic configuration, two or more switches or hubs may be connected to one another, but all computers and printers connect to these switches. Following the pattern of interstates, cities, and towns, you will create a network environment (using switches, not hubs) that effectively isolates traffic and improves overall traffic flow or network performance.

The two figures identify several items of which you should have a basic understanding in order to make proper decisions on network design. Those items are the switches themselves, firewalls, routers, and Internet connections. Each network component invites a certain amount of security

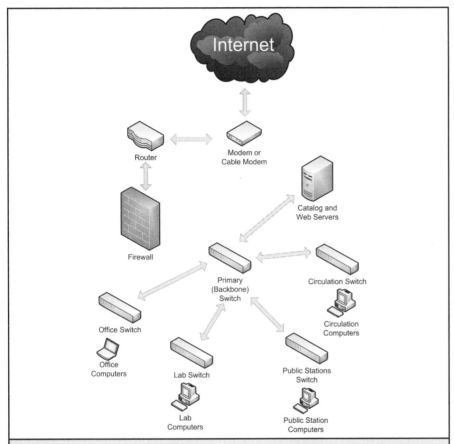

Figure 1-5. A Larger Public Library Layout, with Multiple Switches in Place to Segment Computers and Their Tasks or Locations

risk, and specific steps can be taken to safeguard each. Again, Chapter 4 treats these elements in greater detail, and Chapters 10 and 11 discuss network security at length.

REVIEW QUESTIONS

Use the following questions as a guideline to evaluate the knowledge you have gained from the chapter:

- What are the common technologies found in libraries?
- What is an integrated library system?
- How does an integrated library system become modular?

- What are the hardware requirements for an ILS?
- What are the requirements for Web access to an ILS?
- Are staff computers required for an ILS?
- Can you describe the technology library staff will utilize?
- What is the purpose of the security policy regarding staff technology?
- What types of technology do libraries make available to the public?
- What is the purpose of the security policy regarding public access technology?
- What are data terminals and how do they relate to public access computers?
- What are the three levels of computer access?
- What data are typically stored on computers?
- How does a computer network compare to driving on the highway system?
- What is a modem?
- What are some other ways we communicate through computer networks?

KEY POINTS AND CONCLUSION

- Libraries are unique in their application of common technology when disseminating information to the public and academic world.
- Access to information through technology (e.g., public stations, OPAC, and subscription databases) should be protected with software and network settings and with physical security measures to ensure continuous availability to all patrons.
- Security principles for both simple and complex networks are easy to understand. With forethought and understanding, any size network can be secured against real world threats.

The diversity of technology, information, and accessibility options offered by most libraries form a powerful combination. However, as we shall see in ensuing chapters, the generosity of information and access provided by libraries leaves them vulnerable to certain types of security threats. Protecting a library's investments—and its patrons and personnel—while offering generous degrees of accessibility to information requires the establishment of well-considered security policies.

Draconian measures are not required to secure library technology. Common sense and foresight are your best tools against information theft, damage to your network and computers, and vandalism or theft of hardware. The remainder of this book is devoted to helping you make the decisions that will best secure your library technology infrastructure.

READINGS AND RESOURCES

Gast, M. 2000. *Network Printing.* Sebastopol, CA: O'Reilly Media.
Preston, W. C. 2002. *Using Sans and NAS.* Sebastopol, CA: O'Reilly Media.

2 EXAMINING LIBRARY SECURITY PRINCIPLES

This chapter offers a broad discussion of security principles, designed to help you understand the reasoning behind the material covered in Chapter 3, "Performing a Technology Inventory" and Chapter 4, "Creating a Network Security Policy." We also briefly examine the three types of security: access, physical, and software.

UNDERSTANDING LIBRARY SECURITY

First, let's discuss what security is not. Security is not restriction of information. Libraries are predicated on the freedom to access information with confidence in its authenticity and without fear of repercussions for having accessed it. Neither is security a black box that miraculously protects everything a library possesses. Security is a mind-set. To be secure is to be aware of your surroundings, of the limitations and weaknesses of the technology you manage, and of threats to all aspects and areas of your library's network, whether those threats are intentional or accidental. Security involves awareness of possible risks and preparation to either prevent threats from occurring or having the capacity to deal with them if they do occur. Security involves willingness to go the extra step in each daily routine and to forgo taking the easy route. Being secure, to be blunt, involves a lot of hard, detailed, underappreciated work. Security is just flat-out inconvenient in the short run.

So why do it? Obviously, the risks of running an insecure library are simply unacceptable violations of professional best practice. The following are some of the more practical reasons for having a secure technology environment:

- *Law*: Almost every state in the Union requires some form of protection for private data (name, address, phone number, date of birth, etc.) against misuse. For example, California has a law that requires a company or organization, whether located in the state or not, to notify California residents when their personal information has been compromised.

- *Liability*: Libraries have never been above or beyond the reach of lawyers. Being proactive in security goes a long way toward reducing liability if a worst-case scenario occurs.
- *Crime*: A secure library network is less likely to be an unwilling participant (liability) in criminal activity.
- *Policy*: Most small government agencies (municipal or county) or governing entities (state or academic) have established policies that requires some form of security to reduce their liability.

Security includes more than software and policy settings on computers; it also includes physical security measures. Being security conscious includes locking doors and locking the desktop of your computer when you leave the room, and paying attention to who is using which equipment. Good security practice will enhance the ability of your technology infrastructure to meet the needs and demands of staff and patrons.

IMPLEMENTING LIBRARY SECURITY

When embarking on a plan to secure library technology, the obvious question is, "Where do I start?" As with any project, you should plan what needs to happen. Two very important questions should be answered before the actual process of securing the technology begins:

1. "What technology does the library have?" You can't secure it if you don't know it's there or what it does.
2. "How secure does this technology need to be?" Your approach to security must strike a balance between protecting the library's investments and resources and allowing reasonably free and flexible access to them. For this, you need a strong, well-written policy, based on a solid understanding of security principles.

> **Media access control (MAC) address**: The MAC address is a specific 16-bit identifier that is viewed in hexadecimal format to identify a specific device on a network. More detailed information on how to obtain this is provided later.

SECURITY PRINCIPLES AND INVENTORY

Why perform an inventory? The most obvious reason for our purposes is that an inventory gives your library the ability to create a tailored security strategy. Additional benefits to having a current and valid inventory include:

- Planning for equipment replacement or upgrade
- Easy access to serial numbers/information for warranty, theft, or criminal investigation
- Value of equipment for replacement from disaster
- Equipment accountability (did the computer have a 40GB or 80GB hard drive?)

Knowing the precise location of equipment as indicated on an inventory roster can be invaluable when troubleshooting a network and when investigating inappropriate use of the network or library resources. Knowing the network address of a computer or device in conjunction with its physical location makes it easy to isolate the time and place at which a specific event occurred and may help to identify who was using the device at the time.

SECURITY PRINCIPLES AND POLICIES

When dealing with colleagues or the public concerning security, one of the most frequently asked questions you will face—and one of the most frustrating—is "Why?" Why is a given policy in place; why are we allowed to do certain things and not others? Without a solid and well-thought-out security policy, the only reply is some variation on "Because I said so." That doesn't usually go over well, and for good reason.

Having a reliable security policy allows the person responsible to properly develop implementation, maintenance, and action/reaction plans during security scenarios. Having a plan and policy in place removes any question of procedure and reinforces proper lines of authority. It also offers a comfort zone to administrators.

Understanding security principles—reinforced by solid security practices such as strong password protection, timed inactivity auto-logoffs, computer setting policy restrictions, or the use of security software—will foster over time an instinctive security-mindedness on the part of staff and patrons. Formal policies also remind users of the negative issues related to a lack of security, such as institutional liability and criminal activity.

POLICY IMPLEMENTATION AND ENFORCEMENT

Moving forward with a security mind-set requires a strategy for implementation and enforcement. Some aspects of these steps may be difficult and result in unhappy or resistant patrons and staff. Not everyone will share the

One example I have dealt with was notification from attorneys for the music and movie industry organization that an IP address that belonged to my library had downloaded a copyrighted movie from the Internet. I was given the date and time, and instructed to locate the computer and ensure that any copy of the copyrighted material stored or created onto CD or DVD was permanently erased or destroyed. As I had static IP addresses for all equipment in the Library, I was quickly able to locate the computer and format the drive to ensure compliance with the request. This allowed me to honestly reply officially through proper channels that their request had been handled immediately, with a description of the steps taken to rectify and comply with their request. Should there ever be a reason to go to court over this, I would be able to testify under oath that the library complied completely with the request. It was completed the same day the notice was received.

—*Paul W. Earp*

When presenting security plans to staff or administration, it would be very helpful to look up current news stories of hacks, security failures, and criminal activity to offer real-world examples. If possible, use library or academic-specific occurrences.

opinion that security is an important part of the services that a library provides. Even while you have a thorough understanding the principles of security, being able to communicate their necessity and importance may be a difficult proposition with some library users.

When implementing a security program, two important concepts will be immensely helpful: patience and buy-in. Strong-arm enforcement generally creates more problems than it solves with both patrons and staff; your best bet is to take things slowly. Security practices are usually best introduced gradually, one at a time, over time. Once staff and patrons become familiar and comfortable with a single aspect, begin implementing the next. In time, it should become easier and easier to implement new policies and procedures.

ACCESS-LEVEL, PHYSICAL-LEVEL, AND SOFTWARE-LEVEL SECURITY

Security requires control of the item you intend to secure. This includes accounting for access to the item (is it kept behind a locked door at all times? Must it remain public at all times?), its physical security (is it physically secured by a cable system or other device?), and the software settings that grant various levels of authority to usage of operating systems and specific programs.

Knowing your audience is important, and a description of your user base will be a key part of the policy that you will develop with the help of this book. The appropriate levels of access for users, both public and staff, should also be considered. How much control should a public user have over basic settings? Should staff be allowed to install programs on their workstations without consulting systems personnel? Answers to those and related questions depend on the software each class of user requires in order to meet specific, well-defined ends.

The library's policy should also identify physical controls that determine where technology assets will be located and who will have access to them. Network closets, for example, should be used only for data infrastructure and not as storage for cleaning goods or other items; this reduces the number of people who need to have access to those spaces. It also reduces the opportunity of accidental damage to equipment.

Security software can be installed on public systems to enhance their availability. Some applications allow a user the freedom to apply quite a few modifications that are erased or reset when the system is rebooted; others lock out everything but select software. The former is good for public stations, and the later is good for computers set up as terminals intended for catalog access only.

Again, for most current issues and versions, a reliable site is www.download.com. Using the search string of "securing desktop users" works well. Always research and experiment with software of this type before purchasing and deploying within the library.

REVIEW QUESTIONS

Use these questions as a guideline to evaluate the knowledge gained from this chapter.

- What is security? What is it not?
- Why is security necessary?
- What are some more practical reasons for having security?
- Where do you start to secure your library's technology?
- How do you answer the question, "What technology does my library own?"
- What is a technology inventory?
- Why is a technology inventory necessary?
- What are the benefits of a technology inventory?
- What is one example of how an inventory was used in a library?
- What is a security policy?
- Why is a security policy necessary?
- What are some considerations when implementing a security policy?
- What is access control?
- What are some levels of access control?
- What tools are available for access control?

KEY POINTS AND CONCLUSION

- The security mind-set is to be aware of limitations and weaknesses of technology, the existence of threats whether intentional or accidental, and having plans and policies in place to deal with them when they occur.
- Knowing what technology the library has by maintaining a valid inventory will help in formulating policies and will help in quickly isolating any compromised technology.
- Having a comprehensive security policy in place will prevent many security issues from occurring and will assist in dealing with security concerns that do arise by having a specific level of authority to deal with them.

The principle of security is an important aspect of any type of technology. In dealing with the double-edged sword of library technology in which one side requires full and unfettered access to information and the other side requires that both hardware and information be protected, the person responsible for security must balance the needs of the patron with the security of the technology. Accomplishing this requires forethought, planning, and careful implementation to be successful.

If you have an accurate inventory of all library technology and have security policies already in place, feel free to skip the next two chapters and move on to the chapters on implementing security in public computers, staff, computers, servers, and the network.

READINGS AND RESOURCES

Lehtinen, R., Russell, D., and Gangemi, G. T. 2006. *Computer Security Basics.* Sebastopol, CA: O'Reilly Media.

Wang, W. 2006. *Steal This Computer Book 4.0: What They Won't Tell You about the Internet.* San Francisco, CA: No Starch Press.

3 PERFORMING A TECHNOLOGY INVENTORY

You can't secure it if you don't know it's there. A good inventory, consisting of detailed information on all of the technology that a library uses, is the foundation of any library technology security strategy. Examples of information you should gather include serial numbers, software versions, operating system information, network addresses, locations, brands, and user information. You might be able to get by with less information, but the more intensive your efforts to properly secure your technology infrastructure, the more important the details become.

Although technology inventories tend to focus on hardware, the record you will develop of the software installed on your library's computers will prove extremely valuable. For instance, when a security patch is issued for a particular program, you will know quickly to which of your computers it applies, saving you time by allowing you to confidently upgrade only those workstations affected.

A reliable inventory also reveals when each device on your network was purchased, and thus will help inform your technology-replacement strategy. With this information, you can hone your technology plan, disaster recovery plan, and technology-investment budget.

BEGINNING THE INVENTORY: WHAT SHOULD BE RECORDED?

To build a viable plan for securing your technology infrastructure, you must first know of what that infrastructure consists. The inventory described in this chapter may be a bit more detailed than you might expect, but such detail will greatly facilitate the development and implementation of your overall network security policy.

What will you be recording in your inventory? Just about everything pertaining to the network—staff and public workstations, servers, simple network devices such as switches and wireless access points, peripheral equipment like printers and scanners—anything that connects in any way to your library's network.

MEDIA ACCESS CONTROL ADDRESSES

Every device that connects to the network is assigned a network interface card (NIC). Each NIC has a unique identifier known as a media access control (MAC) address. This number in hexadecimal format will look like this: **00-14-2A-00-3D-3E**. The first six digits identify the brand of the NIC, and the second six are specific to that individual NIC. MAC addresses allow computers, printers, and other devices on your network to identify one another readily and to communicate efficiently. Ethernet switches feature a table built in short-term memory that keeps track of which MAC address is on what port of the switch, and the port won't receive any traffic that isn't specifically for that MAC address.

MAC addresses provide vital information when tracking security problems or resolving bandwidth issues on your network. They are also necessary if you wish to exert fine control over your network, as when you lock a switch port to a specific computer (this prevents patrons from gaining unauthorized access to your network by unplugging a public workstation's Ethernet connection and using it to connect a laptop computer).

Exhibits 3-1 and 3-2 explain how to locate MAC addresses on the Windows XP and Macintosh OS X operating systems.

Another way to obtain the MAC address on a Windows XP system is to right-click on the icon "My Network Places" (or use the "Start" menu to access the selection to right-click), and in the resulting drop-down menu to select "Properties." Right-click on the Local Area Connection

---

Hexadecimal

0 = 0	4 = 4	8 = 8	12 = C
1 = 1	5 = 5	9 = 9	13 = D
2 = 2	6 = 6	10 = A	14 = E
3 = 3	7 = 7	11 = B	15 = F

Windows XP/2003 Server

1. At your Start Menu select "Run"

2. Type into the text box "cmd" and click on OK.

3. You will get a window with a black screen and white text within it, allowing you to manually type in commands at the command prompt. It will have similar text to the following: "C:\Documents and Settings\User>"

4. At your command prompt (at the >) will be a flashing cursor bar. Simply type in "getmac" and hit the Enter key. The next screen you see will appear like this one:

```
Microsoft Windows XP [Version 5.1.2600]
© Copyright 1985-2001 Microsoft Corp.
C:\Documents and Settings\User\getmac
Physical Address      Transport Name

================  ===================================
00-14-2A-00-3D-3C     Media disconnected
C:\Documents and Settings\User>
```

The series of alpha-numerics immediately below the "Physical Address" will be the MAC address for that computer. In this particular instance, the MAC address is **00-14-2A-00-3D-3C**.

Exhibit 3-1. How to Use the Windows Command Prompt to Obtain the Computer Network MAC Address

---

Apple Mac OS X

Click on the Apple in the upper left corner, and select **System Preferences** in the drop-down menu.

A window will appear with several groups of icons. In the group of icons under the heading **Internet & Network** open the **Network** icon.

A new window will appear titled **Network**. Change the **Location** bar to **Automatic**, and the **Show** bar to **Built-in Ethernet**.

The menu bar below these two will have the following:

TCP/IP   PPPoE   AppleTalk   Proxies   Ethernet

Select **Ethernet** so that it is highlighted. The MAC address will be located just below:
Ethernet ID: 00:14:51:2d:d3:57

Note: Apple does not show the MAC address in all caps the way Windows does.

Exhibit 3-2. A Walk-through on Obtaining the Computer Network MAC Address on a Macintosh OS X Computer

---

icon, and again select "Properties." The Properties window will have two tabs, "General" and "Support." Bring the Support tab to the front, and click on the "Details" button. You should now see a window that looks like Figure 3-1. The first line, labeled "Physical Address," contains the computer's MAC address.

MAC addresses are just one example of the information you will collect toward creating a full inventory of the library's technology infrastructure.

COMPILING A COMPREHENSIVE TECHNOLOGY INVENTORY

A clear, comprehensive inventory of the technology in your library is crucial for several reasons (Exhibits 3-3, 3-4, and 3-5 are forms for compiling a thorough, accurate inventory). You need an inventory to develop a technology maintenance plan: knowing what you currently own will help you determine the schedule for assessing and replacing devices on your network. An inventory is also vital in case you ever suffer a material loss due to disaster or theft; your library's insurance carrier may even require that an accurate inventory be maintained for this purpose.

For the purpose of this book, the most important reason to keep an inventory is the insight it provides on how best to secure a network against various forms of attack. With a sound inventory at hand, you can better map what defensive strategies to employ; some preventive measures, such

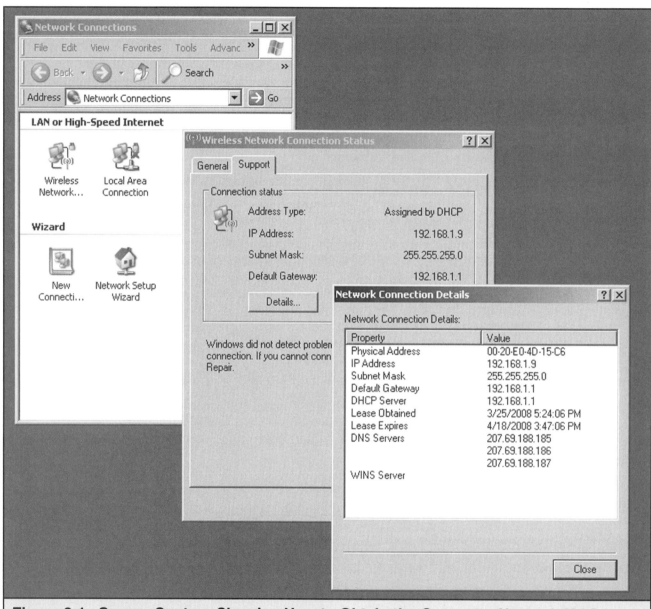

Figure 3-1. Screen Capture Showing How to Obtain the Computer Network MAC Address through the Windows Graphical User Interface

as timely updating and patching of your system's software, can introduce performance benefits as well.

An inventory will also allow identification of compatibility issues when purchasing new equipment. As an example, one library recently purchased an expensive new book scanner for its interlibrary loan department. The department intended to use its existing workstations with the new scanner. These had worked adequately in the past, but upon installing the new scanner, the department learned that it was completely incompatible with their existing workstations. After having spent so much on the scanner, the department was left with little choice but to purchase a compatible computer system, a large and unexpected expenditure in an already tight budget. An inventory would have revealed that the workstations' physical capacity (memory, hard drive capacity, processor speed, video card), their operating systems, and their capability to install the hardware required by the new scanner, rendered them inappropriate for use with the new scanner.

Computer Inventory					
Brand	**Model**	**Processor & Speed**	**HD Capacity & RAM**	**Serial or Service Tag**	**Local ID #**

Exhibit 3-3. Sample Inventory Sheet: Computers

Network Computer Information					
Brand & Model	NIC & Speed	CPU Name	Operating System	MAC Address	Static IP ADX (if applicable)
Exhibit 3-4. Sample Inventory Sheet: Network Computer Information					

Network Equipment Information					
Brand & Model	**Device Type (i.e., Switch or Router)**	**Device Name**	**Operating System & Version**	**MAC Address**	**Static IP ADX (if applicable)**

Exhibit 3-5. Sample Inventory Sheet: Network Equipment Information

There are two basic ways to perform a technology inventory: manually, on paper, or digitally, using a word processor, spreadsheet, or database program. Exhibits 3-3, 3-4, and 3-5 provide templates that can be used directly for manual inventory-taking or adapted for use with a spreadsheet or database.

Whether the inventory is compiled manually or digitally, include at a minimum the following items:

1. Product brand name
2. Serial number
3. MAC address (for network equipment there may be more than one)
4. Operating system, version, and any service packs installed
5. Software installed and its version/issue
6. Category
   - Public station
   - Staff
   - Server
   - Computer lab
7. Location
8. Internet connection
9. Network equipment
   - Router
   - Hub or switch
   - Firewall

> Automated network-inventory programs include Spiceworks IT Desktop, Network Inventory Manager, Belarc, and SysAid Helpdesk & Inventory

Listing all of the software installed on the network will help in determining whether someone has installed unauthorized (and thereby potentially harmful) software onto a computer. Such a list also helps ensure compliance with licensing terms governing some programs. When programs need to be patched or otherwise updated, this list will allow you to quickly locate every computer affected.

The simplest way to list software installed on a Windows computer is to go to the Control Panel and view the list in the "Add/Remove" function. You can also use the Explore option to view the C: Drive root and Programs Folder. Most programs provide version and service pack information through the "About" menu option under the Help menu bar.

> www.webjunction.org offers TechAtlas, a comprehensive and easy-to-manage Internet inventory tool that has the ability to comprehensively inventory your library network. The latest version, released in 2008, allows downloading inventory information as an Excel spreadsheet.

Several programs are available that perform automated technology inventories of your network. Many of these tools can be expensive, but some offer free trial versions.

TechAtlas, in conjunction with Webjunction.org, offers a free inventory tool. This tool requires that you log into WebJunction, but there is no cost to the library.

REVIEW QUESTIONS

Use these questions as a guideline to evaluate the knowledge gained from this chapter.

- What are some of the benefits of a reliable library technology inventory?
- What should be included in an inventory?
- What is a network interface card?
- What is media access control number?
- Why is a MAC address important for a computer inventory?
- How do you acquire the MAC address on an Apple computer?
- How do you acquire the MAC address on a Windows-based computer?
- How do you perform a technology inventory in your library?
- What is one example of when an inventory was valuable in a situation other than a security policy?
- What are the two ways to conduct a technology inventory in a library?
- What are some of the software tools available to assist in a technology inventory?

KEY POINTS AND CONCLUSION

- Inventory is the backbone when creating a reliable security policy. The more detailed the inventory as it relates to specific technology information, such as computer name, MAC address, or TCP/IP address, the more apparent its value will be when a security concern actually occurs.

- Much of the inventory process can be automated through software that is available online at no cost to libraries, or software can be purchased that will audit all networked technology.

Do not be intimidated by all of the data that we recommend be collected for your inventory. Pick and choose the items to be inventoried in such a way that extensive information is interspersed with easily obtained information. As an example, obtaining the location and user information can typically be done in a couple of days or less. Having this information will allow you to divide it into sections and then tackle the more detailed requirements a group at a time. This information will prove invaluable over time.

READINGS AND RESOURCES

WebJunction. www.webjunction.org. This organization works as a unified access portal for library support in training, knowledge, and information for all levels and types of libraries and librarians. Its Web site is designed to assist librarians and libraries find what they need to accomplish projects in technology through a combined social network of librarians and services offered through partnered vendors.

4 CREATING A NETWORK SECURITY POLICY

Library network security policy may already be addressed, particularly at school and academic libraries, by policies governing the host institution. These broader policies should be incorporated into the security policy for your library, but they seldom take into consideration the unique purpose that a library serves. Most policies handed down to libraries in this way do not address the blend of staff-specific and public functions hosted by your network, and may seem to offer—whether intentionally or not—limited room for adaptation to your library's specific needs.

Personalizing these broader policies for your specific library will require forethought and effort, and may quite possibly be subject to review by the administrators responsible for the policies being adapted. But the reward for establishing a tailored policy instead of relying on your institution's generic policy will prove itself invaluable in the future.

BUILDING A WRITTEN POLICY FOR LIBRARY SECURITY

An important point to consider when building any policy dealing with network security is that technology is constantly changing, even though security principles do not. An annual review and revision of your policy should be conducted to keep the policy's terminology and conventions current.

Building a policy specific to your library is the foundation for all security practices. Without an explicit description of the rules governing use of library digital technology, security efforts will have no authoritative iteration, and ultimately very little power.

Quite a few questions must be asked before creating effective policies governing library technology security. Understanding your library's technology, as discussed in Chapter 3, will help you make policy decisions appropriate to your library's specific technological infrastructure. The model policy in this chapter builds on the inventory outlined in Chapter 3, and is structured as follows:

Classifying information: Confidential, mission critical
Servers: Web, catalog, domain, and all other servers
Staff: Desktops, laptops, printers
Public: Desktops, laptops, printers
Network: Routers, firewalls, switches, wireless, monitoring software/appliances

Again, this policy is not intended to create an atmosphere in which networked technology is difficult to use; its intent is to protect the library's technology investment and to allow staff and patrons uninterrupted and unhindered freedom to pursue their work. An example of this policy as it applies to a public library is presented throughout the chapter in Exhibits 4-1 through 4-5.

CLASSIFYING INFORMATION

Before moving into policies, the library must define the types of information stored on its computers, and should identify the relevance of that information to the library's mission. State and local laws may require compliance in this regard, especially if the library is a public institution.

For our purposes, a simple and prudent working definition might describe "confidential information" as any nonpublic information necessary for the establishment and maintenance of library records. This includes descriptive personal information, such as a patron's home address and driver's license number, and also includes book-borrowing records.

Mission-critical information is the data a library needs in order to function. A library's Web site is important, but in most cases it is not strictly mission critical: in the event of a Web site crash, most core operations within the library can still proceed. If the same library's ILS were lost, say, due to hacking, core library functions such as cataloging and OPAC searching would be severely compromised or simply impossible. The ILS, then, contains mission-critical information.

1. CLASSIFICATION OF INFORMATION

1.1. *Confidential information*: Information that is excepted from disclosure requirements under the provisions of <your state law on public information or privacy> or other applicable state or federal law <including the Family Educational Rights & Privacy Act (FERPA) (if applicable)>.

Authors' Note

All types of libraries must have policies regarding confidential information. A library must locate applicable laws and place them in the section to account for their confidential information agreement. This advice pertains to all libraries, regardless of size.

> 1.2. *Mission-critical information*: Information defined by the library director/dean as essential to provide <academic or public> and administrative computing services and that would cause severe detrimental impact if the data/systems were lost and unable to be restored in a timely fashion (i.e., in less than two days).

Authors' Note

For a public library, the following might be used:

> Information that is defined by the library director or executive management to be essential to provide IT services. The library director should provide guidance in a separate policy or rule on causes of severe detrimental impact if the data/systems were lost and unable to be restored in a timely fashion (i.e., in less than two days).

Small public libraries without an IT department would not need this section, but need a clear separate definition on what is considered to be mission-critical information:

> Mission-critical information is defined as any information, if lost, that results in the ceasing of library operations.

For an academic library of any size, the policy could read:

> Information that is defined by the library dean to be essential to provide academic and administrative computing services and would cause severe detrimental impact if the data/systems were lost and unable to be restored in a timely fashion (i.e., in less than two days).

For an example network security policy, see Exhibit 4-1.

The Anytown Public Library is a fictional library in north Texas. It is a medium-sized public library serving a community of 10,000. The library administration recently developed some security policies. Throughout this chapter, we refer to Anytown PL's security policy as an example of how a library might fit the broader sample policy to its particular needs.

NETWORK SECURITY POLICY

1. Anytown Public Library Classification of Information

   1.1. *Confidential information*: The Anytown Public Library adheres to the information disclosure requirements under the provisions of applicable laws in the state of Texas or other applicable federal law.

   1.2. *Mission critical information*: The Anytown Public Library utilizes Book System's Concourse product as its integrated library system (ILS). Any data stored within the ILS database is defined by the library director to be essential to provide public services and would cause severe detrimental impact if the data were lost and unable to be restored in a timely fashion.

Exhibit 4-1. Anytown Public Library Network Security Policy

SERVER POLICY

Server policy is very important, but relatively simple. The policy will determine the levels of access and authority are granted to various library personnel

Servers should be housed in a dedicated, locked server room. They should never be housed on a staff desk, even if that desk is in a locked room. Allowing servers to remain on a staff desktop invites unauthorized access—and even when such access is unintentional or well-meaning, it can have dire consequences. In any case, when servers are properly configured, administrators will be able to do 90 percent of their work from desktop workstations.

It is dangerous to invest only one person with server-administration responsibilities: sharing administrative responsibility allows for greater responsiveness in times of crisis and helps to ensure a continuation of institutional memory when system administrators leave their jobs.

The generic policy provided here is organized specifically to meet the needs of libraries, and may not work well in other settings. Some aspects of this policy may not suit your particular library's needs; feel free to adapt this model as needed.

2. LOCATION AND ACCESS

2.1. All servers will be located in a secure room with appropriate air and humidity control. This room will be at least one layer from public access, that is, in a room off of restricted office area that is not open to the general public. See Figure 4-1 as an example. (*Note*: Locating servers in the same room as the network equipment, if properly located and secure, is acceptable, as long as the room is not a closet space.)

Authors' Note

The section as presented is appropriate for any medium or large academic or public library. For a small library, either academic or public, the following might be sufficient:

All servers will be located in a secure room, or within easy reach of the library director's desk. When feasible, an appropriate air and humidity control should be utilized. If possible, the servers should reside in a locked room when the library is closed.

2.2. Server rooms will not have a window, but may have a secondary door if it is keyed the same as the primary door. The door(s) will have business or industry class doorknobs and keysets, with additional protection of a metal plate extending over the gap between the door and doorjamb. The door(s) must open outward from the room. (Additional forms of access control such as keypads or swipe cards are acceptable.)

For an example diagram of a server room's location, see Figure 4-1.

Authors' Note

The section as presented is appropriate for any medium or large academic or public library. For a small library, either academic or public, the section is not feasible as most do not have the servers in a separate room and are limited financially in modifying a room to host a server like in the larger library settings.

2.3. Server room access will be relegated to a single key, not part of a series that has a master key.

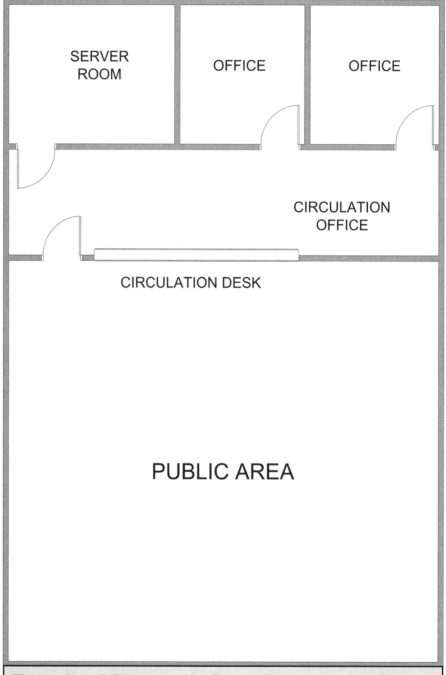

Figure 4-1. A Diagram of a Server Room Located One Layer Away from Public Areas

Authors' Note

The section as presented is appropriate for any medium or large academic or public library. For a small library, either academic or public, this section is not feasible. However, small library directors might make a concentrated effort to keep the server in a locked room during hours the library is closed.

    2.4. Keyholders will be the library director/dean, assistant director/dean, and server administrators.

        2.4.1. A reserve key may be made and kept in Director's/Dean's office.

        2.4.2. On keyholder termination or departure, key/lock will be changed.

Authors' Note

The section as presented is appropriate for any library type.

3. SERVER ADMINISTRATORS

    3.1. Designated administrators will maintain respective servers. This will include:

        3.1.1. Managing users for the designated server

        3.1.2. Managing user security/authority levels

        3.1.3. Managing updates and security patches of all installed software

        3.1.4. Supervising/managing hardware repairs or up-grades

    3.2. Maintain procedures manual and inventory/logs on:

        3.2.1. Backup procedures

        3.2.2. Restore procedures

        3.2.3. Disaster recovery procedures

        3.2.4. Maintain administrative passwords log

            a. Log is not to be stored on any computer.

            b. Log will be kept in locked drawer or safe.

            c. Updated copy will be kept in locked drawer or safe in director's/dean's office.

        3.2.5. User maintenance procedures

3.2.6. Common update/recurring maintenance procedures

3.2.7. Repairs, both warranty and out of warranty

3.2.8. Installed software and related licensing

Authors' Note

The section as presented is appropriate for any library type. Although
some might seem excessive for smaller libraries, it is recommended all
server administrators, even if it is the library director, perform the tasks
listed previously.

3.3. Communications

3.3.1. Server administrators will communicate regularly (designate time frame here—weekly, bi-
monthly, etc.) with director/dean and assistant
director/dean the status of updates, projects, etc.

Authors' Note

For the smallest libraries, in which the library director could be the server
administrator, the following statement might be more appropriate:

The server administrator must keep a weekly log of all tasks
performed in maintaining the server.

3.3.2. Communicate events affecting users and patrons
to include the following:

a. Planned server outage (when possible at least
two weeks in advance)

b. Status of unplanned server outages with brief
nontechnical explanation of outage

c. Upgrades with possible adverse effects on
user software, when suspected as a possibility

3.3.3. Communicate password policies: If minimal requirements and time limits are adopted on passwords, responsible server administrator will
give adequate warning to all users that passwords will expire.

Authors' Note

The section as presented is appropriate for any library type.

3.4. Server passwords will be changed quarterly

3.4.1. Passwords must contain both alpha and numeric characters.

3.4.2. Passwords cannot be family names, pet names, or easily recognizable names such as the street the library is located on or the brand of the server. Random identifiers or uncommon acronyms are acceptable.

3.4.3. Passwords will be a minimum of eight characters and contain at least one nonstandard character, such as the & or $ symbols (only when the software or operating systems are compatible with that usage in their password fields).

Authors' Note

The section as presented is appropriate for any library type.

3.5. Log on and screen savers

3.5.1. Server administrators will log off or lock the terminal when leaving the room for any reason.

3.5.2. Screen savers will be set between 10 and 30 minutes, with password required for access.

Authors' Note

The section as presented is appropriate for any library type.

3.6. Remote access

3.6.1. Remote access will be limited to within the building unless an encrypted virtual private network (VPN) is in place for out-of-building access.

3.6.2. Any computer used for remote access must comply with Section 3.4 passwords and Section 3.5 log on/screen savers policy.

3.6.3. Any computer used for remote access must have the Web browser used for access cleared of history, cache, passwords, on completion of remote connection to server.

3.6.4. Any computer used for remote access must have the document and command line history erased on completion of remote connection to server.

3.6.5. Passwords are not to be stored locally on any user computer for access to edit Web pages, catalog entries, or related servers.

Authors' Note

The section as presented is appropriate for any library type. However, the smallest libraries might not have a need for remote access. If this is the case, this section could be omitted from the policy.

3.7. Logs will be maintained for a period of no less than one month but no more than one year. No log may be erased or deleted prior to creating a backup and storing that backup in a secure location. Backups more than one year old may be destroyed.

Authors' Note

The section as presented is appropriate for any library type.

4. BACKUPS AND RESTORE

4.1. Backups

4.1.1. Catalog server

a. The server will be completed daily for patron and book data and any other fields or areas that change more than once a week.

b. The entire server will be backed up at least monthly and both prior to and immediately following any upgrades, patches, or serious change to any aspect (including hardware) of the server.

    c. Backup copy will be stored offsite in secure location. It may be uplinked to a secure hosting service only if the backup is encrypted and password protected.

    d. Backups should be stored for no more than two years, unless state or federal law requires longer periods.

Authors' Note

The section as presented is appropriate for any library type. However, smaller libraries might not have a need for the second sentence in paragraph *c*.

    4.1.2. Web server

        a. Entire Web site will be backed up weekly by the server administrator.

        b. A copy will be stored off-site in secure location or uplinked to a secure hosting service. Encryption is not required if no patron or sensitive data is stored within backup.

        c. Authorized Web editors will maintain a copy on their office computers of the pages they are responsible for prior to making any changes and on completion of those changes.

        d. Backups should be maintained for no more than one year.

Authors' Note

The section as presented is appropriate for any library type. However, smaller libraries might not have the ability to uplink the backup so this part of the first sentence in paragraph two could be deleted.

    4.1.3. Domain controller and all other servers

        a. Entire domain controller or other server will be backed up quarterly and before any patches or upgrades are performed.

b. Users, groups, access policies and related settings, and stored data (such as e-mail or calendar) will be backed up daily on an incremental backup system.

c. Backups that contain sensitive data will be encrypted.

d. A complete backup copy will be stored off-site or uplinked to a hosting service, and must be encrypted if there is sensitive information within the backup.

Authors' Note

The section as presented is appropriate for a medium or large public or academic library. Smaller libraries would have a shorter section.

4.1.3. Domain controller and all other servers

a. If present, entire domain controller or other server will be backed up quarterly and before any patches or upgrades are performed.

b. Users, groups, access policies and related settings, stored data (such as e-mail or calendar) will be backed up daily on an incremental backup system such as tape backup or flash drive.

c. Backups that contain sensitive data will be encrypted.

d. A complete backup copy will be stored off-site.

4.2. Restore/testing

4.2.1. All backup processes will be tested annually to ensure that there are no flaws in the procedure. Testing will be conducted during library downtime <to be determined by library> by performing a backup of the server and then restoring the system with that backup. (*Note:* If a restore fails, with the possible exception of the catalog server, it is recommended that the administrator install the operating system and software from original CD, and then use the most recent settings/data backups to restore the service.)

Authors' Note

The section as presented is appropriate for any library type.

5. SECURITY PATCHES AND SOFTWARE UPGRADES

5.1. Server administrator is responsible for monitoring for security patches, software patches, and software/hardware updates.

5.2. Security patches will be installed within four days from date of notification from software/hardware manufacturer, unless a critical flaw is reported that will adversely affect the functionality of that particular server or software package as configured for library use.

Authors' Note

The section as presented is appropriate for any library type.

6. AUTHORITY AND RESPONSIBILITY DELEGATION

6.1. The server administrator will designate and train at least one person to perform basic duties of user and group administration, password resetting, backups, and restore functions.

6.2. The server administrator may designate and train personnel to perform limited user and group administration within the department that person(s) has responsibilities, such as adding new patrons in the catalog.

Authors' Note

The section as presented is appropriate for a medium or large public or academic library. For a smaller library, the following might be more appropriate:

6.3. User (staff) and patron access and authority

    6.3.1. Users will have access and authority only to the level required to properly and efficiently perform their job requirements and duties.

    6.3.2. Patrons will have access and authority to view their own account information and to change their own account settings and personal information such as phone number, address, e-mail, etc.

Authors' Note

The section as presented is appropriate for any library type. However, smaller libraries might not have software sophisticated enough to allow patrons to interact directly with their stored information. In these cases, the smaller libraries can delete section 6.3.2.

7. PERSONNEL ADDITIONS, DEPARTURES, AND TERMINATIONS

7.1. New personnel will not be granted access, user accounts, e-mail, or server authority or access of any level until appropriate training and policies are reviewed and signed by same.

7.2. Departing personnel will be reduced in authority and access not more than one week prior to leaving, unless the director/dean expresses in writing either full lockout or full access, depending on the needs or concerns of the library. Arrangements will be made for removal/offloading of personal data or information prior to departure.

7.3. Terminated personnel will be locked out immediately from all access and authority on all servers by the server administrator(s) on notification from the director/dean of the termination.

Authors' Note

The section as presented is appropriate for any library type.
For an example server policy, see Exhibit 4-2.

2. Location and Access

   2.1. All servers will be located in a secure room with appropriate air and humidity control. This room will be at least one layer from public access, that is, in a room off of the restricted office area that is not open to the general public.

   2.2. If feasible, the server rooms will be located in a room with no window, but may have a secondary door if it is keyed the same as the primary door. The door(s) will have business or industry class doorknobs and keysets, with additional protection of a metal plate extending over the gap between the door and door-jamb. The door(s) must open outward from the room.

   2.3. Server room access will be relegated to a single key, not part of a series that has a master key.

   2.4. Keyholders will be the library director/dean, assistant director/dean, and any server administrators.

      2.4.1. A reserve key may be made and kept in director's/dean's office.

      2.4.2. On keyholder termination or departure, key/lock will be changed.

3. Server Administrators

   3.1. Designated administrators will maintain respective servers. This will include:

      3.1.1. Managing users for the designated server

      3.1.2. Managing user security/authority levels

      3.1.3. Managing updates and security patches of all installed software

      3.1.4. Supervising hardware repairs or upgrades

   3.2. Maintain procedures manual and inventory/logs on:

      3.2.1. Backup procedures

      3.2.2. Restore procedures

      3.2.3. Disaster recovery procedures

      3.2.4. Maintain administrative passwords log

         a. Log is not to be stored on any computer

         b. Log will be kept in locked drawer or safe

         c. Updated copy will be kept in locked drawer or safe in director's/dean's office

      3.2.5. User maintenance procedures

      3.2.6. Common update/recurring maintenance procedures

      3.2.7. Repairs, both warranty and out of warranty

      3.2.8. Installed software and related licensing

   3.3. Communications

      3.3.1. Server administrators will communicate with the library director when tasks were carried out in maintenance of the server.

      3.3.2. Communicate events affecting users and patrons to include the following:

         a. Planned server outage (when possible at least two weeks in advance)

         b. Status of unplanned server outages with brief nontechnical explanation of outage

         d. Upgrades with possible adverse effects on user software, when suspected as a possibility

      3.3.3. Communicate password policies: If minimal requirements and time limits are adopted on passwords, library director or assistant director will give adequate warning to all users that passwords will expire.

Exhibit 4-2. Anytown Public Library Server Policy

3.4. Server passwords will be changed quarterly

    3.4.1. Passwords must contain both alpha and numeric characters.

    3.4.2. Passwords cannot be family names, pet names, or easily recognizable names such as the street the library is located on or the brand of the server. Random identifiers or uncommon acronyms are acceptable.

    3.4.3. Passwords will be a minimum of eight characters, and contain at least one nonstandard character, such as the & or $ symbols.

3.5. Log on and screen savers

    3.5.1. Server administrators will log off or lock the terminal when leaving the room for any reason.

    3.5.2. Screen savers will be set between 10 and 30 minutes, with password required for access.

3.6. Logs will be maintained for a period of no less than one month but no more than one year. No log may be erased or deleted prior to creating a backup and storing that backup in a secure location. Backups more than one year old may be destroyed.

4. Backups and Restore

4.1. Backups

    4.1.1. Catalog server

        a. Will be completed daily for patron and book data, and any other fields or areas that change more than once a week.

        b. Entire server will be backed up at least monthly and both prior to and immediately following any upgrades, patches, or serious change to any aspect (including hardware) of the server.

        c. Entire server backup copy will be stored off-site in secure location.

        d. Backups should be stored for no more than two years.

    4.1.2. Web server

        a. Entire Web site will be backed up weekly by the server administrator.

        b. A copy will be stored off-site in secure location

        c. Assistant director will maintain a copy on their office computers of the pages they are responsible for prior to making any changes, and on completion of those changes.

        d. Backups should be maintained for no more than one year.

    4.1.3. Domain controller and all other servers

        a. Entire domain controller or other server will be backed up quarterly, and before any patches or upgrades are performed.

        b. Users, groups, access policies and related settings, stored data will be backed up daily on an incremental backup system.

        c. A complete backup copy will be stored off-site.

4.2 Restore/testing

    4.2.1. All backup processes will be tested annually to ensure that there are no flaws in the procedure. Testing will be conducted during library down time by performing a backup of the server and then restoring the system with that backup.

Exhibit 4-2. Anytown Public Library Server Policy (*Continued*)

5. Security Patches and Software Upgrades
   5.1. Assistant director is responsible for monitoring for security patches, software patches, and software/hardware updates.
   5.2. Security patches will be installed within four days from date of notification from software/hardware manufacturer, unless a critical flaw is reported that will adversely affect the functionality of that particular server or software package as configured for library use.

6. Authority and Responsibility Delegation
   6.1. The assistant director will designate and train at least one person to perform basic duties of user and group administration, password resetting, backups, and restore functions.
   6.2. User (staff) and patron access and authority
      6.2.1. Library staff will have access and authority only to the level required to properly and efficiently perform their job requirements and duties.

7. Personnel Additions, Departures, and Terminations
   7.1. New personnel will not be granted access, user accounts, e-mail, or server authority or access of any level until appropriate training and policies are reviewed and signed by same.
   7.2. Departing personnel will be reduced in authority and access not more than one week prior to leaving, unless the library director expresses in writing either full lockout or full access, depending on the needs or concerns of the library. Arrangements will be made for removal/offloading of personal data or information prior to departure.
   7.3. Terminated personnel will be locked out immediately from all access and authority on all servers by the server administrator(s) on notification from the library director of the termination.

Exhibit 4-2. Anytown Public Library Server Policy (*Continued*)

STAFF TECHNOLOGY POLICY: DESKTOPS, LAPTOPS, PRINTERS

If a library has never had a formal, comprehensive policy governing staff computer use, some colleagues may resent what they see as an imposition on their freedom to use their workstations as they choose. Some complaints will be grounded in reasonable arguments. People tend to work more productively and more happily when they have control over some aspect of their environments, and some colleagues may well be savvy enough to be trusted with more authority over their workstations than the library's policy allows. It is crucially important when introducing a security policy to fellow library staff members that you acknowledge the trade-offs involved, and that you not be seen as heavy-handed or presumptuous. Following are some tips for broaching the new policy with colleagues.

1. *Be frank and honest with staff about the changes wrought by the new policy.* Where the new policy

requires changes to established workflows, train staff in whatever new techniques may be necessary; enforcement of the new policy should not be a focus of these training sessions. The best time to begin this training schedule is when the inventory is taken.

2. *Inventories are rarely completed in a day; do not rush this process.* Consider gathering information about staff workstations while colleagues are present, giving them a chance to ask questions and allowing an opportunity to explain what is taking place and why. This also creates an opportunity to listen to their concerns. You may not be able (or willing) to indulge a given colleague's requests, but sincere attention to staff concerns can help ensure a smooth implementation of the new policy.

3. *Emphasize personal responsibility as the key to establishing solid workplace security.* This message should inform every bit of staff training provided, and may be reinforced by encouraging staff to sign an agreement or acknowledgment of the new policies. During training sessions devoted to the new security policy, reserve time for a question-and-answer exchange at which staff can voice their opinions and concerns. This training combined with the individual attention offered during the inventory process will help smooth out the transition to a more secure technology foundation.

Enforcement is a critical aspect of any security policy; the policy should specify a person or office responsible for enforcing technology security. The policy presented here does not provide for sanctions. This element touches on factors unique to each library and requires support from the director/dean and possibly the human resources/personnel department.

8. TECHNOLOGY SECURITY LEADER

8.1. The library director/dean will designate a staff member to be responsible for coordinating security training, implementing security policies, and regularly reviewing policies and procedures to ensure compliance to and effectiveness of policy. In addition, this staff member will regularly check computers and laptops to ensure patches and versions are up to date, that no unauthorized software has been installed that may jeopardize the security of library technology, and that virus and security software are up to date.

8.2. <Determine and name position (not person's name) of staff member assigned this responsibility.>

Authors' Note

Although not specifically required in the policy, the section as presented is appropriate for any library type. However, a smaller library can reduce this section to the following statement, which allows the security leader to be the dean/director:

The library director/dean will designate a staff member, if available, to be responsible for coordinating security training, implementing security policies, and regularly reviewing policies and procedures to ensure compliance to and effectiveness of policy.

9. APPROPRIATE COMPUTER USE

9.1. *Authority*: Staff, by position of being employed, are authorized to use library technology in the performance of assigned duties and job responsibilities.

9.2. Staff are required to use their assigned user ID for logging onto their office computer or any computer that they will be working on in the performance of their job. The user ID password should not be shared with any other person.

9.3. During the performance of their duties, staff may incur incidental computer usage. This is defined as checking personal e-mail, weather, or minimal time in news/related Web site.

9.4. Staff will not perform any action that may compromise the security of the network, computers, or allow a nonauthorized person to use a computer while that staff member is logged on with his or her personal ID.

Authors' Note

The section as presented is appropriate for any library type. Smaller libraries might not see a need for separate user accounts, but this best practice is recommended as a way to track possible security threats.

10. STAFF COMPUTERS

10.1. *Log on*: All staff computers will require a log-on screen, either local log on or a network log on.

10.2. *Tracking*: Network or server administrators may use this unique ID to assist in isolating security issues or logging inappropriate or unauthorized activity that could jeopardize the security of the library technology.

10.3. Passwords

10.3.1. Staff log-on passwords must be a minimum of eight digits, include alpha and numeric values, and should not be a name or term commonly known or easily found that is identified with the user. Additional nonstandard characters such as $ or # are encouraged but not required.

10.3.2. Passwords are not to be shared with anyone.

10.4. *Security settings*: Staff will not change any computer security setting without prior approval from the appropriate authority, <the technology security leader>.

10.5. *Software installation*: Staff will not install any software, Active X controls, Java controls or software, menu bars (such as Google or Yahoo), screen savers, alert systems (air fare notification, weather alert notification, etc.), or any software downloaded from the Internet or installed from CD not purchased by the library. Many such software have built-in tracking or stealth software that will compromise the security of the network and computers.

10.6. *Screen savers*: The screen saver that is part of the operating system will be set to no more than 20 minutes, and will require password to wake up.

Authors' Note

The section as presented is appropriate for any library type.

11. STAFF LAPTOPS

11.1. Staff using laptops will comply with all portions of section 11 of this policy.

11.2. *Physical security*: Staff will keep the security cable attached to the laptop at all times that the laptop is in its office docking station if one is supplied, or at all times the laptop is in the office of the staff member if a docking station is not supplied.

11.3. *Information security*: Staff will not download and store any information that is considered confidential or mission critical on the laptop unless the folder in which the data is stored on the laptop is encrypted. Previously described data may be stored separately on a jump drive or key if the key is encrypted with a separate password than that used on the computer.

Authors' Note

The section as presented is appropriate for any library type. If smaller libraries do not utilize laptops this section is irrelevent.

12. PRINTERS

12.1. Printers attached directly to a computer or laptop will not be shared for network access.

12.2. Network-ready printers, copier/printers, or copier/ scanner print systems will have password protection for setup, changes, or addition of users. (*Note*: 12.1 will reduce cross traffic and prevent unnecessary wear and tear on a computer as well as remove a layer of vulnerability from the sharing process. 12.2 will add a layer of protection from outside and unwanted access to print systems.)

Authors' Note

The section as presented is appropriate for any library type. Smaller libraries might not have a choice on whether to share printers directly attached to a computer if this is the only option available. In these cases, every security precaution should be taken by the library before sharing out the printer.

For an example of a staff policy, see Exhibit 4-3.

8. Technology Security Leader

  8.1. The assistant director will be responsible for coordinating security training, implementing security policies, and regularly reviewing policies and procedures to ensure compliance to and effectiveness of policy. In addition, the assistant director will regularly check computers and laptops to ensure patches and versions are up to date, that no unauthorized software has been installed that may jeopardize the security of library technology, and that virus and security software are up to date.

9. Appropriate Computer Use

  9.1. *Authority*: Staff, by position of being employed, are authorized to use library technology in the performance of their assigned duties and job responsibilities.

  9.2. Staff are required to use their assigned user ID for logging onto their office computer or any computer that they will be working on in the performance of their job. The user ID password should not be shared with any other person.

  9.3. During the performance of their duties, staff may incur incidental computer usage. This is defined as checking personal e-mail, weather, or minimal time in news/related Web site.

  9.4. Staff will not perform any action that may compromise the security of the network, computers, or allow a nonauthorized person to use a computer while that staff member is logged on with his or her personal ID.

10. Staff Computers

  10.1. *Log on*: All staff computers will require a log-on screen, either local log on or a network log on.

  10.2. *Tracking*: Assistant director may use this unique ID to assist in isolating security issues or logging inappropriate or unauthorized activity that could jeopardize the security of the library technology.

  10.3. Passwords

    10.3.1. Staff log-on passwords must be a minimum of eight digits, include alpha and numeric values, and should not be a name or term commonly known or easily found that is identified with the user. Additional nonstandard characters such as $ or # are encouraged but not required.

    10.3.2. Passwords are not to be shared with anyone.

  10.4. *Security settings*: Staff will not change any computer security setting without prior approval from the assistant director or library director

  10.5. *Software installation*: Staff will not install any software, Active X controls, Java controls or software, menu bars (such as Google or Yahoo), screen savers, alert systems (air fare notification, weather alert notification, etc.) or any software downloaded from the Internet or installed from CD not purchased by the library. A lot of software have built-in tracking or stealth software that will compromise the security of the network and computers.

  10.6. *Screen savers*: The screen saver that is part of the operating system will be set to no more than 20 minutes, and will require password to wake up.

11. Printers

  11.1. Printers attached directly to a computer or laptop will not be shared for network access.

  11.2. Network-ready printers, copier/printers, or copier/scanner print systems will have password protection for setup, changes, or addition of users.

Exhibit 4-3. Anytown Public Library Staff Policy

PUBLIC TECHNOLOGY POLICY: DESKTOPS, LAPTOPS, PRINTERS

This is the real test of a sound, well-balanced library network security policy. Granted, there are obvious differences between public and academic libraries in their missions and patrons.

Academic libraries often have the capacity and right to limit access, in some cases by legal agreement to protect subscription contracts with online information vendors. In many academic contracts with large data vendors only registered students and faculty will be allowed access to certain library databases.

Public libraries are generally chartered to provide freer access to information, while serving a larger and broader user base, than their academic counterparts. This mandate makes it more difficult for most public libraries to justify an investment in, for example, a single-seat license to an expensive scientific database. On the other hand, many public libraries do subscribe to costly databases whose licenses must guarantee more generous terms of access than those required by academic institutions.

Public libraries strive to remove bars from information access, often as part of their charter. They cannot afford to purchase a single seat to a scientific database for $10,000 a year. Fortunately, their patrons will seldom need access to such a specific product.

Despite these differences, the goal of the public security policy in both settings is to protect the library technology from multiple threats, be it hacking, vandalism, theft, or illegal conduct. Often these threats are nothing more than curious youth exploring and experimenting with freely accessible technology. Unfortunately, these explorations often cause headache and loss of service to other patrons and library staff. Competent policy will balance freedom to explore with protection of services offered, regardless of the mission of the library that adopts it.

Modifying this portion will require work on the part of the library director/dean and the technology staff to ensure that the measures do not stifle curiosity or legitimate access to knowledge, and yet protect library technology, assets, and reduce liability.

Note: In the following sections, several examples are presented based on the type of library.

13. DEFINITION OF VALID PATRON OR USER

13.1. *Public*: Any and all persons residing within or visiting the district or geographical location that the library resides in or who have privileges to check out library material, excluding those who for any reason have been barred access due to conduct

13.2. *K–12*: Faculty and staff employed at the school and students registered with and attending classes at the school or students covered under agreement between schools or districts who are authorized to check out library materials

13.3. *Academic*: Faculty and staff employed at the academic institution <name>, students currently registered and attending classes, or students covered under reciprocal agreements between specified institutions, and all other persons authorized to do research at the institution <name>

13.4. *Corporate*: Employees authorized to use resources in the performance of their assigned duties

Authors' Note

If a definition already exists that is approved by the proper authority within the organization, use that instead.

14. PATRON RIGHTS

14.1. *Public and K–12*: Access to Internet and technology within the library for any reason is considered a privilege and not a right. As a privilege, access may be denied for violating any policy regarding its use.

14.2. *Academic*: Access to Internet and technology within the library for faculty, staff, students is necessary for research and completion of assignments for degrees. Violation of appropriate use policy, vandalism, or criminal behavior will be referred to the appropriate administrative office with a request for denial of access to technology within the library.

14.3. *Corporate*: Library services to employees are offered as a tool to fulfill their job duties. Company policy dictates appropriate behavior and use of technology and equipment.

15. PATRON AGREEMENT

For access to Internet and computer technology, patrons must sign the following agreement/acknowledgment, or to log in be required to read a statement that indicates they agree and accept the terms of use policy of the library. (*Note*: This may not apply to all circumstances; however, it does present an opportunity to remind the user.)

> *Agreement*: By logging onto and using this computer or technology the user agrees to abide by all policy and rules regarding its use. Abuse or misuse of the equipment, or using it for inappropriate or criminal activity will result in action being taken in accordance with stated policy(s).

16. PROPER USE OF TECHNOLOGY

Note: Choose only those sections that apply in your situation.

16.1. *Appropriate use*: Research, education, document processing, communications (e-mail or instant messaging), maintaining personal Web space

16.2. *Accessing publicly offensive material*: Access to sites or material that the general public may deem offensive (as defined by state law) or criminal in content is not authorized. Patrons requiring access to such material for legitimate research must make arrangements with library administration and offer valid documentation that access is warranted in the process of research.

16.3. *Physical abuse*: Physical abuse is defined as causing any physical damage to technology through neglect or by intention.

16.4. *Bypassing software security*: Patrons are not authorized to bypass installed security software, security settings, or physical security devices related to software or security settings.

16.5. *Changing software settings*: Patrons may not change preset standard settings or profile settings. Should these settings inhibit or restrict otherwise authorized use, the patron should seek assistance from staff.

16.6. *Installing software*: Patrons are not authorized to install any software. This includes server side software, Java applications, Active X applications, freeware, shareware, or other similar software products.

16.7. *Games* (if authorized or installed): Use of noneducational games must be discontinued if all other computers are in use and other patrons are waiting to use a computer for anything other than playing a game.

16.8. *Criminal activity*: Activity as defined by federal and state law that is considered criminal in nature will be referred to the appropriate law enforcement agency for review or investigation.

Authors' Note

The previous sections cover all activity on both desktops and laptops that are property of the library and offered or issued to patrons.

17. PERSONALLY OWNED COMPUTERS/LAPTOPS/ WIRELESS PRODUCTS

Note: Choose accessibility.

17.1. Patrons do not have authority to connect to the wireless or wired network with personal property of any type. (*Note*: No further policy required if connection to network is denied.)

17.1. Patrons will have access to the library wireless network, but may not directly connect their computer or other technology onto the network through physical cable (Ethernet).

17.2. Patrons wishing to access the wireless network must comply with all applicable sections in Section 16, and prior to gaining access should be required to sign or acknowledge electronically the agreement listed in Section 15.

18. PRINTING

Note: Place any existing policy on patrons using printers here, with the addition of wireless access as part of the policy if the library offers wireless access.

19. SANCTIONS

Note: These should reflect sanctions existing for noncomputer or non-technology-related offenses, ethics policies, or policies and guidelines currently existing on behavior/conduct of patrons.

19.1. *First offense*: Warning

19.2. *Second offense*: Technology/Internet privileges lost for six months

19.3. *Third offense*: Technology/Internet privileges lost for one year

19.4. *State/federal criminal activity*: Referral to appropriate law enforcement agency for review, investigation, or action

For an example of an access to technology policy, see Exhibit 4-4.

NETWORK POLICY: ROUTERS, FIREWALLS, SWITCHES, WIRELESS ACCESS, MONITORING SOFTWARE/APPLIANCES)

> **Wireless access point**: These devices are radio network devices that use radio waves directed through attached antennae to provide connectivity for like hardware, such as laptop computers or PDAs (personal digital assistants). These will be physically connected in some form to the library local area network (LAN), most commonly either through Cat 5 cable or Cat 6 cables.

Creating a network policy requires a basic knowledge of networks and how they function. Policy will cover who gets to access the network, how they can access it, and what types of security protocols should be in place. Network policy will also cover allowed network use from a network administrator position.

A network is composed of several items: firewalls, routers, switches, wireless access points (WAPs), and monitoring software or appliances. See Figure 4-2 for the common layout of a network.

Looking at all the different possible points of access to the network, it becomes obvious that a network can become quite large, and therefore it is difficult to locate and isolate problems when they occur. There are many ways to enhance a network, to monitor its activity, and to automatically correct for issues that negatively impact the network and its users. Some of these items, which physically connect to the network, are called appliances, and others are software packages that can be installed on computers connected to the network.

A network administrator should have the tools in place to monitor traffic and ports to determine when a computer is acting inappropriately and to be able to isolate that computer or technology to prevent damage or degradation of services for other users. This same technology also allows a network administrator, by its very nature, to be able to see and monitor what users are doing. The degree to which a network administrator can view activity with basic tools is limited by experience and the software being used.

These software tools look at information traveling over the network at a level well below programming or software such as instant messaging or an e-mail client. In a simplified explanation, data travels across the Internet in binary—a value of 0 or 1—much like Morse code. To compare computer network data to Morse code is really an oversimplification, but it will

12. Definition of valid patron or user

   12.1. Any and all persons residing within or visiting the district or geographical location that the library resides in or have privileges to check out library material, excluding those that for any reason have been barred access due to conduct

13. Patron Rights

   13.1. Access to Internet and technology within the library for any reason is considered a privilege and not a right. As a privilege, access may be denied for violating any policy regarding its use.

14. Patron Agreement: For access to Internet and computer technology, patrons must sign the following agreement/acknowledgement, or to log in be required to read a statement that indicates they agree and accept the terms of use policy of the library.

   Agreement: By logging onto and using this computer or technology the user agrees to abide by all policy and rules regarding its use. Abuse or misuse of the equipment, or using it for inappropriate or criminal activity will result in action being taken in accordance with stated policy(s).

15. Proper Use of Technology

   15.1. *Appropriate use*: Research, education, document processing, communications (e-mail or instant messaging), maintaining personal Web space.

   15.2. *Accessing publicly offensive material*: Access to sites or material that the general public may deem offensive (as defined by state law) or criminal in content is not authorized. Patrons requiring access to such material for legitimate research must make arrangements with library administration and offer valid documentation that access is warranted in the process of research.

   15.3. *Physical abuse*: Physical abuse is defined as causing any physical damage to technology through neglect or by intention.

   15.4. *Bypassing software security*: Patrons are not authorized to bypass installed security software, security settings, or physical security devices related to software or security settings.

   15.5. *Changing software settings*: Patrons may not change preset standard settings or profile settings. Should these settings inhibit or restrict otherwise authorized use, the patron should seek assistance from staff.

   15.6. *Installing software*: Patrons are not authorized to install any software. This includes server side software, Java applications, Active X applications, freeware, shareware, or other similar software products.

   15.7. *Games*: Use of noneducational games must be discontinued if all other computers are in use and other patrons are waiting to use a computer for anything other than playing a game.

   15.8. *Criminal activity*: Activity as defined by federal and state law that is considered criminal in nature will be referred to the appropriate law enforcement agency for review or investigation.

16. Personally Owned Computers/Laptops/Wireless Products

   16.1. Patrons do not have authority to connect to the wireless or wired network with personal property of any type.

17. Sanctions

   17.1. *First offense*: Warning.

   17.2. *Second offense*: Technology/Internet privileges lost for six months

   17.3. *Third offense*: Technology/internet privileges lost for one year

   17.4. *State/federal criminal activity*: Referral to appropriate law enforcement agency for review, investigation, or action

Exhibit 4-4. Anytown Public Library Public Access to Technology Policy

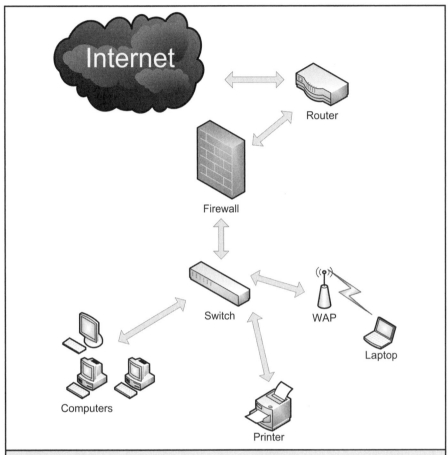

Figure 4-2. Visual Description of the Common Items in a Library Network

build a foundation for the nontechnical person to understand the working level of the software tools being discussed.

Morse code allows communication over a wire by a series of short and long beeps, which are actually electrical signals. The listener on the other end determines whether the beep is a short beep or long beep, and then translates the pattern according to a standardized code. Almost everyone remembers that three short beeps followed by three long beeps and then three short beeps will spell SOS, a request for help.

Data, in essence, travels over the wires (or radio waves) in the same format, as a beep, or 1. Timing is critical for data, because it determines what is a short beep, a 1 for example, and what is a long beep, or a 0. We will say that a data packet is 10 seconds long and contains 10 bits of data. The sending computer will send 10 bits of data, and the first bit will always be a 1 so the receiving computer knows when to start counting. For a visual depiction of this transmission, see Figure 4-3.

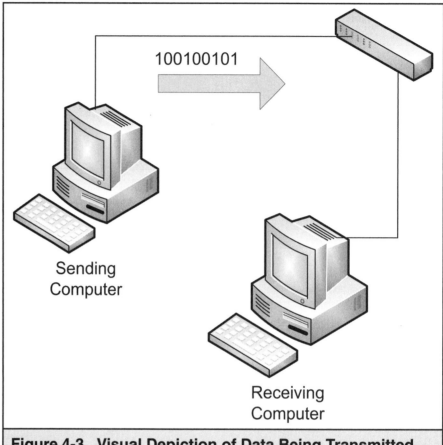

100100101

Sending
Computer

Receiving
Computer

Figure 4-3. Visual Depiction of Data Being Transmitted over a Network

A beep will equal 1, and no beep will equal 0 for our explanation. The receiving computer in Figure 4-3 will see the very first beep, and know that data is coming for 9 more seconds (the first beep taking up the first second). The computer doesn't hear a beep in the next second, and knows that is a 0. Then there are two beeps, two seconds of silence, a beep, two more seconds of silence, and a final beep for a total of ten seconds. So a data packet of "1001001101" is being received by the second computer.

To take the example further, although not entirely accurate, the ten-second data packet will be associated with a letter or character on the keyboard. We'll say that the data packet we used equals the letter "S." It should become clear that if a third computer attached to the switch is just listening in (Figure 4-4), it will know the same Morse code, and can begin to read any SOS message being sent from one computer to another.

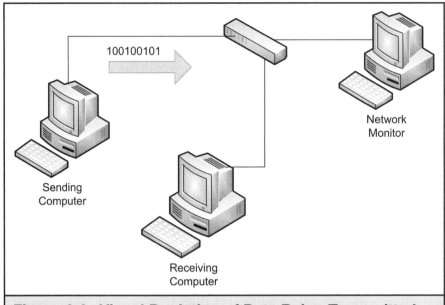

Figure 4-4. Visual Depiction of Data Being Transmitted over a Network, with a Network Traffic Monitor

The purpose of monitoring data on a network isn't one of voyeurism or eavesdropping, although both can be done in this way. The purpose of having a network monitor or appliance is to scan for data that has become corrupted and floods the network, effectively shutting down all traffic and network access. The network monitor sends an alert to a manager, or automatically shuts down the port in the switch that the problem computer is connected to, isolating it from causing further problems.

Similarly, a network monitor can look for specific packets or types of data packets that are known to be destructive, such as a worm or virus. The network monitor is able to remove the dangerous packet(s) from the network before they can do any real damage, or even block the offending computer from any further access to the network.

A network monitor can also determine the health of a network by the quantity of healthy versus corrupt data packets traveling the network. If a computer is only sending corrupt data packets occasionally, the network monitor will be able to isolate the computer that isn't performing at 100 percent and notify the network administrator that the computer needs attention or repair.

A data packet contains much more than ten bits in ten seconds. It will contain a specific identification number that we have already discussed, the MAC address. The MAC address in the inventory will assist the network administrator in tracking down problem computers or network ready devices to repair them.

Because this software or network appliance is so powerful, network policy will also provide guidance for network administrators in the performance of their duty. It will limit the scope of what they are, by policy, authorized to do with such powerful tools. To remove these tools completely would remove the most effective network management and troubleshooting tool available.

20. NETWORK POLICY

20.1. Objective: Provide efficient and reliable network access, Internet access, and access to network features, servers, appliances, printers, or shared storage.

20.2. Network administrator will ensure that all aspects of the network are available and functioning. Through training and review, will ensure that users (staff, patrons) are security conscious and aware/understand policy regarding network access.

21. NETWORK HEALTH TOOLS

Note: These are appliances, software, or hardware that monitor the network for errors, viruses, or other security or traffic efficiency issues.

21.1. The network administrator may use network health tools in the course of maintaining a reliable and secure network.

21.2. These tools may not be used to view or record data being passed on the network for any other reason than that listed in 21.1.

21.3. Any information viewed through the software in the course of legitimate troubleshooting or maintenance must be considered as confidential, and will not be shared with anyone.

22. ROUTERS

22.1. Routers will be password protected, with a minimum of an eight-digit password containing both alpha and numeric characters. The password will not be a specific word but may be an acronym if the acronym is not related to library terms or technology terms.

22.2. A copy of the password will be delivered to the director/dean for safekeeping.

23. FIREWALLS

23.1. The firewall will be set to allow outgoing traffic to initiate contact, but deny all other incoming contact initiation.

23.2. Network address translation (NAT) will be set for all intranet (networked devices within the library, computers, laptops, printers, etc).

23.2.1. Static IP address assignment: Printers and servers will be the only devices with a specific assigned IP address. Documentation must be provided on static IP assignments. (See Exhibit 4-5.)

23.2.2. Static IP address request for other items should be considered on a case-by-case basis, justification required, submitted on form. (See Exhibit 4-6.)

23.2.2. All other network devices will be assigned by NAT, and set to release/renew every 24 hours so that any network accessible device will not retain the same IP address for more than one day.

23.3. Firewall settings will be documented and files stored in a secure, locked file cabinet.

23.4. Firewall settings/trivial file transfer protocol (TFTP).

23.4.1. Firewall settings will be backed up prior to and after any changes to a secure TFTP server.

23.4.2. TFTP server may be on the network administrators computer, but the service must be turned off when not being used.

24. SWITCHES

24.1. Switches will be password protected, with a minimum of an eight-digit password containing both alpha and numeric characters. The password will not be a specific word but may be an acronym if the acronym is not related to library terms or technology terms.

24.2. A copy of the password will be delivered to the director/dean for safekeeping.

Computer Name		Serial #/Tag	
MAC Address			
User Name/Department			
Location			
Purpose			
Services (Web, Domain, DNS, etc.):			
Software Installed (OS, Productivity, etc.) and version			

Exhibit 4-5. Static IP Address Documentation

Computer Name		Serial #/Tag	
MAC Address			
User Name/Department			
Location			
Purpose			

Exhibit 4-6. Static IP Address Request

25. WIRELESS ACCESS

25.1. Wireless access points (WAPs) will be secured using wired equivalent privacy (WEP).

25.1.1. WEP will be changed monthly, requiring staff and patrons utilizing WAPs to renew/obtain new access codes.

25.1.2. Patrons will be given instructions on accessing the WAP, with policy agreement and notice that the access codes change monthly.

25.2. WAPs will issue their own IP addresses through NAT, and should be on a separate subnet from staff and public stations.

25.3. WAPs will be password protected, with a minimum of an eight-digit password containing both alpha and numeric characters. The password will not be a specific word but may be an acronym if the acronym is not related to library terms or technology terms.

25.4. A copy of the password will be delivered to the director/dean for safekeeping.

Authors' Note

The sections as presented are appropriate for any library type. If the library director/dean is the server administrator then the sections will need to be modified to reflect this situation.

26. INAPPROPRIATE EMPLOYEE OR PATRON CONDUCT

26.1. Employees/staff/faculty

26.1.1. If during the course of legitimate troubleshooting or maintenance, activity is observed that negatively affects the network, its security, or is in obvious violation of employee policy, the instance will be documented and a memo sent to the library director/dean.

26.1.2. Documentation must include a description of the routine or legitimate troubleshooting or maintenance that occurred, verifiable by an outside source if challenged.

26.1.3. Library director/dean will follow appropriate policies in documenting incident with staff member or in notifying immediate supervisor of staff member for action.

26.1.4. If activity is repetitive or appears to be occurring at multiple staff locations, training should be implemented to correct the deficiency in security awareness.

26.1.5. If the activity poses an immediate threat to the network or the institution, network access of that computer should be stopped immediately, and the previous procedures on documentation followed with haste.

Authors' Note

The section as presented is appropriate for medium and large library settings. In smaller libraries with few employees, this section would be reworked to accommodate the setting. For example, section 26.1.1 might be the following instead:

> If during the course of legitimate troubleshooting or maintenance, activity is observed that negatively affects or impacts the network, its security, or is in obvious violation of employee policy, the instance will be documented.

26.2. Patrons

26.2.1. If during the course of legitimate troubleshooting or maintenance, activity is observed that negatively affects the network, its security, or is in obvious violation of the user agreement, the network administrator will document the incident and deny further network access of the station/computer.

26.2.2. Appropriate reference or circulation supervisors (department with responsibility for public computers/supervision) should be notified immediately so that they may identify and notify patrons of the impact of their activity.

26.2.3. All incidents should be documented.

Authors' Note

The section as presented is appropriate for any library type. However, smaller libraries will not report to a department head. Instead, the library director will be informed if the network administrator and the library director are different individuals.

27. CRIMINAL ACTIVITY

27.1. If during the course of legitimate troubleshooting or maintenance, criminal or suspected criminal activity is observed, the network administrator will immediately contact the library director/dean, report the suspected activity, and allow a determination of whether it is valid research of a known party or possible criminal activity.

27.2. The library director/dean upon determining intent of activity will document for liability or contact appropriate authority and notify appropriate administrative personnel.

Authors' Note

Once again, the section as presented is appropriate for any library type except smaller libraries. Because the library director is often the network administrator, subsections 27.1 and 27.2 could be combined.

28. OFFICIAL LAW ENFORCEMENT INVESTIGATION

28.1. On instruction from director/dean, or competent legal authority with proper documentation (subpoena or court order), network administrator will cooperate with law enforcement officials as required by law.

28.2. On conclusion of investigation, all documentation related to the investigation will be turned over to the director/dean for safekeeping. No related material will be kept by the network administrator. Materials related to the investigation not submitted to the director/dean should be destroyed or secured in accordance with appropriate policy or by instruction from legal authority.

Authors' Note

The section as presented is appropriate for any library type except smaller libraries. Since the library director is often the network administrator, subsections 28.1 and 28.2 could be combined.

For an example of a network policy, see Exhibit 4-7.

---

18. Network Policy

    18.1. Objective: Provide efficient and reliable network access, Internet access, and access to network features, servers, appliances, printers, or shared storage.

    18.2. Assistant director will ensure that all aspects of the network are available and functioning. Through training and review, will ensure that users (staff, patrons) are security conscious and aware/understand policy regarding network access.

19. Network Health Tools: Appliances, software, or hardware that monitors the network for errors, viruses, or other security or traffic efficiency issues.

    19.1. The assistant director may use network health tools in the course of maintaining a reliable and secure network.

    19.2. These tools may not be used to view or record data being passed on the network for any other reason than that listed in Section 19.1.

    19.3. Any information viewed through the software in the course of legitimate troubleshooting or maintenance must be considered confidential, and will not be shared with anyone.

20. Routers

    20.1. Routers will be password protected, with a minimum of an eight-digit password containing both alpha and numeric characters. The password will not be a specific word but may be an acronym if the acronym is not related to library terms or technology terms.

    20.2. A copy of the password will be delivered to the assistant director for safekeeping.

21. Firewalls

    21.1. The firewall will be set to allow outgoing traffic to initiate contact, but deny all other incoming contact initiation.

    21.2. Network address translation (NAT) will be set for all intranet (networked devices within the library, computers, laptops, printers, etc).

        21.2.1. Static IP address assignment: Printers and servers will be the only devices with a specific assigned IP address. Documentation must be provided on static IP assignments.

Exhibit 4-7. Anytown Public Library Network Policy

21.2.2. All other network devices will be assigned by NAT, and set to release/renew every 24 hours so that any network accessible device will not retain the same IP address for more than one day.

21.3. Firewall settings will be documented and files stored in a secure, locked file cabinet.

22. Switches

22.1. Switches will be password protected, with a minimum of an eight-digit password containing both alpha and numeric characters. The password will not be a specific word but may be an acronym if the acronym is not related to library terms or technology terms.

22.2. A copy of the password will be delivered to the director/dean for safekeeping.

23. Inappropriate Employee or Patron Conduct

23.1. Employees/staff/faculty

23.1.1. If during the course of legitimate troubleshooting or maintenance, activity is observed that negatively affects the network, its security, or is in obvious violation of employee policy, the instance will be documented and a memo sent to the library director.

23.1.2. Documentation must include a description of the routine or legitimate troubleshooting or maintenance that occurred, verifiable by an outside source if challenged.

23.1.3. Library director will follow appropriate policies in documenting incident with staff member.

23.1.4. If activity is repetitive or appears to be occurring at multiple staff locations, training should be implemented to correct the deficiency in security awareness.

23.1.5. If the activity poses an immediate threat to the network or the institution, network access of that computer should be stopped immediately, and the previous procedures on documentation followed with haste.

23.2. Patrons

23.2.1. If during the course of legitimate troubleshooting or maintenance, activity is observed that negatively affects the network, its security, or is in obvious violation of the user agreement, the assistant director or librarian in charge will document the incident and deny further network access of the station/computer.

23.2.2. All incidents should be documented.

24. Criminal Activity

24.1. If during the course of legitimate troubleshooting or maintenance, criminal or suspected criminal activity is observed, the assistant director will immediately contact the library director, report the suspected activity, and allow a determination of whether it is valid research of a known party or possible criminal activity.

24.2. The library director upon determining intent of activity will document for liability or contact appropriate authority.

25. Official Law Enforcement Investigation.

25.1. On instruction from the library director or competent legal authority with proper documentation (subpoena or court order), assistant director will cooperate with law enforcement officials as required by law.

25.2. On conclusion of investigation, all documentation related to the investigation will be turned over to the library director for safekeeping. No related material will be kept by the assistant director. Materials related to the investigation not submitted to the library director should be destroyed or secured in accordance with appropriate policy or by instruction from legal authority.

Exhibit 4-7. Anytown Public Library Network Policy (*Continued*)

REVIEW QUESTIONS

Use these questions as a guideline to evaluate the information gained from this chapter.

- What is a security policy?
- What roles do the various stakeholders play in developing a security policy?
- What are some questions to ask about a security policy before it is developed?
- Why is classifying information necessary in a security policy?
- What is confidential information? What is mission-critical information?
- What is role of the "Server" section of a security policy?
- What are some of the parts of the "Server" section of a security policy?
- What is the "Staff" section of security policy?
- How should staff be introduced to the security policy?
- What is the "Public" section of a security policy?
- What is goal of the "Public" section? What parts should be included?
- What is the "Network" section of a security policy?
- How is a computer network set up and what are some main of its components?
- What are some parts that need to be included in the "Network" section of a security policy?

KEY POINTS AND CONCLUSION

- Written policies are designed and intended to improve the security of library technology, ensure uninterrupted access for patrons and staff, and protect access to information and the privacy of patrons.
- The policy example provided here can be easily modified to benefit either public or academic libraries, and with consideration toward the specific library's mission it provides protection of the technology investment.

- Should the library already have a written policy in place,
  it can be compared and contrasted to what is offered here
  to enhance and improve the existing policy.

This policy is a building block, a starting foundation for a library to develop and tailor security to fit their needs. Without policies in place, there is no central theme to securing technology. This will create boundaries of safety around the network, computers, and wireless technology that are used to assist patrons in achieving their goals.

In addition to the policy as offered, define criminal activity specifically by using the state law's definitions. This will help clarify a user's responsibility and understanding of what is expected of them. Appendix A provides links to the state laws concerning crimes and penal codes. Please use these links to enhance the policies.

5 UNDERSTANDING THREATS FROM HACKERS AND MALCONTENTS

In the first four chapters we covered the basic managerial functions of good network security: how to conduct an inventory, develop security policies, and conduct a security audit. Having introduced those preparatory steps, in this chapter we introduce the enemy by examining hackers, viruses, malware, and other threats. We highlight how these enemies pose various threats to a library's technological infrastructure. We realize that new threats develop every day, and do not pretend to offer comprehensive, timeless coverage of these threats. However, by the end of the chapter, you should have a good understanding of the threats existing as of this writing. We also suggest some additional resources to help you track new and developing threats.

HACKERS 101

Hacker: A person who enjoys exploring the details of computers and how to stretch their capabilities. A malicious or inquisitive meddler who tries to discover information by poking around. A person who enjoys learning the details of programming systems and how to stretch their capabilities, as opposed to most users who prefer to learn only the minimum necessary. (Williams, 2001)

The definition (see sidebar) from Williams's book is broader and gentler in nature than the popular conception of "hacker": most people identify hackers as criminals, pests, troublemakers, and so on. This dim view grants hackers a certain perverse mystique, though most of the trouble hackers cause is ultimately harmless. When malicious intent motivates hackers though, their impact can be devastating: hacking has become such a problem that the federal government has created a department just to assist in tracking down hackers who are considered to be threats to national security.

Libraries are not immune to hackers. What do hackers do with library computers? What interest might they have in hacking into a library server? What information could they possibly steal from a library?

Here are some examples, drawn from various (necessarily anonymous) libraries:

- A library had someone walk in and hook a laptop directly into the network using an Ethernet connection. Before library staff identified this user as a threat and got him off the computer, he had compromised the library's Web server. It was not until a concerned patron told staff that the library's Web site was down that they discovered that the hacker had managed to install software on the library's Web server, essentially turning their Web server into a chat-room server. The chat-room software installed on the Web server could not be uninstalled, and the library had to bring in an IT specialist to completely reconfigure the server. A week of library service was lost because of the hacker.

- Another library found its Web server suddenly performing sluggishly. The library's IT staff spent considerable time diagnosing the problem and discovered that someone had hacked into the server through its FTP (file transfer protocol) service and turned the Web server into a spam server. Thousands of e-mails were being sent through the server's simple mail transfer protocol (SMTP) service to destinations throughout the world. Once the intrusive software was removed from the Web server, it began to function normally again. About a week of service was lost to the hacker.

- An academic university library found that computer science students liked the challenge of attempting to hack into the library's network infrastructure. Servers went down regularly because no matter what protections were in place, the students found a way around them. It took thousands of dollars in security software and hardware and security cameras strategically placed around the library to reduce the hacking to a manageable level.

A HISTORY OF HACKING

Libraries need to be as concerned about hackers as mainstream businesses. Before we describe in more detail how hackers do their mischief, let us examine the history of hacking.

1960S: THE DAWN OF HACKERS

The 1960s were considered the dawn of the hackers, when computers first began to become mainstream. The first self-described hackers were MIT students who took their name from a model train group who used to "hack" the electric trains, tracks, and switches to make them run faster. These early hackers decided to see how they could utilize their talents in improving the performance of the mainframe computers found on campus (PCWorld.com staff, 2001).

Richard Stallman became the most famous person to come from this initial group.

> In 1971 when I joined the staff of the MIT Artificial Intelligence lab, all of us who helped develop the operating system software, we called ourselves hackers. We were not breaking any laws, at least not in doing the hacking we were paid to do. We were developing software and we were having fun. Hacking refers to the spirit of fun in which we were developing software. The hacker ethic refers to the feelings of right and wrong, to the ethical ideas this community of people had—that knowledge should be shared with other people who can benefit from it, and that important resources should be utilized rather than wasted. (Heaton, 2000)

Although we acknowledge the legitimate and productive nature of benign hacking, in this book we are concerned primarily with the effects of malicious hacking. Therefore, we often refer simply to "hackers" in its current popular sense, describing those who engage in hacking with malicious intent.

1970S: INNOVATION AND CREATIVITY

The 1970s saw a flowering of the innovation and creativity often associated with hackers. For example, hackers began to break into phone networks to make free phone calls. These hackers were labeled phreaks. John Draper, one such hacker, famously discovered that a whistle included as a prize in boxes of Cap'n Crunch cereal made the precise sound frequency needed to access AT&T's switching equipment. Draper built a blue box that used the whistle to allow him to make free phone calls. *Esquire* magazine featured the blue box in an article, and wire fraud escalated. Future Apple Computer founders Steve Jobs and Steve Wozniak created a home-based business selling versions of the blue box (PCWorld.com staff, 2001).

1980S: HACKER CLUBS AND MOVIES

In the 1980s, hackers increasingly banded together to share knowledge, forming clubs. Electronic bulletin board system (BBS), a precursor to discussion forums and usenet groups, sprang up with hackers sharing tidbits of knowledge such as stolen passwords and tips on how to break computer security. Two of the more famous hacker clubs were the Legion of Doom in the United States and the Chose Computer Club in Germany (PCWorld.com staff, 2001).

Electronic bulletin board system (BBS): A simple database, stored on a server, of postings by persons allowed to dial in to the server via a modem.

As personal computers grew in popularity during the 1980s, hacking became more widespread. Many people who had never had access to computers now had it, and with greater computer power being made more affordable to meet market demands, hackers had more powerful tools at their disposal. Hollywood took advantage of the phenomenon by releasing movies centered on hacking; *War Games* (1983) was one example.

The first arrest for hacking was made in 1983 when six teenagers, calling themselves the 414s after an area code in Wisconsin, were charged with breaking into computer systems including the one at Los Alamos National Laboratory. One of the six was given immunity for his testimony while the other five received probation.

To help combat the rising costs associated with hacking, Congress passed the Computer Fraud and Abuse Act of 1986, which, among other things, made it illegal to use another person's password to gain access to a computer system. A 17-year-old hacker named Herbert Zinn was the first person prosecuted under the law, for breaking into computers owned by AT&T.

1n 1988, Robert Morris, a graduate student at Cornell University, released the first worm on the Internet. The worm caused an estimated $15 million to $100 million in damages by exploiting security holes in the UNIX operating system. Morris was sentenced to five years in prison and fined $250,000.

1990S: RAIDS AND ARRESTS

In the 1990s, authorities began to take the hacking community even more seriously. Operation Sundevil was a Secret Service operation featuring multiple early morning raids in 14 U.S. cities targeting well-known hackers. The formerly close-knit hacking community began to fall apart as hackers turned on each other to gain immunity from prosecution.

One hacker who escaped the first wave of arrests, Kevin Poulsen, was caught in 1993 after hacking into a radio station's computer system to allow him and his friends to win two cars and thousands of dollars in cash. Poulsen had rigged the computer system to allow only specific phone numbers (known only to him and his friends) to get through to the radio station. Poulsen served three years in prison and now works as a freelance journalist covering computer crime.

In 1994, the Web had begun to gain popularity, and the easy exchange of information became an increasingly important consideration. The old BBS were abandoned and new tools for widespread communication were developed. Credit card numbers were increasingly used as means of payment on the Web, and were increasingly stolen by hackers. In the mid-1990s, $10 million was stolen from Citibank by Russian hackers who transferred the money to accounts all over the world. Vladimir Levin was the ringleader of the outfit responsible, and served three years in prison as a result. All but $400,000 of the money was recovered.

In the late 1990s, Microsoft became a prime target of hackers when they released Windows 95 and Windows 98, which were not designed with security primarily in mind and provided hackers with numerous security vulnerabilities. Hackers had a field day exploiting these operating systems; Microsoft released thousands of patches over several years to help stem the attacks.

HACKERS OF THE TWENTY-FIRST CENTURY

Numerous people have sought fame (and infamy) by becoming hackers. One has even written a successful book on his particular specialty, social hacking, a means of obtaining information through friendliness or intimidation that allows the hacker to gain access to victims' accounts and restricted data.

As with the 414s attacking Los Alamos, hackers continue to target large quarry. Yahoo!, Amazon.com, Buy.com, eBay, and CNN.com have each at some point been compromised by denial of service (DoS) attacks. An exponential growth in blackmail via threats of denial of service attacks has become very popular among economically motivated hackers. We will discuss what the denial of service attack is in the next section on what hackers do to break into computer systems.

Despite the malicious intent of some hackers, many in the hacking community continue to be motivated by benign curiosity. The legitimate hacking community hosts Web sites and publishes periodicals that make it easy to stay up to date with new developments . . . and to hone your awareness of developing threats. You might read publications like *The Hacker News Network*, or visit an industry news site like Network World.

HACKER MIND-SET

When it comes down to it, malicious hackers are nothing more than sophisticated criminals who think like thieves. With this in mind, you can develop a decent general picture of the hacker's mindset. For instance, hackers tend to focus on discovering a system's smallest weaknesses and tend to prefer avoiding detection rather than drawing attention to their exploits. Here are some examples of how a hacker might think when exploiting a library's network:

- Performing an attack from a library's wireless network, which makes it difficult for the authorities to track.
- Bypassing a library's security system by doing something as simple as unplugging a camera found on the system.

- Via social networking services, acquiring sensitive information by befriending a library employee, acquiring the employee's log-in and password, and then downloading patron data.
- Volunteering at the library to help with the computer network, then violating that trust by leveraging it to exploit information found on the system.
- Setting up a "wireless clone" in a library's network that patrons use, thinking that it is the library's own wireless network.

Hackers are motivated by a variety of factors. Some do what they do for the simple thrill of it. Some do it to get attention for themselves, or for a cause. Other hackers have more serious intentions, attacking government and public utility networks in the hopes of causing widespread disruption.

Hackers know that most organizations, including libraries, do not manage their computer security perfectly well, and that it is nearly impossible to keep up with the many different vulnerabilities present in computers, networks, and organizational structure.

HACKER ATTACK MODES

As mentioned earlier, hackers are constantly thinking of how to exploit computer systems, both through technical attacks and through social networking. Hackers are constantly devising new techniques, but their methods tend to describe five categories.

1. *The personal approach.* Through social networking applications, a hacker will gain the trust of someone on the library staff and gain access to sensitive information.
2. *The direct approach.* Hackers will observe an organization to gain an understanding of its computer security policies. When a hacker acquires a good understanding of a library's security practices, he or she may choose to make bold use of that knowledge by breaking into buildings, computer rooms, or other areas where sensitive information is kept. Some hackers will resort to outright theft of computer equipment to get what they want. Dumpster diving, the act of going through someone's trash, is another common practice of hackers.

3. *The backdoor approach.* Hackers can gain covert access to a library's network in several ways:

- Using a rogue modem to get to a computer behind the library's firewall.

- Gaining access through an unsecured wireless network.

- Installing a network analyzer on an unsecure public computer station to record all traffic on a network in a simple text file. Hackers will then use additional software to survey the data captured.

- Creating a DoS on a server by flooding the network with requests until the server protests. Once the DoS occurs, all traffic gets turned back, including legitimate requests.

- Network protocols, the language computers use to talk to one another on the network, have some inherent weaknesses that hackers can exploit.

4. *The application-based approach.* Applications on computers, such as e-mail clients or office productivity software, are also inviting targets for hackers:

- Hackers often exploit inherent weakness found in database applications. Database applications, in this context, refer to applications such as Microsoft Access and Microsoft SQL Server, along with an ILS's patron database.

- Voice-over Internet protocol (VoIP) is a technology that allows users to make phone calls over the Internet. As more libraries adopt this technology, they should be aware that hackers will attack this protocol to gain access to their networks.

- In order to allow staff and patrons to access the Web and e-mail, most libraries will leave open the ports on their firewalls to all for full access. Libraries need to be aware that hackers realize that hypertext transfer protocol (HTTP) and SMTP are not closed off so the hackers will take advantage and break into a library's network.

5. *The OS approach.* All operating systems have inherent weaknesses that can be exploited, even relatively secure ones such as Unix. Most hackers focus on vulnerabilities in Windows, since it is the most popular

> **Rogue modem**: A modem illicitly placed on a staff member's computer and phone line; this allows a hacker access to the network by dialing in from home.

OS. The most common hacks to an operating system include:

- Exploiting specific network protocols
- Breaking into an operating system's authentication system
- Cracking file system security
- Determining passwords and logins

ADDITIONAL HACKER METHODOLOGY

Each type of hacker attack will attempt to exploit a particular vulnerability. The following are some of the more common vulnerabilities that hackers will seek out.

Passwords

Left entirely to their own devices, most users choose simple, easy-to-remember passwords; in many cases, these are proper names or common English words. This limits the universe of possible passwords, which gives hackers an important advantage when staging a brute-force attack against password security. Using programs that generate every possible combination of characters (usually weighted toward patterns commonly found in passwords), hackers can automate the process of simple guesswork, a process that in theory guarantees a successful breach of password security.

Libraries can frustrate this approach by insisting that users choose difficult-to-guess passwords, and can further mitigate the possibility of a successful brute-force attack by forcing users to change their passwords often. Please refer to Chapter 4 for more information on how to establish a policy for passwords.

Other types of password hacks include:

- *Dictionary attacks*: This attack uses software that quickly compares a set of common words with a database of passwords. Hackers download a dictionary file that lists a range of words for the password-cracking software to use; the software then uses each of these common words to generate possible passwords (by adding numbers, changing the case of individual letters, and so on).
- *Rainbow attacks*: This approach reduces the inefficiency of brute-force attacks by using a collection of known passwords to establish a table of likely entries. In this way, the 218 trillion possible eight-character passwords are narrowed to the likeliest four million.

For more information on rainbow style attacks, visit http://lasecwww.epfl.ch.

NETWORK INFRASTRUCTURE VULNERABILITIES

The network is the backbone of technical infrastructure; it is also one of the more vulnerable parts of that infrastructure. Hackers know this and will make direct attacks on your network before blindly attempting more roundabout approaches such as password-cracking.

Hackers will try to first gain information about your network, and then will map its configuration. Once the network map is known, a hacker will see what devices are accessible and what applications are running on each. Finally, the hacker will attempt to penetrate the vulnerable devices most likely to grant free access to network resources. The following are some of the tools hackers will use to assess and penetrate a network.

HACKER METHODS AND TOOLS

Port Scanner

Port scanners are discussed in more detail in Chapter 6. Hackers use them to find out which ports are available on your network.

ARP Poisoning

Address resolution protocol (ARP) is a language used by network routers to map IP addresses to media access control (MAC) addresses. Hackers can use programs like Cain and Abel, dsniff or ettercap to change the ARP tables on a router so that it sends network traffic to the hacker's computer before the intended host receives it. The hacker thus becomes a middle-man, automatically privy to all network transmissions. The hacker can record all of the traffic going between the router and the requesting computer without either being the wiser.

MAC Address Spoofing

Hackers can also trick network switches into thinking that the hacker's computer is a proper network device like a router or a hub. Again, all network traffic is sent to the hacker's computer.

Ping Sweeping

Through a command prompt, a person can find out which devices on the network are currently active. When a hacker gains access to a computer, a

Why would anyone want to hack into a library network? What does a library have that a given hacker could possibly be interested in? This isn't so much a question of what a library has, but what can the network be used for. Patron information stored in a library's ILS is often a prime target. In addition, servers can be used for storing illegal software or pirated movies and music, computers can become clones for DoS attacks, and some hackers actually attack library networks in order to get freer access to library resources than their library cards might allow.

ping sweep will be used to find out what is available to exploit. Ping sweeps can be generated using NMap.

SNMP Scanning

Simple network management protocol (SNMP) is built into every network device. This protocol allows network management programs to control a network device remotely. Most network devices will leave this protocol enabled by default, and hackers know it. When they find a SNMP port open, they will use it to gather information on such things as user names and TCP (transmission-control protocol) connections. Several software packages exist that will assist a hacker in scanning SNMP, such as Solar-Winds, Getif, and SNMPUTIL.

Network Analyzer

Also called sniffers, these programs do what their name implies: capture and report on network traffic. Hackers might attach a sniffer to a network to find out what activity is being conducted on it. This sometimes results in the direct divulging of sensitive information, but network analyzers can provide damaging information simply by providing clues as to a network's composition and traffic patterns.

Banner Grabbing

This is a process hackers use to capture welcome screens, which will often reveal information about the software such as the type of operating system, version number, and which service packs have been applied. Many hackers use telnet to do this. To see what information is revealed through banner-grabbing, you can go to a Windows command prompt and type in telnet <ip address>; this will provide a welcome screen that shows a version number. Figure 5-1 is an example of what this screen looks like. This banner tells the hacker which Web server is being used, IIS (Internet Information Services), and what version.

Denial of Service

DoS attacks are the most famous of all network attacks, because they have been used to inconvenience some major corporations, such as Microsoft and Yahoo!. Using freely available software, hackers can generate so many requests to a server that it disallows further requests, effectively shutting it down.

```
HTTP/1.1 400 Bad Request
Server: Microsoft-IIS/5.0
Date: Sun, 28 Sep 2008 03:42:37 GMT
Content-Type: text/html
Content-Length: 87

<html><head><title>Error</title></head><body>The parameter is incorrect. </body></html

Connection to host lost.

C:\Documents and Settings\User>
```

Figure 5-1. Screen Capture of a Command Prompt Showing a Queried Web Server Response and Version of the Web Server

War Dialing

War dialing is the act of using a computer to find accessible modems. Using freely available software, a hacker can automatically call multiple numbers over a period of time to find these vulnerable modems. This method is akin to brute-force password hacking: both use freely available software to automate what would be an unviable and inefficient approach. And they are often used in tandem: after targeting a modem, a hacker often uses a brute-force password attack to gain access to the network.

WIRELESS LOCAL AREA NETWORKS

Wireless networks offer a whole different challenge for libraries on the security side. Wireless networks have never been very secure, and hackers know this. The following are examples of the ways in which hackers can take advantage of wireless networks.

Denial of Service (DoS) Attack

Much in the same way as with traditional networks, hackers can flood a library's wireless network with requests that will bring the network to a crawl and may eventually shut it down.

Man-in-the-Middle Attacks

These are used in conjunction with software like Gspoof and LANforge, which force wireless access points to fail. Hackers can then place a rogue access point on the wireless network, which the wireless clients will believe is the legitimate one. The rogue wireless access point can be used to capture and/or redirect network traffic.

Eavesdropping

Unencrypted wireless network traffic can be recorded as clear text by a network sniffer. Even some encrypted traffic, such as WEP (wired equivalent privacy), can be cracked and recorded by a hacker.

It must also be pointed out that even with MAC controls in place, a hacker can use programs such as NetStumbler to find out which MAC addresses are being allowed various types of access and then to spoof selected MAC addresses to gain access to the wireless network.

OPERATING SYSTEM HACKS

Windows

Microsoft is the largest software vendor in the world. Because of this, hackers love to find security flaws in their products, especially the Windows Operating System. A basic introduction to some Windows hacks follows.

Nbtstat. This is a built-in Windows program that is used to gather NetBIOS name table information. By using the command nbtstat –A, a hacker can find out a computer's name, domain name, and MAC address. Hackers can use this information to dig deeper into a network.

Scanning for Shares. It is common for staff using Windows-based workstations to share folders or drives with colleagues. However, most do not set the permissions on these shares correctly. Hackers will take advantage of this error to discover what rogue shares are available to penetrate. Software programs like Legion, NetScan, and ShareEnum will find the poorly secured shares on a Windows network.

Remote Procedure Call (RPC). Windows applications make calls with one another using internal protocols such as RPC. Hackers love to exploit RPC. Using a built-in tool like Rpcdump, hackers can find out what applications are running on a host. Once they have found out what is running, they can build a strategy on how best to attack the host.

Null Sessions. A vulnerability on older Windows operating systems, pre–Windows XP and Server 2003, is the ability to map a null session—an anonymous connection—to a hidden share called IPC$. Once a hacker has done this, Windows host configuration information can be discovered; even the registry can be accessed and, within limits, edited.

Taking Full Control. In today's world, it is very important to keep your operating system's patches up to date; if you don't, a hacker can use applications such as Metasploit or CORE IMPACT to take complete control of your computer. These programs allow a hacker to upload some stored code to a compromised computer. The code will take advantage of the unpatched vulnerability and may give the hacker complete ownership of the computer.

VULNERABILITIES OF OTHER OPERATING SYSTEMS

As much as attention Windows gets from hackers, other operating systems have their share of vulnerabilities. We will make a short introduction to vulnerabilities to two operating systems: Linux and Novell Netware (a popular network operating system).

Linux

This flavor of Unix has become very popular in the last ten years. Relatively few libraries use Linux, but the ones that do should be aware of what hackers will look for in a Linux system.

File Transfer Protocol (FTP). If this is not set up properly on a Linux computer, the hacker can easily access files and download sensitive information. Log-ins can be cracked through a brute-force method.

Telnet. Network analyzers can easily capture the text from telnet sessions. Logins can also be determined through the brute-force methods described previously.

Sendmail. This is the world's most popular e-mail server software, and it has its share of vulnerabilities that hackers will exploit. As with Windows, it is important to patch this software as often as needed.

File Systems. Linux, as a flavor of Unix, is a file-based operating system; hackers will attack Linux machines at the file level. Certain files contain information describing which users of the local Linux computer are trusted. Hackers will look for this information in the hosts.equiv and .rhosts files after they have gained access to a given workstation.

Network File System (NFS). The NFS of Linux is similar to the Windows shares system, and like Windows shares has a fair number of security weaknesses. The etc/exports file contains a setting that if adjusted correctly by a hacker will provide access to the entire file system. If the command / rw is included in this file, the hacker will have free rein over the entire computer.

Buffer Overflow. This is a popular form of attack. A buffer overflow attack will send strings of information—often nonsensical instructions—to the Linux machine, causing an overflow in the machine's data buffer. This overflow causes the Linux box to give the hacker root-level permissions.

NETWARE VULNERABILITIES

Netware is one of the more secure network operating systems available today. However, it has its share of vulnerabilities that hackers like to use. Similar to Windows Terminal Services, Rconsole is a tool in Netware that allows remote access to a Netware server; a hacker who has cracked the appropriate password can gain control of a Netware server through the rconsole. These passwords are easily found in files on the server (sys:\system\ autoexec.ncf or sys:\system\ldremote.ncf). Netware has the same vulnerabilities as Windows when it comes to capturing network activity. With a network analyzer, a hacker can capture sensitive information that may later be used to break into the Netware server. Finally, be careful of rogue NLMs (NetWare Loadable Modules), as hackers will load them quickly if console access is granted.

APPLICATION HACKS: E-MAIL, INSTANT MESSAGING, VOICE-OVER INTERNET PROTOCOL (VoIP)

Hackers can have a field day with applications that deal directly with library servers. Communication applications such as e-mail clients are prime targets.

E-mail

E-mail can be fertile ground for hackers. E-mail attachments are particularly effective. Some malicious attachments contain executable files designed to collect sensitive information or to send large volumes of phony messages. In the latter case, the local e-mail server may not be able to handle the increased traffic; the bandwidth consumed by this type of attack also causes hassles for network administrators.

SMTP is full of weaknesses that hackers will use to their advantage. A hacker can use the VRFY or EXPN command to discover what users, or e-mail lists, exist on a server. Once hackers know this information, they can use it to send spam. Hackers can also use the SMTP relay to send external e-mails through an e-mail server. If the library leaves the SMTP relay open, a hacker might use it to send spam and other messages through the library's e-mail server.

E-mail headers contain a wealth of information about an organization, including the internal IP address of your e-mail client, its hostname, and the versions of the e-mail clients being used by your staff and patrons. With this information, a hacker can begin to plan what to do to further infiltrate network infrastructure.

Instant Messaging (IM)

Instant messaging has several security vulnerabilities of which library network administrators must be aware. Name-hijacking, for example, allows a hacker to take over someone else's IM identity. Hackers can launch a DoS attack on an IM client to allow complete control of a computer, and can capture internal IP addresses through an IM client. The most simple IM hack involves convincing a victim to click on a link that leads to a Web site that installs malicious software such as spyware or a virus. If you allow IMing in your library, be sure that no one is sharing your library network drives on the IM client. If they are, then a hacker could easily gain access to these network shares through the IM client.

Voice-over Internet Protocol (VoIP)

An approach to making phone calls over the Internet, VoIP is a relatively new target for hackers.

As mentioned previously, VoIP is not widely adopted by libraries, but a library should be aware of the security issues involved before investing in any technology. Bear in mind that VoIP is no more or less secure than any other network service. For instance, VoIP can be hit with a DoS attack, which will cause the service to stop functioning. VoIP transmissions are not encrypted, so anybody with the right software or hardware can listen, and even record, phone conversations. Be careful if you decide to implement this technology.

VULNERABILITIES OF WEB SERVERS

Because Web servers perform a specialized function, they present unique security vulnerabilities. Here are few methods that hackers might use to gain access to a Web server.

Although some software probably *shouldn't* be installed on any computer in your library, that doesn't mean that it isn't. Peer-to-peer (P2P) clients such as Limewire or eDonkey are typically very susceptible to hacking and viruses. Not always because the client itself contains malicious code; rather, the software downloaded through these programs is often infected. Hackers and well-intentioned staff members alike may seek out ways of installing these programs despite warnings from network administrators.

Voice-over-Internet protocol. Network quality and speed improvements have recently made feasible the conversion of an analog signal (voice, video, music) into a digital signal for transmission over the Internet. Previously, the process of transferring the digital data stream containing the converted analog voice signal resulted in the loss of too much information to be successfully converted back to analog with any quality. New compression techniques have allowed an analog-digital-analog translation to be achieved with greater fidelity, allowing VoIP to become quite popular.

VoIP can be a bandwidth hog, and with software programs like Skype, which are virtually undetectable by network monitoring devices, a network of moderate capacity could be negatively affected. Some organizations devote a discrete, physically separate network to VoIP.

Spoofing Log-ins

Poorly written Web applications invite a variety of Web hacks. Log-in pages in particular can reveal damaging information to hackers. For instance, the error message presented to users upon an incorrect log-in attempt may inadvertently confirm, through phrasing like "the password entered is not valid for this account," that a hacker has uncovered a valid user name. Make sure to make your log-in page error messages as generic as possible.

Directory Browsing

Web sites that enable directory browsing can provide hackers with compromising information. With directory browsing enabled, anyone can type in a URL such as http://secure.library.us/downloads/ and be presented with all the files in the appropriate directory on the Web server.

Buffer Overflows

Web applications are notorious for allowing hackers to give them too much information to process. Web servers will attempt to process any kind of data, and when that data becomes too much, or too confusing, it can crash the server. Hackers will inject automated input or attempt to take over a Web server by changing the code in the data string sent back to the Web server.

Hidden Field Information

Some Web-based forms will use hidden field variables. Hidden fields often hold data needed for a Web application to perform properly. Too often, this information is sensitive in nature—names of databases, credentials to administrative accounts, and the like. With the right software, hackers can record all the hidden variables being sent between a client and a Web server.

VIRUSES

Viruses are small software programs designed to cause mischief with computer systems and to spread themselves from one computer to another. In much the same way as their biological counterparts, viruses exist to replicate and destroy.

Today, viruses are usually spread through e-mail and Internet downloads. Antivirus software is generally sufficient to combat the threat, but should not be seen as a perfectly adequate safeguard. The following guidelines should be presented to staff and patrons for use when surfing the net and reviewing e-mail.

1. Never open an e-mail attachment unless you know the sender and were expecting an e-mail from that person. If you were not expecting an e-mail, it may be wise to contact the sender via an entirely different message or even via the telephone to confirm the e-mail was actually sent to you before you open any attachments.

2. Use the software made available to your workstation, including your local firewall and antivirus software.

3. Keep all your computers' operating systems up to date with the latest patches.

4. Be careful when visiting unfamiliar Web sites.

VIRUS HISTORY

Viruses have been around for more than 20 years. Here is a quick history.

1986: The first PC virus appears. Known as the Brain virus, it infected the boot record of floppy disks. It was also the first stealth virus, as it would never show itself if you tried to view it on the disk's boot record.

1987: This year saw the rise of the memory file resident virus. This virus ran executable files, and when opened would install itself in resident memory. Lehigh and Jerusalem were two examples of memory file resident viruses.

1988: The media started to pay attention to viruses, which made headlines in several mainstream magazines. The first antivirus program was written to detect and remove the Brain virus. A new type of virus was also introduced: the Cascade virus was the first virus written in encrypted code.

1989: Media reported heavily on the DataCrime virus. The Data Avenger Virus was also introduced. This virus was especially nasty, as it destroyed data over a longer period than previous types; victims did not realize they were infected until it was too late.

1990: The competition for the antivirus market heated up as several new products hit the market. Virus authors nodded to history by blending the characteristics of various long-standing viruses. For example, an encrypted virus written in a fashion that did not allow it to be decrypted.

1992: The Michaelangelo virus was introduced to great alarm. It did not do nearly as much damage as originally feared, and very few infections took place.

1993: The SatanBug virus was written by a child, and infected numerous computers in the Washington, DC, area. Symantec Corporation, a major antivirus vendor, helped the FBI to track down SatanBug's creator.

1995: With the release of Windows 95, it was thought that viruses might be rendered moot. This hope was shattered with the introduction of macro viruses that used productivity applications such as Microsoft Word as their hosts.

1999: The Melissa Virus was introduced and spread by via e-mail attachments.

2000: The "I Love You" virus was introduced; it replicates itself by sending e-mails to everyone in an infected computer's Outlook address book.

It should be pointed out that unlike previous versions of the Macintosh operating system, Apple's OS X is based on a Unix kernel, making it susceptible to many of the virus attacks to which Linux-based computers might be susceptible.

CURRENT TOP VIRUS THREATS

To get an idea of what virus can do to you, here is a listing of the top virus threats in mid-2007 as indicated by Microsoft's Live One Care.

Worm:Win32/Sober.AH@mm

This worm is a mass-mailing virus that will send out massive amounts of e-mail once it is engaged. It does so in both English and German. The virus will also download other files to the infected computer for the purposes of sending out spam. You can find out if you are infected by looking for specific files and folders on your computer's hard drive. Most worms will also make changes to the registry.

Exploit:Win32/Anicmoo.A

This type of software will detect whether a particular vulnerability exists in the Windows Operating System. Anicmmo.A looks to see if the vulnerability exists in the way in which Windows handles animated cursor files. If the vulnerability does exist, a hacker could take control of the infected computer by running some scripts.

Worm:Win32/Nuwar.N@mm!CME711

This worm is also a mass-mailing virus. It carries with it a Trojan horse, a piece of malicious software that hides within a seemingly innocuous object (like an e-mail message). When opened, this Trojan horse will install a peer-to-peer client, which will then download the worm to the infected computer. The worm will then keep itself in memory in order to download updates at a later time.

Win32/Stration

This is a family of viruses, members of which usually disguise themselves as failed delivery messages or as virus-scanning tools. These worms will also attempt to download additional software to an infected computer. These worms are especially dangerous because they will attempt to turn off security programs and disable Windows Update functionality.

W97M/Kukudro.A

This is a Microsoft Word virus. These viruses work by embedding binary code into a Word macro. When the macro is engaged, the binary is loaded into memory. The binary executes and loads additional software from the Internet. Microsoft Word 2003 and subsequent versions will detect the macro and ask permission to run it; older versions of Word will ignore it. Firewalls and antivirus packages are also very good at catching these types of viruses.

Worm:Win32/Bagle.EG@mm

This is yet another mass-e-mailing worm. Most of these worms use the address book assigned to the host's e-mail client to send out batches of e-mails. This particular worm disguises itself as a love message. When opened, the attached zip file will cause additional software to be downloaded. This Trojan horse then listens on a particular port for additional information.

Exploit:Win32/Wordjmp

This virus exploits another vulnerability found in Word, specifically one that exists in Word 2002 and 2003. When exploited, this vulnerability allows full control to an infected computer by uploading scripts. Many different viruses attempt to exploit this vulnerability. Here are known attacks as copied from the Microsoft Web site:

- *TrojanDropper:Win32/Starx.A*

  http://www.microsoft.com/security/encyclopedia/details.
  aspx?Name=TrojanDropper:Win32/Starx.A&view=en-us

> Worms are engaged when an e-mail attachment is opened. The e-mails usually carry a subject line that is generic in nature but specific enough to lure the reader to open the attachment. Some examples include:
>
> - 230 dead as storm batters Europe.
> - A killer at 11, he's free at 21 and kills again!
> - British Muslims Genocide
> - Naked teens attack home director
> - Re: Your text
> - Russian missile shot down USA satellite
> - U.S. Secretary of State Condoleezza Rice has kicked German Chancellor Angela Merkel

- *Backdoor:Win32/Ginwui.A*

  http://www.microsoft.com/security/encyclopedia/details.
  aspx?Name=Backdoor:Win32/Ginwui.A&view=en-us

- *Backdoor:Win32/Ginwui.b*

  http://www.microsoft.com/security/encyclopedia/details.
  aspx?Name=Backdoor:Win32/Ginwui.B&view=en-us

Worm:Win32/Mywife.E@mm

This worm, another mass e-mailer, takes a slightly different approach to disguising itself. First, it uses an icon similar to the zip icon. Second, it adds two extensions to itself to disguise the fact that is an executable file. This virus promises pictures from the *Kama Sutra* and will infect files on the third day of every month. This worm also uses writable network shares to spread itself.

Win32/Sober.Z@mm

As you have probably noticed, many worms consist of e-mail attachments programmed to mail copies of the same virus-laden message to large numbers of recipients. Almost all of them deal with vulnerabilities present in Windows. This virus makes particularly good use of its host's operating system. Once it infects a computer, it will download some additional software and then every two weeks do so again. This gives it a degree of persistence not found in many other viruses, and you have to be very diligent to remove it completely from your computer. Virus writers may not be terribly admirable, but they can be deviously creative. Here are a couple of examples of e-mails that might contain this worm.

From: *<spoofed>*

Subject: hi, ive a new mail address

Message body:

hey its me, my old address dont work at time. i dont know why?!in the last days ive got some mails. i' think thaz your mails but im not sure!

plz read and check …

cyaaaaaaa

Attachment: *<random>*.zip

From: *<spoofed>*

Subject: Your IP was logged

Message body:

Dear Sir/Madam,

we have logged your IP-address on more than 30 illegal
Websites.
Important:
Please answer our questions!
The list of questions are attached.

Yours faithfully,
Steven Allison
*** Federal Bureau of Investigation -FBI-
*** 935 Pennsylvania Avenue, NW, Room 3220
*** Washington, DC 20535
*** phone: (202) 324-3000

Attachment: *<random>*.zip

Win32/Mytob

This virus resembles its mass-mailing cousins described previously, except
for one significant difference: it can spread itself through MSN Messenger
and Windows Messenger.

Win32/Netsky

This family of worms works just like all the other mass mailing bugs, but
they will also launch DoS attacks that will quickly shut down a server or
computer. They also propagate across network shares. An interesting feature
of this worm is that it comes with its own e-mail server.

SPYWARE

Spyware is a type of software that is downloaded to a person's computer
covertly, without the user's consent. The software then performs data-gath-
ering operations on the infected computer, such as tracking Web sites visits
and invoking advertisements in Web browsers. As spyware has evolved, it
has become less an annoyance than a dangerous threat.

Some spyware is installed when you install a legitimate product, such as Real Player. Most spyware, however, is downloaded when visiting a Web site. Here are some ways that you can tell if your library has spyware on its computers.

- You get a lot of pop-up ads (or attempts at pop-ups if you have a pop-up stopper).
- Your browser's default home page has changed, and you cannot change it back to the one of your choosing.
- Your bookmarks change on their own.
- When searching the Internet, a new search engine executes the search for you.
- Unexplained phone calls are made from your computer.
- You lose your ability to control your browser.
- You see ads all the time even when you are not surfing the Net.
- Your computer generally slows down.

SPYWARE HISTORY

The first use of the term "spyware" occurred in 1995 in a usenet group; the term was coined during a criticism of Microsoft's business practices. In 1999, an article appeared promoting a new software firewall. This is the first recorded instance of spyware being used in the context it is today. In the same year, the first explicit spyware product was released as a free, user-friendly game called "Elf Bowling." Spyware has since evolved to meet the growing demand for detailed consumer computing information. Some of the more well-known spyware programs are Xupiter, Gator, XXXDial, DirectRevenue, Euniverse, CoolWebSearch, 180 Solutions, Bonzi Buddy, and Cydoor.

Soon after spyware's widespread appearance, the first antispyware software program was released. OptOut was released by Steve Gibson, followed shortly by Lavasoft's Ad-Aware product. Spyware is now on about 80 to 90 percent of the computers on the Internet, according to a survey performed by AOL and the National Cyber-Security Alliance. Over 90 percent of affected users did not give permission for this software to be installed on their computers, and even more did not even realize that the spyware was present. It has become such a problem that some states are developing legislation banning the use of spyware.

TYPES OF SPYWARE

As with viruses, some spyware is considered more dangerous than others. Here are the top threats in mid-2007, according to pcsecuritynews.com.

CoolWebSearch Spyware

This family of spyware is revised every two to three weeks so that new infections can spread more easily. This spyware is especially tough to get off a computer once it does its business. The symptoms you will face if attacked by this spyware include the spontaneous redirection of your Web browser to sites chosen by CoolWebSearch and placement of pornographic sites in your favorites list, along with the installation of a new toolbar. As with all spyware, your computer will also slow down considerably because of the new actions being carried out.

Autosearch

This type of spyware first came into prominence in 2004 and since then has inspired several copycat efforts. It will install a new toolbar into your browser window, change your homepage, and redirect you to www.tunders.com whenever you mistype a Web address.

BARGAINBUDDY

This spyware can be especially annoying. It monitors what you do on your computer and tracks your Web movement; it does this so it can better serve advertisements to your browser. For example, if you mistype a Web address, this software will recognize this fact, redirect your request to a Web site of its choice and then flood your computer with advertisements.

Claria

Claria was formerly known as Gater. Users are infected with this software when they install an application that has been built by the parent company. The Gator Advertising Information Network consists of a series of software vendors who have paid to join the network. Once the spyware is installed on the victim's computer, it will send a barrage of ads directly to the user through pop-up ads. Before long, the software has eaten up megabytes of your hard drive.

CYDOOR

This software will hijack your browser, redirect your requests, and track your Web-surfing habits. It also puts up more ads than any other spyware. The neat addition to this package, however, is a couple of viruses that take advantage of Windows vulnerabilities.

Spyware is more common in a Windows environment using Internet Explorer than with other OS/browser combinations.

REVIEW QUESTIONS

Use these questions as a guideline to evaluate the knowledge gained from this chapter.

- What is a hacker?
- What is the history of hacking?
- What are some of the hacker techniques used today?
- What would a hacker do to a library's computer network?
- What is a hacker's mind-set?
- What are some wireless network hacks?
- What are some operating system hacks?
- What are some application hacks?
- How do hackers take advantage of Web servers?
- What are viruses?
- What is the history of viruses?
- What are some examples of viruses?
- What is spyware?
- What are some examples of spyware?
- What is the history of spyware?

KEY POINTS AND CONCLUSION

- Knowing what to expect will help the library better prepare to ward off unwanted attention from malicious hackers or accidental damage from overly curious patrons.
- It isn't a matter of *if* a library will be attacked or be affected by virus or hackers, it is a matter of *when* a library will be attacked or be affected by viruses or hackers, and to what extent the damage will be.
- New viruses, Trojan horses, and operating system or software weaknesses are discovered every week. It is a primary cause of the loss of data, loss of network and Internet accessibility, and loss of productivity.

In this chapter, we have introduced the dangers faced regarding library technology. Appendix A lists resources used to track the growing number of threats. In the following chapters, we show you how to protect yourself against the threats introduced in this chapter.

READINGS AND RESOURCES

Gralla, P. 2005. *PC Pest Control.* Sebastopol, CA: O'Reilly Media.

Heaton, Jordana. 2000. "Hacker History." Available: www.slais.ubc.ca/people/students/student-projects/J_Heaton/.

PCWorld.com Staff. "Timeline: A 40-year History of Hacking." Available: archives.cnn.com/2001/TECH/internet/11/19/hack.history.idg/.

Wang, W., and Bullfrog, J. 2004. *Steal This File-sharing Book: What They Won't Tell You About File Sharing.* San Francisco, CA: No Starch Press.

Williams, Robert. 2001. *Computer and Network Security in Small Libraries: A Guide for Planning.* Available: www. tsl.state.tx.us/ld/pubs/compsecurity/index.html. Austin, TX: Texas State Library and Archives Commission.

PLANNING FOR SECURITY IMPLEMENTATION AND AUDITING WEAKNESSES

You now have a good idea of how to perform an inventory of the technology within your library, and of how to write policies that dictate use and protection of this technology. A reliable, complete inventory and a robust set of policies is the first step toward securing your technology. You also have a good overview of the threats facing your library technology. The next step is to begin the process of actively locking down your technology.

This approach assists you in protecting your technology from malware, software viruses, and hackers. The rest of the book discusses in detail how to make this happen by describing the tools and processes necessary. In this chapter we show how to plan security strategy through what we call a security audit. A security audit inspects policies and inventory to reveal vulnerabilities that can be used to compromise technology.

We provide a checklist of questions to answer about your current library technology profile (see Exhibit 6-1). This checklist makes it much easier to determine the steps needed to secure your technology. Because libraries come in different types and sizes, we have outlined a general security audit that works for large, medium, and small sized libraries. The latter part of this chapter shows how to implement the required actions indicated by the security audit. We provide hints on the best ways to carry out this plan of action by reviewing a case study.

Question	Yes or No or N/A
Does the library have disclosure statements for confidential information?	
Does the library have an inventory of all of its critical data as defined by the library administration?	
Are the library servers located in a locked room?	
Are the library servers located in a room with atmospheric controls?	
Is the server room removed from public access?	
Are there no windows in the server room?	
Exhibit 6-1. Library Security Checklist	

Question	Yes or No or N/A
Is there a secondary door in the server room?	
Do the server room doors have business or industry class doorknobs and keysets, with additional protection of a metal plate extending over the gap between the door and doorjamb?	
Do the server room doors open to the outside?	
Does the server room have a key swipe or a security touch pad?	
Does the server room's key have a designated separate key from the master key series?	
Does every member of the library administration team have a key?	
Is a copy of the server room key easily available?	
Is a library policy in place to change the server room locks if a key personnel leaves the library?	
Do separate server administrators exist for: • Managing users for the designated server? • Managing user security/authority levels? • Managing updates and security patches of all installed software? • Supervising/managing hardware repairs or upgrades?	
Are procedures manuals and inventory logs available for: • Backup procedures? • Restore procedures? • Disaster recovery procedures? • Maintaining administrative passwords log? • User maintenance procedures? • Common update/recurring maintenance procedure? • Repairs, both warranty and out of warranty? • Installed software and related licensing?	
Is the administrative passwords log kept on one computer?	

Exhibit 6-1. Library Security Checklist (*Continued*)

Question	Yes or No or N/A
Is a copy of the administrative passwords log kept in a locked drawer in the library director's office?	
Are there regular meetings between the library administration and the server administrators?	
Is there a plan in place to communicate to users and patrons about planned down time?	
Is there a password policy in place?	
Are passwords changed quarterly?	
Do passwords contain both alpha and numeric characters?	
Are the passwords not something easily recognizable such as a pet name, library name, or street library is on?	
Are passwords at least eight characters with one unique special character such as $,@%?	
Do server administrators log off or lock down a server when leaving the room?	
Are screen savers set for 10 to 20 minutes with passwords to access the computer?	
Is there a policy for remote access?	
Is there an encrypted virtual private network in place?	
Are browsers used for remote access cleared of history, cache, and passwords on completion of remote connection to server?	
Do the computers used for remote access have the document and command line history erased on completion of remote connection to server?	
Are passwords stored locally when access to edit Web pages, catalog entries, or related servers?	
Are logs kept for a period of one month to one year?	
Is the circulation and patron data backed up daily?	
Is the entire automation server backed up monthly? Is it backed up after each maintenance task such as patches, etc.?	

Exhibit 6-1. Library Security Checklist (*Continued*)

Question	Yes or No or N/A
Is a copy of the backup kept off location at a secure remote site?	
Are the backups kept for a minimum of two years?	
Is the Web server backed up once a week?	
Do the Web editors have working copies of the Web site on their computers?	
Is the domain controller backed up once a quarter?	
Are users, groups, access policies and related settings, and stored data (such as e-mail or calendar) backed up daily?	
Are backups containing sensitive data encrypted?	
Are backup restores tested annually?	
Are the patches for servers monitored daily?	
Are new patches installed within four days of release?	
Is there at least one backup for the server administration who knows how to perform basic server maintenance?	
Are permissions given out to staff relevant to the job duties of the staff? In other words, staff should receive permission to do only what is necessary for the job.	
Are the patrons allowed to access their own accounts on the automation system?	
Are new employees properly trained in security procedures?	
Are departing employees' security authority and access reduced one week prior to leaving the library?	
Are terminated personnel locked out immediately?	
Is there a staff member assigned to train library staff on the security policy?	
Do staff use computers only to perform their job duties?	
Do staff use their assigned log-in and passwords to access their computers?	

Exhibit 6-1. Library Security Checklist (*Continued*)

Are staff using the computers to compromise the security of the network?	
Are user IDs used to track usage of computers if a security concern is raised?	
Are passwords at least eight characters long and contain a mixture of letters and numbers?	
Are these passwords shared among staff?	
Are staff allowed to change their passwords?	
Are staff allowed to install new software applications on their computers?	
Are screen savers set for 20 minutes and with a password to turn off the screensaver?	
Are library laptops secured with a security chain at all times they are in a docking station?	
Do staff store personal sensitive information on the library's computers?	
Are printers shared with other computers?	
Is a log-in required to change printer settings?	
Is there a computer usage and Internet usage policy for patrons?	
Is there a network policy for staff?	
Are network health tools utilized?	
Is information gleaned from network health tools kept confidential?	
Are network hardware appliances such as router switches protected with a password?	
Does the library employ a firewall?	
Does the library use network address translation for all internal staff computers?	
Are the library wireless networks using wired equivalent privacy for traffic?	
Do the wireless routers exist with their own IP address?	

Exhibit 6-1. Library Security Checklist (*Continued*)

DETERMINING SECURITY NEEDS

SECURITY AUDIT: FINDING SECURITY WEAKNESSES

Joe Smith was the director of information systems for the Anytown Public Library. Joe was also the assistant director and main reference librarian. Joe had recently started a campaign to better secure his library's technological investment by establishing a good inventory of the library's technology and creating a baseline security policy. He was proud of his support staff for being able to compile such a comprehensive list. As he looked over the inventory list, he was displeased to see some software on the public computers that he did not authorize. The strong possibility existed that this software was installed by a hacker using the library's technology infrastructure to perform mischief. He decided it was best to take the next step in his plan: a security audit.

A security audit gauges the strength of one's technology security. Joe knew that he needed to evaluate his security capabilities against a set of criteria. This evaluation would look closely at his physical and network arrangements, software, information processes, and user activities. Since Joe already knew he had an issue with unauthorized software, he decided to begin his audit with tests for any additional software vulnerabilities. He would then focus his efforts on the physical and network arrangements. Since his library was relatively small, he felt he could wait to assess his library's information-handling processes and user activity until later in the security audit.

Like Joe, you can perform a security audit. To help you better understand a security audit, here is a definition from Robert Williams, an IT consultant for libraries.

> A *security audit* is the process of assessing the various components and the operating environment of a computer network for vulnerabilities. The audit may be either casual or formal, superficial or detailed, onsite or conducted entirely over the Internet. An in-house self-audit can be conducted when the library employs technically trained personnel, but this is unusual. These audits work well in a security project where the library is assessing what security measures may need to be implemented. As a final audit, however, a self-audit loses the benefit of an independent, objective view. (Williams, 2001)

As you can see, Williams stresses the need to bring in an outside auditor to gauge technology vulnerabilities. Although this would be nice in a world where libraries were properly funded, the reality is that most libraries simply cannot afford outside help. In this book we provide a baseline plan to find security holes, but it cannot be stressed enough that all security holes will not be found without outside help. If all else fails, bring in a colleague from another library to look over conclusions from the security audit, or if you are lucky enough to have the services of a state or regional entity to provide technical support, bring its expert into the mix to get opinions on conclusions. Of course, if funds are available for an independent security consultant to assist with an audit, we recommend budgeting for one.

SECURITY AUDIT TOOLS AND TECHNIQUES

Security experts use several proven techniques to perform security audits. Although you will not be able to discover every last one of the latest security threats using these tools, because new threats are being developed all the time and the newest ones tend to be known only to the most sophisticated security experts, you can find holes caused by historical threats.

PORT SCANNERS

Port scanners can be used to scan your library's technological infrastructure from a remote location. The purpose of a port scanner is to discover what services are available on your network. All networks will have basic services available to the outside world. Some examples of these services include simple mail transport protocol (SMTP), file transfer protocol (FTP), hypertext transfer protocol (HTTP), and so forth. These protocols use communication paths called ports. On routers, these ports are closed unless opened by users.

Port scanners survey the available ports on a router, or computer, to discover what services are available. If hackers discover a service to compromise, chances are that they found it using a port scanner. To assess your network's vulnerability, try emulating a hacker to see if any vulnerable ports are available. Port scanners can also detect operating systems of computers on the network and even the operating system's version.

NMap

NMap is a free open-source utility used for network exploration and port scanning. NMap will discover the following about your network: hosts available on the network, services these hosts are offering, operating systems, firewalls/packet filters, and so on.

> **SMTP (simple mail transfer protocol)**: The protocol used by most e-mail servers. Many server packages (Microsoft Server 2003 as an example) have the ability to act as an SMTP server; alternately, vendors offer stand-alone software packages supporting SMTP.
>
> **FTP (file transfer protocol)**: This protocol allows servers to host files for uploading and downloading. FTP clients can efficiently manage the upload and download of files without the need for a Web browser.
>
> **HTTP (hypertext transfer protocol)**: This is the protocol of the Internet, the World Wide Web. It is designated to use port 80 of a networked computer, and is the designated and default listening port for all Web servers (unless specifically set otherwise).

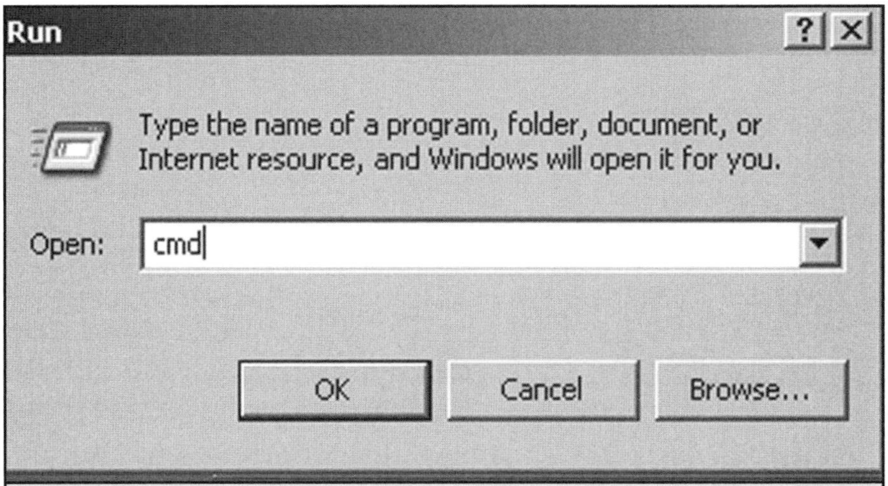

Figure 6-1. Screen Capture of the Window That Allows Use of the Command Prompt

To use NMap for a security audit, first download the open source package from the Web. It can be found at insecure.org. Download the Windows self-extraction file, which will allow easy installation of the software on a computer. You may need to log off of your network and log back in under an account with administrative rights in order to use NMap.

NMap does not have a graphical user interface, so you will need to use the command prompt to launch the program. Open a command prompt by entering Start>Run>type in "cmd" as shown in Figure 6-1.

After this, a DOS command window will appear on your screen, similar to the one in Figure 6-2. Using the command "CD\" to move to the root directory of C:\>, change to the directory in which you stored the NMap files (probably c:\program files\Nmap\) by simply typing in "CD program files\nmap" and hitting "Enter." Then launch NMap by typing in nmap.exe. However, in order to get NMap to target certain computers, you must specify which IP addresses to scan.

The easiest way to do this is to specify a range of IP addresses. For example, if your library's computers are numbered using the reserved internal IP range of 192.168.0.1 to 192.168.0.254, type in "nmap 192.168.0.1-254" at the command prompt. This command will instruct NMap to scan all of your library computers.

You need to add one more argument in order to get the output in a file for easy reading. This is done by adding "–oN libraryoutput.txt" to the end of the command prompt: nmap 192.168.0.1-254 –oN libraryoutput.txt. This command tells NMap to scan the specified range of IP addresses and put the scan results in *libraryoutput.txt* file. It will put the file in the same directory as the nmap files are found.

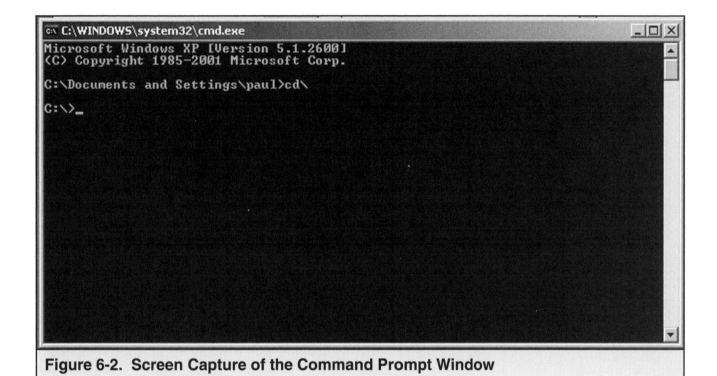

Figure 6-2. Screen Capture of the Command Prompt Window

The following example shows Joe's results:

Interesting ports on 192.168.0.90:

Not shown: 1687 closed ports

PORT STATE SERVICE

21/tcp open ftp

23/tcp open telnet

53/tcp open domain

110/tcp open pop3

113/tcp open auth

139/tcp open netbios-ssn

445/tcp open microsoft-ds

6543/tcp open mythtv

8082/tcp open blackice-alerts

10000/tcp open snet-sensor-mgmt

MAC address: 00:0B:3F:90:0E:AD (Anthology Solutions)

NMap provides this readout for every computer within the IP range specified. It tells Joe what ports are open on each computer and which application is using each port. For the example, ports 21, 23, 53, 110 are basic communication ports used by computers. Port 80 is also a standard port. Ports 113, 139, 445 are used for network communications and may be safely left open. Ports 6543 and 8082 concern Joe as these ports are not usually open ports. Joe will need to do more research to discover more about these ports.

Joe goes to Google first to see what others have put on the Web about the suspicious ports. If Google does not link to the answers, Joe uses sites such as auditmypc.com or Network Ice's Port Knowledgebase to find the port numbers. Using this method, Joe discovers that a library staff member downloaded Black Ice security software illegally and installed it on his computer. Joe also learns that the same staff member has downloaded a program, MythTV, to record television shows to his PC. According to their security policy, this employee is in violation of several rules. Joe goes to his director with his report.

VULNERABILITY SCANNERS

Vulnerability scanners offer automated or manual means of discovering where vulnerabilities lie in your computer network. The main difference between a vulnerability scanner and a port scanner is that a vulnerability scanner will find available services and attempt to exploit them. A port scanner just inventories available services on ports. Vulnerability scanners work from a database of security defects; common configuration errors and unpatched servers are the usual suspects found in vulnerability testing.

Nessus

Nessus is a free vulnerability scanner for download. A fee (as of this writing, $1,200 a year) provides access to all of the updates as they are released. If you decide not to pay the fee, you will get the updates seven days after they are released. You must register to receive the download. Once you download the installation file to your desktop, you can then begin to run scans.

Joe decides to scan his Web server to check for vulnerabilities. His Web server actually existed behind a router configured to send port 80 traffic to the Web server and port 8080 traffic to a calendar server.

To use Nessus, click on Start Scan after starting the program. Next, input the external IP address of the router in which the Web server is connected. On the screen, select the default setting, which scans for vulnerabilities but does not use "dangerous plug-ins" to accomplish the task. Dangerous plug-ins will attack your designated target in a way that could harm your computer. Do not attempt the dangerous scans before performing a safe scan first. The final step is to select the location from which you want to scan. Choose a remote computer or the computer on which you are working, named the localhost.

Joe selects the localhost because he had installed Nessus there. He receives a nicely formatted report from Nessus about his Web server and its vulnerabilities.

> Tenable Nessus Security Report
>
> Start Time: Fri Mar 30 10:41:40 2007
>
> Finish Time: Fri Mar 30 10:56:12 2007
>
> 65.65.127.82
>
> 65.65.127.82
>
> 4 Open Ports, 20 Notes, 2 Warnings, 2 Holes. 65.65.127.82 [Return to top] http-alt (8080/tcp) The "nph-test-cgi" CGI is installed. This CGI has a well known security flaw that lets an attacker get a listing of the /cgi-bin directory, thus discovering which CGIs are installed on the remote host.
>
> Solution: remove it from /cgi-bin.
>
> Risk Factor: High
>
> CVE: CVE-1999-0045
>
> BID: 686
>
> Plugin ID: 10165 Port is open
>
> Plugin ID: 11219 A Web server is running on this port
>
> Plugin ID: 10330 The following directories were discovered:
>
> /public, /shared
>
> While this is not, in and of itself, a bug, you should manually inspect these directories to ensure that they are in compliance with company security standards
>
> Other references: OWASP:OWASP-CM-006
>
> Plugin ID: 11032 The following CGI have been discovered: none

The links in the report take Joe back to the Nessus Web site, where more detailed information is available. Using this tool, Joe discovers important information about his Web server and lays the groundwork for implementing a network security plan. The next section provides details concerning a security implementation plan.

APPLICATION SCANNERS

Application scanners take the idea behind vulnerability scanners one step further and try to exploit weaknesses found in actual Web-based applications. Of course, if your library does not offer any Web-based applications, this step can be skipped. However, if you offer any whatsoever, it is a good idea to proceed with an application scan. The application scanner

> Other vulnerability scanners to consider include Core Impact, QualysGuard, and Internet Scanning.

determines which applications are running and then launches typical attacks against the application. The quality of the scan is only as good as the scanner's database of actions to be taken against a specific application.

Two examples of application scanners are AppScan and WebInspect. Neither is free, so it might be better for a library to use a Web application assessment proxy, which is explained in the next section.

WEB APPLICATION ASSESSMENT PROXY

Another form of application scan, an assessment proxy, creates a version of itself between the Web server and the browser. The proxy will then track all data moving from the Web server to the browser. A comprehensive scan of this data may lead to the discovery of security weaknesses in the Web application.

Paros Proxy

OWASP's WebScarab is another possible tool in this area.

Paros Proxy is freely available on the Internet; a Google search should quickly point you toward the download page. Setup takes only a few seconds.

SECURITY PROCEDURE AUDIT

Chapter 4 introduced a security policy. Establishing such a policy is preferred, but to fully realize the value of any policy, you must ensure that it is being followed in practice by library staff and patrons. Toward this end, we highly recommend that some time be budgeted for running through the following security procedure audit.

Please refer to Chapter 4's policy examples. Your task in conducting a security procedure audit is to ensure that staff are following established policy as closely as possible. This involves meeting with the library staff and asking them a list of questions (see Exhibit 6-1). These questions can be guided by using a checklist built directly from the written policy. From the staff's answers, you should be able to ascertain how closely the library's security is being honored by staff.

Joe reviewed the manual security check and discovered the following regarding his library's security.

No disclosure statements concerning library security

No locked room for the servers

No atmospheric control for the server room

No secondary door in server room

No separate administrators for the various servers (only poor Joe)

No log for administrative passwords

No strong passwords

No policies for remote access

No working copy of Web site on computers

No monitoring of server patches

No training of staff on library security matters

No firewall to protect the network

Overall, Joe was pleased with existing security. However, he had some major security holes to fill, so his next step was to build a plan to remedy the situation.

BUILDING A PLAN TO IMPLEMENT THE AUDIT

The next step is to build a plan to fill the holes revealed by the security audit. The easiest way to do this is to look at each of the weaknesses revealed during the security audit and to prioritize them according to their difficulty and cost. When considering the costs, examine the security risks if the weakness is not addressed. If the risk is considerable, then the relative cost of failing to act is high. Consider creating a chart based on the following categories:

Easy to do/Low cost   Easy to do/High cost

Difficult to do/Low cost   Difficult to do/High cost

The time and effort it will take to address each item on your list will vary widely from library to library. If your library does not employ full-time IT staff, research the task online to get an idea of the cost in time and funds required to do the task.

You can be relatively certain that if you have discovered the task during your security audit, someone else has written about it. Try Google Groups (http://groups.google.com) as a starting point.

Joe prioritized his tasks by using the chart:

Easy to do/Low cost

Fix the security weaknesses discovered by Nessus.

Fix the security weaknesses discovered by NMap.

Create a log of administrative passwords and keep it in a secure place.

> Seek help from state and national organizations for libraries, such as the American Library Association (ALA), by joining a technology-oriented blog for libraries.

Instruct staff to create stronger passwords for their computer workstations.

Create stronger passwords for servers.

Easy to Do/High Cost

Create a disclosure statement for the library security. (high labor required)

Create a policy for remote access. (high labor required)

Create a plan to monitor server patches. (high labor required)

Install locks on the server room.

Install a firewall for the library. (expensive)

Difficult to do/Low cost

Install a working copy of the library Web site on staff computers. (no expertise in this matter)

Provide security training for staff.

Difficult to do/High cost

Install atmospheric control in the server room.

Install a secondary door in security room.

Install security technology in the server room.

Assign servers to staff. (would require hiring more staff?)

Once Joe had prioritized the work needed to shore up his network, his next step was to write a plan for undertaking that work. The resulting task timeline should be reasonable and should include time to communicate with staff about the steps necessary to complete each prioritized section. Early in this process, you may want to gather information toward a report justifying the time and money necessary to address the expensive-but-required tasks on your list. This report should be written while the other less expensive tasks are being completed. Joe's plan follows:

1. Install a firewall in library. (*Note*: This is the biggest security threat for Joe's library, so although the costs are high, Joe makes the right decision to do this first.)
2. Eliminate the security weaknesses discovered by Nessus.
3. Eliminate the security weaknesses discovered by NMap.
4. Create a log of administrative passwords and keep it in a secure place.
5. Instruct staff to create stronger passwords for the computer workstations.

6. Create stronger passwords for servers.

7. Install a working copy of the library Web site on staff computers. (no expertise in this matter)

8. Provide security training for staff.

9. Create a disclosure statement for the library security. (high labor required)

10. Create a policy for remote access. (high labor required)

11. Create a plan to monitor server patches. (high labor required)

12. Install locks on the server room.

Joe determined that the following tasks must be approved by the library director and/or are too expensive for the time being:

1. Install atmospheric control in the server room.

2. Install a secondary door in security room.

3. Install security technology in the server room.

4. Assign servers to staff. (would require hiring more staff?)

REVIEW QUESTIONS

Use these questions as a guideline to evaluate the knowledge gained from this chapter.

- What is a security audit?
- Why is a security audit necessary?
- What are some security audit tools?
- What are some security audit techniques?
- What is the difference between a port scanner and a vulnerability scanner?
- What is an application scanner?
- What is a security policy audit?
- What is a security audit scorecard?
- What questions should be part of a security audit scorecard?
- How does one build a plan from a security audit?
- What is one technique to gauge the needs of a security plan?

KEY POINTS AND CONCLUSION

- To find and implement solutions in securing library technology, an accurate assessment must first be accomplished. This is completed with an audit of existing technology with an eye toward identifying weaknesses.
- With a significant segment of technology connected to the network, a security audit of the network and items connecting to it are required for a comprehensive review of network security prior to creating an implementation plan.
- Once security concerns are identified, evaluate the cost, time required, skill required, and priority of each. A plan will fall into place based on those components that can be implemented in stages, including addressing fiscal and skill issues in future budgets and training or outsourcing.

Some freely available tools were presented that can be utilized to perform a security audit of your library. In addition, you have learned how to create a checklist of security items to look for in your library. With this information, you can begin the task of creating a plan to reduce the security risks and begin implementing the plan based on a working inventory and updated security policy.

READINGS AND RESOURCES

Cranor, L. 2005. *Security and Usability: Designing Secure Systems that People Can Use.* Sebastopol, CA: O'Reilly Media.

Dhanjani, N., and Clarke, J. 2005. *Network Security Tool.* Sebastopol, CA: O'Reilly Media.

McNab, C. 2007. *Network Security Assessment.* Sebastopol, CA: O'Reilly Media.

Williams, Robert L. 2001. *Computer and Network Security in Small Libraries: A Guide for Planning.* Austin, TX: Texas State Library and Archives Commission. Available: www.tsl.state.tx.us/ld/pubs/compsecurity/index.html.

7 IMPLEMENTING POLICIES FOR SECURE PUBLIC TECHNOLOGY

Securing public stations is a challenging task. Public workstation security requires striking a delicate balance between security and access. Locking down public workstations too severely will create frustration for patrons and may ultimately send them elsewhere for their research and information needs. Having workstations open to risk will invite the necessity for daily repair tasks just to keep them operational, which also creates frustration for patrons.

Balancing security and access can be accomplished with some forethought and a bit of effort. In this chapter, we consider the threats posed to library networks through public workstations and discuss ways in which you can ensure the security of your library's technical infrastructure without unduly inconveniencing your patrons.

BACKGROUND FOR A SOUND SECURITY FOUNDATION

Libraries tend to face more threats to public systems than do office computers because of one significant wildcard: patrons. Patrons are the library's lifeblood. Without them, there would be no reason to keep the doors open. However, in regard to public systems, patrons can be a library's biggest liability. Most patrons will not set out to hurt the public systems, but they seldom worry about the library's equipment or security concerns. Instead, they will often make inadvertent security mistakes while using library computers. Many of them will not know that visiting an unknown Web site might be a first step to downloading an unwanted virus or spyware on the computer. Many will not realize that opening an e-mail with a virus through a Web-based e-mail provider will have the same affect on the library's public access computers as it does in their homes.

On the other hand, some patrons will know exactly what they are doing. How many teenagers have tried to change public computer settings to show their preferred desktop or screen saver? How many technology-savvy users have gone into public computers hoping to fix a perceived

115

BIOS (Basic Input/Output System): A computer BIOS is the interface to the motherboard that tells it what hardware is attached immediately to it, i.e., the hard drive, CD-ROM drive, and memory. As it relates to security, it also details the order in which boot devices (hard drive, CD-ROM, USB port) are looked at. Setting it to boot only from the internal hard drive protects both the computer and the network from someone using a bootable CD or USB drive to bypass the computer's operating system to have uncontrolled access to the network. Using the BIOS interface, a password can be set to prevent patrons from modifying those settings.

problem? How many expert users have launched attacks from public computers? Even if you do not have quantifiable answers to these questions, chances are that these or similar events have occurred at one time or another in your library.

Their public-service mission makes libraries somewhat unique in the IT (information technology) world. Because they are in the business of providing generous public access to computer workstations, libraries must consider issues that most IT administrators do not normally encounter when planning and managing their IT infrastructures. Most IT administrators are concerned only about securing the office systems.

LIBRARY SECURITY PROFILE AND CHECKLIST

Checklists can provide invaluable assurance that you have addressed every important element of your library's public workstation security strategy. When developing your checklist, you should consider which parts of your security profile should be represented. See Exhibit 7-1 for an example of a security checklist. Next, we address actions that allow these items to be checked off the list. Finally, we briefly introduce solutions that exist today to help in securing your investment in public access computing.

- Does the library have disclosure statements for confidential information?
- Is a plan in place to alert patrons about scheduled downtime?
- Does the library have a computer usage and Internet usage policy for patrons?
- Are library laptops physically secured with security chains when placed in docking stations?
- Are the library wireless networks using wired equivalent privacy (WEP) protection?
- Does every staff and public workstation have firewall protection?
- Is each public and staff computer up to date on its patches? For all its software?
- Has the library taken measures to protect computer users from phishing and identity theft?
- Have proper measures been taken to secure each public workstation's Internet browser?
- Do the public computer stations have their BIOS (Basic Input/Output System) access password protected?

Exhibit 7-1. Sample Security Checklist

PUBLIC ACCESS COMPUTING POLICIES

USAGE POLICIES

Every library should have a computer usage policy in place for the public. This policy should clearly outline acceptable behavior while using the library's public workstations. Here are some items to consider for inclusion in a usage policy. Not all items in this list deal directly with securing library technology, but all should be considered when writing a computer usage policy.

- Tell patrons what services are being provided to them and why. If computers are provided solely for Internet-based research, then this should be explicitly stated in the policy.

- Tell patrons which policies are not allowed and why. If the library does not allow patrons to chat and use e-mail from public computers, the policy should clearly state this fact. As a bonus, you might explain the reasoning behind the restriction. For example, chatting might invite online predators to the library, and the library does not wish to promote or be held liable for such activity being conducted on its network.

- Tell patrons what credentials are needed to use a computer at your library. For example, many libraries today have reservations systems in place, both automated and manual, that require a library card.

- Provide disclaimers on privacy and accuracy of information found. It is wise to inform patrons that their privacy is not protected when using public computers, and also to warn patrons to not trust unknown Internet sources.

- Define inappropriate material.

- Give patrons time limits for computer use.

- Inform patrons about provided training. If no training is provided, tell them so.

- Tell patrons how they can retain work and data. Most patrons will want to save their work. Tell them what is allowable. Most libraries will not allow outside storage mediums to be used. In today's Web 2.0 world, however, plenty of free storage is available. Tell them about box.net or a similar service that gives away storage space.

- Specify any age restrictions. If you have a different policy in place for youth and teens, make sure to include a section addressing this in the written policy.

- Inform patrons that abuse will not be tolerated and that the library reserves the right to deny access to the computers for any violation discovered. Abuse includes physically harming the computer or attempting to download unwanted software and/or trying to launch a malicious attack from a library computer. Abuse also includes engaging in a restricted activity.

- Insist that patrons respect the privacy of others.

- If laptops may be checked out in your library, inform patrons regarding where the laptop can be taken and used in the library. Make sure laptop users know that they are held to the same computer usage policies as those using the library desktop computers.

- Inform patrons about applicable local, state, and federal laws regarding the usage of the library's computers.

> Use the actual state law language and refer to the code—it has a stronger effect in catching the attention of the user. Links to state sites are provided in Appendix A.

PUBLIC ACCESS SECURITY FOR PATRON LAPTOPS

Many libraries today provide laptops for use by patrons. Libraries often charge a deposit fee as collateral guaranteeing return. Some libraries put security devices on their laptops that will trip their security system if the individual attempts to leave with the laptop.

Technology exists for tracking laptops. This software has various names, but works the same way as LoJack does for automobiles. The software is loaded on the laptop and immediately begins to track its location. The software works silently in the background, and is not intrusive. If a laptop is stolen, a call can be made to a monitoring center to report the theft. As soon as the laptop is plugged into any Internet connect, the monitoring center will receive a message from the laptop revealing its location. The vendor will then work with the local authorities in an attempt to recover the laptop. If the laptop is not recovered, various software vendors have specific guarantees in place. For example, one vendor will give a full refund for the security software. One vendor even gives a $1,000 guarantee if the laptop is not recovered.

> Visit the LoJack for Laptops Web site at www.lojackforlaptops.com for more information. Also available are Inspire Trace (www.inspice.com), PC Phone Home (www.pcphonehome.com), and X-Tool Laptop Tracker (www.xtool.com).

How does it work? How does the software know where the laptop is located? If the computer uses a dial-up modem, the software will report the modem's phone number to the software vendor's monitoring center. This phone number can lead to the thief's address. If the computer uses an Ethernet connection, the IP address can be traced to the Internet service provider (ISP), who can then trace it to the thief's location. Of course, the drawback to this arrangement is that tech-savvy thieves will realize that they don't need to plug it into the Internet before collecting sensitive information off the computer's hard drive and reformatting the drive to erase all traces of the security software. However, the industry claims that it recovers three out of four laptops that are stolen if LoJack-type software is installed.

PHISHING

Phishing is a criminal activity using social networking techniques. Phishers attempt to fraudulently acquire sensitive information, such as usernames, passwords, and credit card details, by masquerading as trustworthy participants in an online communication. Often, this involves sending phony e-mails that may appear to originate from trustworthy sources. Two of the most frequently targeted companies are eBay and PayPal, and online banks are also common targets. Phishing is typically carried out by e-mail or instant messaging, and it often directs users to provide details at a Web site, although phone contact has been used as well. Attempts to deal with the growing number of reported phishing incidents include legislation, user training, and technical measures.

Phishing should be a major concern for patrons using the library's public access computers. Education about phishing techniques is the most direct route to helping your patrons protect themselves. A simple sign near the computers might alert patrons to be wary of any of the following behavior.

LINK MANIPULATION

Link manipulation is the most common form of phishing. A hacker will place a link in an e-mail or on a Web site that leads to a phony Web site where users are encouraged to provide sensitive data. Most of these links will lead to mock-ups of financial institutions or other places where money is exchanged, such as eBay. Some hackers will also attempt to gain information through such tricks as claiming that a user's account has been locked and can be reopened only by providing a Social Security number.

PHONE PHISHING

Some hackers have used the old trick of getting an individual to call a number to reopen a closed account. The number is usually given in an e-mail received by the victim. This is a variation on a trick that is unfortunately tried and true.

WEB SITE FORGERY

These phony Web sites are the mainstay for many of the hackers using phishing as a means to retrieve sensitive information. Many hackers have realized that most individuals will look at the various aspects of a Web site to tell whether the Web site is legitimate. Hackers will embed code into their phony Web sites that will do everything from changing the browser's address bar to using the built-in security features of the browser to make the site seem legitimate. If this is the case, how does one protect library patrons from phishing practices?

When informing patrons about phishing, tell them what to do to avoid being victimized. Here are some general pointers:

1. Never respond to an e-mail that encourages you to answer it to avoid account closure.
2. Never respond to an embedded HTML form within an e-mail. This information would be sent in clear text and could easily be copied.
3. Do not e-mail personal, sensitive information.
4. Always look for the lock on your Web browser—your guarantee that you are using a secure connection—before submitting sensitive information.
5. Double-click on the lock to see the secure socket layer (SSL) certificate. This ensures that the certificate was issued by a trusted source such as Network Solutions.
6. Check your credit card statements regularly to ensure that no unauthorized transactions have taken place.
7. If an offer is too good to be true, it probably is.

SOFTWARE FOR PHISHING PROTECTION

Software exists that will also help with the phishing problem. Here are some examples.

Internet Explorer 7.0

This most popular browser has a built-in phishing filter. A phishing filter is a device the browser uses to detect phishing Web sites. It does this in three ways. First, it checks the Web sites visited with a database Microsoft has compiled. If the Web site is in the database, the filter will let the user know. Second, the phishing filter takes a look at the Web site to see if certain features exist that normally reside on a phishing Web site. Third, it will send addresses to Microsoft of sites you visit to compare it with the company's database. The phishing filter must be turned on under the Tools menu. If you do not want to turn it on, you can always ask Internet Explorer to check a specific Web site by selecting this under the Tools Menu, Phishing Filter.

Firefox 2.0

If you do not like Internet Explorer, you can try loading Firefox on your public access computers. Firefox offers the same level of protection as Internet Explorer regarding phishing. The antiphishing device is turned on by default in Firefox, and will check visited Web sites with a database maintained by the browser. The database is updated regularly, so you should not have any fears about having outdated material. As with Internet Explorer, Web sites may be checked individually to ensure their validity.

Google Toolbar

Google Safe Browsing is a feature within the Google Toolbar. This is an extension that can be used with a browser to help discover fake Web sites. Google Safe Browsing uses an algorithm to determine whether a page is the real deal or a fake. Google has even allowed developers to create their own versions of Google Safe Browsing so they can embed it in other applications outside the toolbar.

Gralicwrap

This is an open source product that can help with protection from phishing. It works in the same manner as the Web browsers mentioned previously in that it checks a Web site against a database to see if it is fraudulent. The makers of Gralicwrap have an interesting list of companies that have been victimized by hackers. PayPal and eBay account for more than 50 percent of the Web sites spoofed.

PROTECTING PATRON PRIVACY WITH LIBRARY TECHNOLOGY

One aspect of providing, and securing, public access computers is protecting patron privacy. Patrons need to be assured that what they view and do on a public access computer is kept confidential. This is necessary because multiple patrons use the same computers. Unless you create log-ins for each patron or reboot the computer to get back to a fresh state if you have a program like Deep Freeze (Deep Freeze is explained in detail in a separate section), you will never be able to fully protect patron privacy. Since both of these solutions are impractical, there are actions you can take with computer files and features to help alleviate some of the privacy gaps.

INTERNET TEMPORARY FILES

When individuals browse the Web, they will create temporary browser files to track the contents of Web sites, also known as the cache. Browsers store this information so they do not have to reload each Web site every time it is visited. Let's call it the browser's memory. Storage space for these temporary files can be limited to one to two megabytes. In this way, long-term history will be erased while enough short-term memory is retained to make browsing more effective.

BROWSER HISTORY

The browser also records every stop you make when browsing the Internet. This is called the browser history. Most patrons will not miss this aspect of their computing experience, so we recommend that this browser feature be turned off.

COOKIES

These infamous files store content. Specifically, cookies store a user's preferences, advertisements embedded in visited Web sites, and other information gathered while browsing. Many Web sites today will use cookies to help customize the browsing experience. It is not a good idea to turn off cookies, as this would make many sites inoperable and not very useful to your patrons. If some patrons are concerned about cookies, they can be turned off and then back on relatively easily. In Internet Explorer, select Internet Options under Tools. Select Privacy at the top. Click on the Advanced button. You can then override your automatic browser cookie settings to the degree the patron requires.

FORM MEMORY

This is a great feature if you hate filling out forms over and over again. However, public access computers should not have this feature enabled. It is the one sure-fire way of violating a patron's privacy because it tracks everything someone does on a Web site form. For example, if someone needs to enter a Social Security number into a form, the Social Security number would be retained for the form field if the form memory feature is turned on. Do everyone a favor, turn this off!

Some software is available to assist with protecting patron privacy. We discuss Deep Freeze in the next section. However, here are some additional options you might want to check out when addressing patron privacy: IClean, Windows Washer, and Internet Privacy Pro.

PUBLIC ACCESS SECURITY SOLUTIONS

Raise your hand if you ever had to do any of the following:

- Clean up a computer desktop after a patron decided to change the wallpaper and screen saver to something inappropriate
- Call a computer technician to come out to work on a computer after a patron accidentally downloaded a virus that made the computer inoperable
- Uninstall a piece of software that froze an older computer and was downloaded by a patron
- Change the monitor settings back to their original state
- Constantly monitor what your teens are doing on the Internet

These are the issues faced by all libraries that provide public access computing to their patrons. Luckily for all of us, some very smart individuals have developed solutions to help us with these inherent issues with providing computers to our communities. Most of the solutions have a cost involved, but one solution comes at no cost to your library: Microsoft's Windows SteadyState.

MICROSOFT WINDOWS STEADYSTATE

SteadyState has several great features that make it much easier to lock down public access computers. The following sections offer a brief overview.

Easy Management of Multiple Users

SteadyState makes managing user accounts much simpler. Since public access computers are shared by multiple users and creating and maintaining separate accounts for each user is untenable and unwise, SteadyState allows you to create a few accounts for many. For example, you can have an adult account and a children account. Each account will have different restrictions and different features active.

SteadyState allows managing these users from a central console. A helpful feature of SteadyState is that users can save profiles to another medium, such as a flash drive, that will persist from session to session. In other words, users can create their own profiles that they can use multiple times.

Locked Down Computers

The ability to restrict profiles to certain programs and features is a very powerful way to secure public access computing. You can get very granular with the restrictions placed on an account from the SteadyState central console. For example, you can place restrictions on Internet usage, the start menu, drives, and programs. You can turn off the shut down, restart, log off, and command windows from the start menu. With drive restrictions, you can deny users from seeing anything but the A drive. The C drive can be hidden so patrons are not tempted to change it and store files on it. Certain programs can be blocked from running if you do not want the patrons to access them.

Disk and System Protection

SteadyState can be downloaded by typing the keywords "steady state Microsoft" into a favorite search engine and selecting the link starting with a "www.microsoft.com." The actual addresses of Microsoft product downloads change quite regularly, so providing a link here would not be valid for very long.

SteadyState has a feature built in that every library should utilize for its public access computers. We want to create a uniform experience for our patrons when they use our computers. We also want to protect our investment by preventing damaging items from being loaded on public computers. SteadyState can return a computer to its original state after each reboot. In this way, a well-meaning patron can adjust a computer's settings, and it will always return to its pristine state.

How does it work? SteadyState will keep a cache of system settings stored on the hard drive. The stored information includes histories, saved files, and logs. SteadyState will keep track of all of the changes made to the computer and then restore the computer to the original state after reboot, referring to its logs to know what to turn off or change back. A library network administrator can actually configure SteadyState to revert to original state at different intervals. This way, if a person does need to retain the changes to the computer after reboot, it can be done.

In the next section, we will discuss a fee-based product, Faronics Deep Freeze, that provides this same functionality and more for public access computers. Deep Freeze is a more robust product that provides more granular control over use of disk and system protection. However, for its cost (none), SteadyState is good at what it does.

In order to use SteadyState, you will need to have a license to Windows XP. Otherwise, it costs nothing other than your time to install it.

Deep Freeze can be downloaded at www.faronics.com as a trial software for you to test out.

DEEP FREEZE

Deep Freeze is a widely used commercial product that provides the same functionality as the disk and network protection component of

Windows SteadyState. Following are some of the highlights of this product and how it differs from Windows SteadyState. This is not an endorsement for the Deep Freeze product, but this product exemplifies a fee-based product's functionality. It is highlighted only for reasons of comparison.

In our opinion, the only reason to purchase a product like Deep Freeze is the ease of maintenance that the Enterprise edition brings to the table as well as the support received with a fee-based product. Deep Freeze Standard is very similar to Windows SteadyState.

Whatever can be done with Windows SteadyState can be done with Deep Freeze Standard. In most cases, Deep Freeze provides stronger support than does Windows SteadyState, but otherwise, we believe that the two products are comparable.

The real jewel is Deep Freeze Enterprise edition. This product makes administering and maintaining public access computers quite easy, and it adds a level of security not realized with less robust products. You can encrypt all of the Deep Freeze components on the network. You can set multiple passwords to be used with each Deep Freeze console. You can create temporary passwords and even disable mouse and keyboard functions from a central console.

Deep Freeze's most powerful feature is the ability to reboot individual computers from a central console. In fact, you can set up a schedule to restart computers and even have them restart automatically if the computer is inactive for a certain time. You can also set the computer to restart whenever a user logs off.

You will not have to worry about Windows Updates not taking place with Deep Freeze. The enterprise edition allows you to schedule times for Deep Freeze to shut off so that operating system updates can take place without interruption and without inconveniencing patrons.

Deep Freeze provides other built-in capabilities not available in other products. For example, you can allocate a certain amount of hard drive space that will allow modification despite Deep Freeze's protection. This allows an individual to add new materials to a hard drive without shutting down the Deep Freeze product first. If you are worried about people gaining access to Deep Freeze, you can configure the software to hide itself from detection. You would then have the only access to the product as you are the only one who knows it exists on the system.

If you use another network management suite, you can integrate Deep Freeze into the suite as a component. With the Wake-on-the-LAN (local area network) function, you can have computers turn themselves on as soon as activity is detected on the network. Deep Freeze works with Active Directory and allows you to create groups and subgroups of workstations; this way, you have to configure the software only once, and then push out the configuration to your network's computers.

Finally, you can send messages to individual workstations. This is useful when you want to let the network know of upcoming network maintenance and planned outages.

THIN CLIENTS

For securing your public access computers, thin clients—networked computers without hard drives or native operating systems—give you another option. Thin clients offer implicitly the security control you get on a desktop only after implementing a software package like Windows SteadyState. Following is a breakdown on the basics of thin clients.

Central Storage

In a thin client network, everything is stored centrally on the server, both data and applications. The thin client is essentially an empty shell that relies on the server for its processing and data.

Central Processing

Since all data and applications are stored centrally at the server, the server is the workhorse of this arrangement. Most thin clients do not even possess enough firepower to turn themselves on. However, some implementations of the network architecture allow thin clients to have some small amount of native processing power.

Printers and USB Devices

Thin clients do typically have some of the standard ports of a traditional desktop computer, such as USB (Universal Serial Bus) ports. This allows them to support items such as floppy drives, CD-ROM drives, and flash drives. Printers must be networked or attached directly to the server.

What are the benefits to having a thin client architecture in your library? First, it is much easier to manage and allows the preservation of disk and network partitions. Patrons will no longer be able to change the computer settings because there are none for them to change; this makes it a significantly more secure environment.

You can also easily update public access computers because you need to update only the central server's operating system. Finally, some believe thin clients ease some of the funding pains with sustaining technology. The total cost of ownership drops because you do not have to replace desktops regularly or purchase licenses for multiple copies of native software. You can also use outdated equipment in a thin client implementation.

REVIEW QUESTIONS

Use these questions as a guideline to evaluate the knowledge gained from this chapter.

- Why is security important for public access technology?
- What threats exist for public access technology?
- What questions must be answered about public access technology security?
- What should be included in a usage policy for public access technology?
- What security measures should be taken with public access laptops?
- What is phishing? Why is it dangerous for patrons?
- How does a library protect patron privacy?
- What options exist for public access computing security?
- What is Microsoft's Windows SteadyState?
- What is Deep Freeze and how does it work?
- What are thin clients?
- Why are thin clients a good choice for libraries?

KEY POINTS AND CONCLUSION

- Before securing public technology, administrative concerns should be addressed that include usage policies, privacy issues, and legal issues such as liability of the library.
- Educating patrons about security concerns that extend beyond the control of the library, about the policies and appropriate usage of technology, and how they can protect themselves is an important part of public technology security.
- Installing hardware, software, or other controls on public technology should be thoroughly tested before full implementation or rollout to prevent patron frustration, additional work, and wasted energy.
- Hardware options other than personal computer stations are available that reduce overhead of technical support

and long-term maintenance costs, but each library should consider its long-term goals and existing budget before purchasing such technology.

After reading this chapter, you should have a better idea of how to begin to secure your public access computers. We have shown you what you need to consider when securing public access computers, and we have introduced some of the ways to do this. Whether using an open source product such as Windows SteadyState or a fee-based product such as Deep Freeze, you should feel assured that solutions are available to assist you in protecting your investments.

READINGS AND RESOURCES

Allen, R., and Hunter, L. E. 2006. *Active Directory Cookbook.* Sebastopol, CA: O'Reilly Media.

Allen, R., and Lowe-Norris, A. G. 2006. *Active Directory.* Sebastopol, CA: O'Reilly Media.

Carter, G. 2003. *LDAP System Administration.* Sebastopol, CA: O'Reilly Media.

Culp, Brian. 2007. *Windows Vista Administration: The Definitive Guide.* Sebastopol, CA: O'Reilly Media.

Frisch, A. 2002. *Essential System Administration.* Sebastopol, CA: O'Reilly Media.

Wang, W. 2006. *Steal This Computer Book 4.0: What They Won't Tell You about the Internet.* San Francisco, CA: No Starch Press.

DEVELOPING SECURITY FOR LIBRARY OFFICE TECHNOLOGY

Chapter 7 introduced the first step in securing library technology by explaining how to secure a library's public computer stations.

In this chapter, we discuss how to best secure office technology. Office technology refers to all library technology that is used primarily by staff. It might seem to make sense to secure public technology and staff technology in the same fashion, and some libraries do indeed take that approach. However, we suggest that each sector of technology be approached in a different way, with tools tailored to each.

Greater pains must be taken to secure public technology because of the multitude of threats that can be introduced by library patrons. A wider variety of individuals will be using public technology, which means a greater chance for malicious factors to be introduced, whether intentionally or not. In the broad view, you will add a significant baseline of security precautions to both your staff and public computers, and then add a little more to your public computers.

To avoid downplaying the importance of securing library office systems, we devote an entire chapter to this effort. In this chapter, we begin with a general overview of our approach to office system security (see Exhibit 8-1). We next introduce some best practices for securing computers against the threats outlined in Chapters 4 and 5. We highly recommend that staff be trained in these best practices and be accountable for their implementation. We then introduce several solutions that you can use against previously outlined threats.

SECURING STAFF COMPUTERS: BEST PRACTICES

PROVIDE SECURITY TRAINING FOR STAFF

We touched briefly on staff training in Chapter 2. In this section, we expand on this information and review some best practices for training staff to use computer security practices.

Library staff need to know what to do to protect themselves (and the library) from hackers, viruses, and other threats. It should be an integral

Here are the issues from various checklists that are addressed in this chapter.

- Is the domain controller backed up once a quarter?
- Are users, groups, access policies and related settings, and stored data (such as e-mail or calendar) backed up daily?
- Do staff use computers only to perform their job duties?
- Do staff use their assigned log-in and passwords to access their computers?
- Are staff using the computers to compromise the security of the network?
- Are user IDs used to track usage of computers if a security concern is raised?
- Are passwords at least eight characters long and contain a mixture of letters and numbers?
- Are these passwords shared among staff?
- Are staff allowed to change their passwords?
- Are staff allowed to install new software applications on their computers?
- Are screen savers set for 20 minutes and with a password to turn off the screen saver?
- Are library laptops secured with a security chain at all times it is in a docking station?
- Do staff store personal sensitive information on the library's computers?
- Are printers shared with other computers?
- Is a log-in required to change printer settings?
- Does every staff workstation have antivirus protection?
- Does every staff and public workstation have antispyware protection?
- Does every staff and public workstation have firewall protection?
- Is each public and staff computer up to date on its patches? For all its software?
- Has the library taken measures to protect computer users from phishing and identity theft?
- Have proper measures been taken to secure the various Internet browsers?
- Has spam control software been installed on each staff workstation?

Exhibit 8-1. Security Checklist for Library Office Technology

part of their everyday routines to help ensure the security of the library technological infrastructure. The following ideas will help you to accomplish this task:

- Always explain why staff need to do something as well as what they need to do. Most people like to feel empowered by being educated on a topic, and empowered individuals are more inclined to follow training. If you simply tell staff members that their passwords need to be 8 to 12 characters with at least one number, they may consider this to be a minor imposition. If you explain to them that a password at this length and makeup is important to keep hackers from accessing their desktop, they are more likely to see it as a security precaution—one that they are being trusted to take themselves.

- If possible, present the training in a classroom setting and give incentives to people who attend. It is a simple, unavoidable fact that people generally find computer security training to be dull. At the beginning of each training session, inform the class that you'll give them an incentive if they pass a short quiz at the end of the session. It does not have to be anything elaborate—cookies are nice—but it will give people a reason to pay attention.

- One-on-one training is important to library settings that do not have formal employee orientation. During these training sessions, make sure to take numerous breaks. It might be advisable to spread the training out over time to avoid overloading the staff member.

- Tell colleagues only what they need to know. When it comes to computer security, what one does not know cannot accidentally be revealed to someone else. Remember, hackers love to use social networking to gain inside knowledge of an organization. Strange as it may seem when speaking of librarians, ignorance is a blessing in this case.

MONITOR COMPUTER ABUSE BY LIBRARY STAFF

Numerous studies that show a significant percent of the workforce will use the Internet at work for their own personal use. Beyond the loss of productivity by the working world, this behavior is a major security concern for IT professionals.

Spyware, viruses, hackers, and phishers all use the Internet as one of their main delivery vehicles. Staff should be educated on the dangers of spyware, viruses, and hackers when they are just surfing the net for the sake of surfing. To reduce the risks a computer security policy should include a statement that library computers should be used only for work. Enforcement of policies by the administration is paramount in preventing these problems.

If abuse does become a problem due to staff having difficulty complying with policies, in addition to administrative action on abusers, the library has the option of implementing user profiles on the network to limit the usage of office computers to assigned duties. For example, the cataloging computer should have software on it that will allow only the library cataloging to be accessed and worked with. In the same way, office productivity workstations should possess only the office software needed to get the

Several software packages exist for this purpose. Web-Watcher (www.webwatcherkids. com) is one such product. WebWatcher is unique because it allows the employer to view the employee's computer usage through a Web browser. The employer can quickly monitor computer usage for an employee by logging into the person's computer via the Internet. Most of this software requires that the employer be present in front of the employee's computer to view the logs of computer activity. Some other titles in this area include eBlaster (www.eblaster. com), Spector Pro (www. spectorsoft.com), and Spy Agent (www.spytech-web.com).

office tasks completed. The step is a bit extreme, but might be necessary with staff who do not understand the importance of security or who refuse to comply with policy.

PROVIDE EMPLOYEE COMPLIANCE CHECKS

As important as it undoubtedly is to respect peoples' personal privacy, employers have legally recognized interests in ensuring that employees make valid use of organizational resources while on the job. Compliance with policies on staff workstation usage must be checked, if only to confirm that appropriate use is being made of library resources.

Library networks should be set up to allow auditing of staff log-in attempts. In this way, IT staff can know when a particular user was on a computer and, if a security hack is made, a virus downloaded, or unauthorized network traffic initiated, network administrators will have a better idea as to who might be the culprit.

On a more aggressive note, software is available that can monitor an employee's computer usage. It can track what sites a library staff person visits while using the library computer and can take screenshots of a person's computer, providing visual proof of an employee's computer usage. Most of these types of software will also track e-mail, instant messaging, and chatting. Some of this software will also include a key logger, which is a software program that records all keyboard impressions.

We do not necessarily recommend that every employee be monitored in this way, especially if the staff is large. However, if security issues do arise and you suspect a library staff member is suspected, a program such as WebWatcher can help to verify or obviate suspicions.

CHOOSE SECURE PASSWORDS

How does one keep up with the passwords? Most security experts will agree today that writing them down is perfectly acceptable. In the past, writing down passwords was considered a security hazard. However, as most people quickly forget long unfamiliar characters, the effort it takes to maintain passwords for staff soon outweighed any security risk the practice might have invited.

Hackers love the fact that most people are complacent when choosing passwords. Most people will pick a personally significant name, date, or number for their passwords. This practice lends itself to easy memorization, but it is a bad idea when it comes to securing library technology.

When providing security training for staff, make sure to include a section on passwords. Explain why it is so important to have a highly secure password. A secure password will have a mixture of alphanumeric characters and will include one capitalized character. It should always be 8 to 12 characters long.

Caution staff to never share their passwords with one another. Sharing passwords puts liability in the hands of the sharer should someone using the password make illegitimate use of networked resources. Second, it becomes difficult for IT to audit network log-ins because several people may be using one user ID and password.

Finally, make it a priority to have staff change their passwords on a regular basis, at least once a year. In this way, a stolen password will not work after a certain time.

EMPHASIZE SAFE INTERNET BROWSING HABITS

Safe browsing habits should be highlighted in your policy and emphasized to the library staff. Here are some tidbits to pass to the staff about browsing the Internet.

Stay away from Web sites that look suspicious. If it feels wrong, it probably is wrong. Look for contact information on the Web site. If the Web site does not provide contact information, or if the information provided seems out of place, leave the Web site and do not go back. Also, do not provide personal information at any time unless you are sure that the Web site is legitimate. Use all of the safety features available through the Web browser. Most Web browsers provide an adequate suite of built-in safety features.

Type in Web addresses only in the browser address bar. If you get a link through an e-mail, do not click on it. Phishers embed these links in innocent-looking e-mails in the hope of getting personal information from you.

BACK UP DATA

The best defense against computer threats is strong offense. Take steps to prevent attack against technological infrastructure. However, even with all of the protection in place, a disaster could still occur. You must have a strong recovery plan in place to restore lost data and services.

In the case of office computers, this disaster recovery plan begins with regular staff training on backing up their workstations. Of course, you can make networkwide backups with a network storage device. You can even, if funds allow, have a storage area network in place that will back up all data in your infrastructure. However, most libraries do not have the budget for this solution, so it is very important for staff members to back up their critical data. Data backup can be achieved in several ways.

Roaming Profiles

Most networks will give users the ability to create profiles. For example, in a Microsoft Windows environment, the network administrator can set up an account for each staff member. This account can include a profile that will contain the user's various files. In most cases, this would be the My Documents directory. The files contained in these profiles are copied to the server every time the user logs off the network.

The network administrator can then back up each profile to another device such as an external hard drive.

External and Network Hard Drives for Archival Purposes

The library can purchase an external hard drive for each staff workstation, which can then be used for archival purposes. A network drive can also be used by the library. These drives reside on the network, and staff members will see them as additional lettered drives, just as if they were connected directly to their workstations. Staff can be trained to back up their vital data directly to the network drive.

Flash Drives for Mobile Storage

With floppy drives on the way out, flash drives have become popular choices for mobile storage. These compact devices can hold gigabytes of data. Each staff member could be given a flash drive and instructed to back up important files daily.

No matter which storage medium is used, it is also a good idea to have a plan in place to quickly restore lost data. A written policy should be created to instruct staff on what to do in the case data is lost or destroyed. All of this should then be conveyed to the staff in the computer security training orientation program.

KEEP THE COMPUTER UP TO DATE WITH PATCHES

> If for some reason you prefer not to use automatic patching mechanisms, at a minimum show staff how to patch their workstations manually through Internet Explorer. It is important to use the Microsoft Update versus the Windows Update because the Microsoft update will catch patches for all Microsoft products on the PC while Windows captures only the ones for the operating system.

The final component of your training module for staff on computer security should be a discussion of keeping computers up to date with patches. If Microsoft Windows is used, we highly recommend that you enable automatic updates and instruct the staff to never disable them. In addition, you should tell the staff to always allow for rebooting after the automatic installation of patches, which occurs when the automatic updates are turned on. Delay in restarting the computer could prevent possible security vulnerabilities from being patched, which means a higher chance of a breach in library security.

Emphasize that all software on computer systems should be patched on a regular basis, as most software companies will release periodical patches throughout the year. Whenever a staff member installs a patch for a software program, he or she should check to see if the patch will cause additional programs to fail. Carnegie Mellon's Computer Emergency Response Team (CERT, 2002) offers the following advice about patching computer software:

> Imagine then that you've either found a patch on the vendor's site or you've received notice that a patch is available.

What do you do next? Follow the steps below to evaluate a patch before you install it:

1. The **<u>Affected</u>** test: Does this patch affect one of the programs on your computer? If it doesn't affect your computer, you're done. Whew!

2. The **<u>Break</u>** test: Can you tell from the vendor's Web site or the patch's description if installing it breaks something else that you care about? If installation does break something, then you have to decide how to proceed. Try notifying the vendor of the program that might break to learn what its strategy is for addressing this problem. Also, use your Web browser to learn if anyone else has experienced this problem and what he or she did about it.

3. The **<u>Undo</u>** test: Can you undo the patch? That is, can you restore your computer to the way it was before you installed the patch? Currently, vendors are building most patches with an uninstall feature that enables you to remove a patch that has unwanted consequences. In addition, some computers also come with features that help you restore them to a previously known and working state should there be a problem. You need to know what your computer provides so that you can undo a patch if necessary.

Finally, always check to see if other patches become available after installing a patch. In other words, if you install a Windows patch, this might cause another vulnerability to appear, thus requiring a check for more patches as a result of the installation of the first patch.

ANTIVIRUS SOLUTIONS

Several antivirus solutions are on the market today. Each one has its strengths and benefits. Our list here does not constitute endorsement; it simply lists a series of popular applications. Whichever antivirus solution you select should enable certain features to ensure its effectiveness.

BEST PRACTICES

Schedule a Regular Scan

Always schedule at least one scan a week to determine if any viruses have infected the computer. These scans should be full in nature—not the "quick scans" offered by some products—and should scan the root directories as well as three levels deep into each computer's file system. Have the software scan your memory, register, and common infection points. It is a good idea to have the software back up files before they are removed. Make sure that the scan will eliminate the threat, and if elimination does not work, quarantine the threat for review. Finally, always have the software inform you of the threats it discovers in its scan.

Have Auto-protect Features in Place

Most antivirus software will scan new files as they are introduced to the computer. Make sure this protection is in place for all for file types on all types of media: floppy disks, flash drives, etc. If possible, it is also smart to configure the software to turn itself back on if disabled. In this way, if you turn it off for some reason and forget to turn it back on, you can still be protected.

Turn on E-mail Protection

Most antivirus software will also scan e-mail. Make sure to scan all attachments, including zip files. This is especially important today when many viruses spread through e-mails. As with the scheduled scan, go three levels deep (this is important for zip archives, which might contain multiple levels).

Instruct the software, if capable, to scan outgoing e-mail messages, as many worms today are designed to send mass mailings. If the e-mails sent match a particular description, the antivirus software can catch the culprit and warn about its actions.

Antivirus software relies on a database of virus definitions, which must be updated on a regular basis. The majority of the available software will have an automatic update mechanism in place so you do not have to worry about doing it manually. Be forewarned, however, that slower Internet connections will experience major performance issues with automatic update software as it will eat up the bandwidth in its effort to download the latest database definitions.

Use Tamper Protection (if available)

Tamper protection means that the antivirus software will monitor processes and internal objects for specific behaviors. If the antivirus software discovers unexpected behavior, it will let you know and ask what to do about it.

Some antivirus software functions will slightly hinder the performance of a computer, and some antivirus programs are more intrusive than others. It is important, then, to make sure that your computer meets the minimum specifications of the antivirus software.

Finally, if the budget will allow, always get the server-based implementations. The maintenance is much easier if done from a centralized server rather than going to each workstation.

ANTIVIRUS SOFTWARE

The following are some possibilities for antivirus software, obtained from *PC World* reviews.

BitDefender

This software package received highest marks from *PC World*. Its biggest plus was its ability to detect malware, while its slow scan speed was its biggest drawback. It was able to detect a larger number of pests than other comparable software. It costs around $40 a license for the individual PC versions. An enterprise version is available that will allow you to manage the software from a centralized location.

Symantec Antivirus

This is our preferred choice as it has always performed quite nicely in our libraries. *PC World* likes its robust features and ease of use. This program has some features not found in the other software packages, such as scanning instant messaging traffic, protecting computers against browser hijacks, and preventing the installation of key loggers. *PC World* is very down on the technical support: cost and quality. It comes in both stand-alone and enterprise edition.

MacAfee Antivirus

PC World ranked MacAfee's product as the second best behind BitDefender. It is reasonable in cost, around $40, but does a good job at all of the required functions for an antivirus package. Phone support is also expensive for this vendor, costing $3.00 a minute. MacAfee offers a wide variety of packages—everything from stand-alone software to centrally managed solutions. If the library chooses with this product, make sure to evaluate each solution closely.

AVG

AVG is an open source solution that comes at no cost to users. However, be forewarned that you get what you pay for. AVG does not have all of the functions of the fee-based solutions and it does only an adequate job of detecting threats, according to *PC World*. It can also be very slow. The upshot is the cost—nothing—so if the library does not have a budget for a more robust solution, then at least provide this level of security to office computers.

Alwil

Alwil is another open source solution. Like AVG, it has questionable performance and reliability according to *PC World*. What sets Alwil apart is its slick interface which is similar to Windows Media Player.

AntiVir

PC World ranks AntiVir as the best open source solution. As with its other free counterparts, it lacks in functions, such as the ability to quarantine virus and scan incoming e-mails. However, it does an adequate job of detecting threats.

All of the open source products come with absolutely no support other than the communities that build and enhance the products. The level of support will depend on the activity level of the community.

ANTISPYWARE SOLUTIONS

As with antivirus solutions, there exist applications devoted to protecting against spyware. Some antivirus programs include antispyware functionality. Dedicated antispyware programs, though, seem to work best, and they should be used in conjunction with antivirus solutions. In fact, it is not a bad idea to use multiple solutions to battle spyware, as no single product will catch everything.

Antispyware programs today will scan the hard drive, Windows registry, and your computer's memory. Have the software scan all of these items on the computer, because spyware can reside on any of them. Also look for a software program that will perform real-time monitoring, which scans URLs and cookies for any suspicious threats, and for one that allows scheduling of scans. As with antivirus packages, update the software's database regularly.

It is difficult to measure the effectiveness of antispyware applications, and benchmarks, base-level expectations for a software package, are hard to come by. However, if after reading reviews and testing the software you do not feel confident that the software will be able to detect at least 50 percent of the possible spyware, then look elsewhere for a solution.

The next criterion to apply when considering antispyware software is how the spyware is removed once it is detected. The application should at the bare minimum erase corrupted registry settings, stop unwanted processes, and delete all offending files.

Antispyware software should also quarantine spyware before deleting it. It should also have built-in recovery systems. Some desktop applications actually check to see if its bundled software is still on the system before it opens. If the software does not find its spyware, it will shut down. If the application is vital, then you will want the ability to get the spyware back (this was actually difficult to write) so the need to quarantine and recover the spyware is important. Not to mention, some antispyware packages make mistakes and attempt to delete perfectly legit software.

If spyware infections have become chronic at your library, find an antispyware package that features the ability to keep a white list, which is a listing of acceptable spyware while summarily deleting the rest. In this way, the software does not continually ask to delete the wanted spyware.

BEST PRACTICES

Instruct the staff to adopt some of the following preventive measures that will reduce the amount of spyware that ends up on the library's computer in the first place.

1. Add known spyware purveyors to your banned URL list in Internet Explorer.
2. Block all Active X controls from running without permission.
3. Reconfigure the Internet Explorer security settings to prevent spyware from running in the first place.
4. Be aware of unfamiliar Web sites.
5. Try a more secure Web browser than Internet Explorer, such as Firefox.

ANTISPYWARE SOFTWARE

Here are some possible antispyware solutions for you to try at your library.

Lava Ad-Aware

This free software does an excellent job of discovering and cleaning up a computer's spyware invasion. However, it lacks any real-time monitoring that is available for free in other products as well as the ability to test rootkits. In the *PC World* tests, it scored very high in detecting inactive spyware samples, which points to a strong signature database. If your library cannot afford to purchase spyware, this is a good product to provide some protection against spyware.

PrevX 2.0

PrevX 2.0 is a relatively new to the antispyware software scene, but it has made a huge impact already. It determines threats and eliminates them like all the other competitors on the market; however, it does include a real-time monitoring component that checks the status of each program starting up on the computer and checks it against its database. If the programming starting up does not compute, then it will flag it and ask the user if it wants it to allow the program to continue.

Since most spyware will install and start itself on a computer with the user's knowledge, this type of software is a big boon to eliminating the threat. Of course, it does have its issues. It can be time-consuming and intrusive in its work. It can also eat a lot of computer resources while it downloads updates to itself. If your library has older computers, it might be a good idea to go with software such as Microsoft Windows Defender that does not have the potential to freeze the computer.

Spybot: Search and Destroy

One of the first antispyware products on the market, Spybot: Search and Destroy has always performed solidly for a price everyone can afford: $0.00. It has a rich interface with a multitude of options that allows a more granular control over the whole detection and removal process. According to *PC World*, it detects a lesser number of spyware threats than other products and offers no real defense against rootkits. It also does not provide any real-time protection.

Microsoft Windows Defender

Windows Defender is the antispyware package that comes embedded in the new Microsoft operating system Microsoft Vista. It does an adequate job of detecting spyware and you can download it at no cost. It has real-time monitoring of spyware so that threats may be caught as they occur.

The product has had some difficulty in the past at actually removing the spyware from the computer once it locates it, so be diligent and use more than one program to comprehensively clean up your library's computer.

Spyware Doctor

This fee-based product ranked second on *PC World* testing. It offers a rich interface and a robust database that detected 90 percent of the spyware on *PC World*'s test computer. *PC World* was impressed with the reporting mechanism of the product because it classifies the threats in a fashion that is easily read. Its main drawback for libraries is that it carries an annual per-workstation subscription cost. If your library's budget allows, this product might be worth the investment.

REVIEW QUESTIONS

Use these questions as a guideline to evaluate the knowledge gained from this chapter.

- Why is security important for office technology?
- What is the best way to secure your library's office technology?
- What questions should you ask concerning your office technology?
- Why is staff training so important?
- What training of staff is required?
- What are the allowable activities for office technology?
- What is needed to check compliance with staff usage policies?
- What software tools are available for the user concerning checking staff usage of technology?
- What are some good guidelines to follow concerning passwords?
- What are some good usage policies for Internet browsing?
- What should be done about backing up office technology data?
- What should be done with patching an office computer?
- What are some antivirus solutions on the market?
- What are some antispyware tools on the market?

KEY POINTS AND CONCLUSION

- Office technology is often overlooked as a security concern, and this oversight can create serious security problems. Due to the greater need for flexibility to maintain better workflow and productivity, office computers are frequently left with only basic virus protection turned on.

- Training of staff in security is extremely important. Having a staff that understands the importance of security measures, their place in daily processes, and each individual's role in security will help reduce friction and resistance to new policies or implementations when they are required.
- Security hardware and software offer tremendous features and are valuable for public station use, and office systems can easily be controlled through a server or local policy settings.

This chapter has described the best ways to secure office systems from attack. It outlined various tips and tricks that can accomplish this task and gave some software choices on protecting computers against viruses and spyware. The next chapter focuses on what can be done to secure servers.

READINGS AND RESOURCES

CERT. 2002. *Home Computer Security.* Pittsburgh, PA: Carnegie Mellon University. Available: www.cert.org/homeusers/HomeComputerSecurity/.

9 ESTABLISHING SERVER SECURITY

Servers are the heart of any network, and securing servers is the ultimate goal of any network security strategy. Servers are available on many different platforms, and in many cases several different versions of the same server exist. It is not the intent of this book to discuss in detail each version of each platform of server software; there are simply too many. Fortunately, all servers are built on the same basic principles and standards of operation. For example, all Web pages are transmitted and received on port 80. The key to securing servers is to understand the way a server functions, what its inherent weaknesses are, and what can be done to protect the server and the data it hosts.

UNDERSTANDING SERVERS AND HOW THEY WORK

To understand how a server should be secured, it helps to first gain a basic understanding of what servers actually do. A server is best defined for the purpose of this chapter as a computer that listens for requests for information from other computers—whether locally (within the building or organization) or globally (the Internet/World Wide Web), locates that information on its storage device or hard drive, and sends that information to the requesting (client) computer.

Originally, mainframe computers were developed to manage and serve data at an acceptable speed for business applications. When personal computers became popular, people quickly discovered that the desktop computer could, with limits, emulate a mainframe's role in managing and serving data for multiple users. The desktop computer did not require a cavernous room with isolated electricity and expensive air-conditioning as mainframes did, and, more important, it did not require a large budget for hardware, software, and expert programmers. The cost-effectiveness of this approach led businesses (and libraries) to begin using personal computers as servers.

As desktop computers grew in popularity, the desire for widespread sharing of data—for networking—increased. Since desktop office computers were not originally designed to work as servers, the need for small,

143

efficient computers devoted to the task of serving information eventually led to the development of so-called desktop servers. These computers can look like traditional desktop machines but are often configured as compact, rack-mounted units. Any desktop computer can act as a server given the proper software, though most personal computers are not specified to handle the demands placed on an average server. In the simplest terms, servers provide information to clients requesting it. This information can include, among other things, e-mail, FTP services, Web sites, or information derived from a library's online catalog.

A server listens for requests, and when it receives one it replies with the appropriate information to the requesting computer. To do this, a server listens to ports 0 to 65535. These ports, as previously explained, are simply channels or tunnels through which data travels from one computer to another. Figure 9-1 is a visual example of how a server handles data and transports it through these ports.

Figure 9-1 deals only with TCP traffic and does not indicate nor include what is known as UDP (user datagram protocol) traffic. For the most part, UDP traffic is dedicated to control channels such as RPC (remote procedure call) and is not a significant part of server functionality as related to this discussion. Some services used by servers do require certain channels

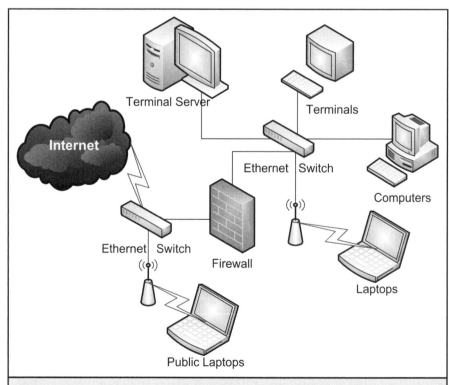

Figure 9-1. Visual of How a Server Handles and Transports Data

of UDP to be available through the firewall, but these UDP ports tend to be devoted to specific software applications.

Figure 9-1 offers a simplified view and does not indicate the deeper levels of Internet traffic. The structure of data sent through the Internet from one computer to another is fairly complex, and understanding that depth is not necessary to determine how best to secure the network and servers.

A Web server deals out Web pages; domain controllers and NISs (network information servers) administer computers and similar devices on local networks; DNS (Domain Name System)/WINS (Windows Internet Name Service) servers act as the phonebook and map to the Internet for computers; and e-mail servers manage calendars and the mail transmitted over the Internet. These different types of servers each transmit data, files, e-mail, and resources to the computers on their local networks and/or the Internet.

WEB SERVERS

A Web server does more than just send Web pages. It is a storage facility for a Web site (or Web sites) and, for our purposes, it is an interface for users to obtain information from online resources a library provides. A functional Web server will always be able to send out pages, even when a site has been hacked or compromised; the need is to ensure that the pages being sent are the ones intended to be sent.

A Web server can be an all-inclusive package of operating system and server, or it can be a software package designed to work, like any other program, on top of a basic desktop computer operating system. Microsoft provides a server operating system known as Windows server 2003, Server Edition, which offers the basic functionality needed for a Web server. Linux in its various incarnations (Cent, Fedora, Red Hat, and others) is an operating system built with network functionality and efficiency in mind, but it still requires an additional software package or "engine," such as Apache, to be installed in order to act as a genuine Web server.

The port that a Web server listens to is 80. When a Web server receives a request for a Web page over this port, the server locates the appropriate file and sends it to the requesting client computer. Of course, Web pages are composed of much more than text files. They often include graphic files and even small embedded programs (such as streaming media content) that provide added functionality. Files that carry suffixes such as PHP and ASX are not traditional, static Web pages. These pages are dynamic; their content changes based on input from the server and/or client.

It is this latter type of Web page that catalog servers tend to use in their Web server interface. A basic "fill in the blank" Web page is provided to a client computer that allows the user to seek information, such as a book or

> Web servers typically have the ability to do much more than send out a Web page. They may request cookies and store the received cookie information in a database for statistical analysis, run server side includes (SSI) (small programs that the server uses to render Web design more efficient), provide an interface through a Web page to a search engine physically located on the server itself or on another server within its network (the catalog Web interface or other database, for example), and provide a secure, encrypted dialogue between server and computer for sensitive transactions such as financial purchases or reference inquiries, to name only a few additional functions.

Table 9-1. Sample Checklist of Services Commonly Provided by Servers

Service	Required	Service On or Off?
Web	Yes	On
Secure Web	Depends	Off/On (for catalog interface if needed)
FTP	Depends	Off/On (download only—use log-ons)
SMTP	Depends	Off (unless using as internal e-mail server)
DNS	No	Off (use ISP DNS servers if possible)

DNS (Domain Name System): Unless the library has multiple Web services and servers, the DNS is provided by the Internet service provider (ISP). All computers on the LAN (local area network) with Internet privileges/access will need to know these IP (Internet protocol) addresses as provided by the ISP. Normally this information is included (if programmed) with the IP address assignment by the DHCP (dynamic host configuration protocol) server.

magazine title. When the user fills in this information and presses the "Search" button, the server receives the request and identifies the words typed into the blanks as keywords.

When these keywords are received, the server then interfaces with the catalog database to request books that are tagged or associated with those words. The catalog returns information to the Web server, which in turn places the information into the format of a reply Web page, generates the Web page "on the fly" so to speak, and sends the new Web page with the requested information to the client computer that originally requested that information.

The details are a little more complicated than this, as the interactions between the client computer requesting information and the Web server receiving the request and interacting with the catalog database to receive that data and plug it into a new Web page to answer the requesting computer has a lot of room for errors and problems.

SECURING THE WEB SERVER

Before deploying *any* server, review the software and examine its default settings. Default settings are seldom sufficient to properly secure a Web server. Anything not required for the intended functionality and for effective management of the server should be turned off. Table 9-1 is a simple checklist listing the most important services offered by most Web servers and the basic recommendations for choices an average library might make regarding each service.

Compromised Web Servers

Web servers can be compromised in various ways. Keeping the server updated with the latest operating system/platform patches and service packs, specific software package updates, and virus protection is extremely important. Untold numbers of Web servers have been compromised because of unpatched weaknesses in their software and in their host machines' operating systems.

Compromised operating systems are the most common problems, but a denial of service (DoS) attack completely (if only temporarily) freezes all services available through the Web server. DoS attacks are usually launched off-site, through compromised computers on the Internet. This approach uses "zombie" computers—home or personal computers that have been compromised and instructed to send bad requests to a Web server for unknown or invalid Web pages. This has the effect of flooding the server with garbage requests that eventually overpower the capacity of the server, preventing legitimate requests from being processed and eventually denying service to all other client computers.

As a precaution, it is safest first to turn off any of your server's options set by default to "On." If the service is required, you can always turn it on after reviewing the server's security settings and determining how badly needed the service is by your user base. Most vendors of Web server software, including Microsoft, provide documentation on their Web sites on further securing their products.

HTTPS: SECURE WEB SERVERS

Secure Web servers require validation before providing access to requesting clients. A common default setting on secure servers is that this validation be completed in "open text" format. This involves the user ID and password being sent over the Internet as a text file, which can be intercepted by hackers. The obvious problem with this is the user ID and password can easily be compromised.

When configuring secure Web servers, always require that the server request a "secure" connection before validating or entering a user ID and password. This adds a layer of security by lightly encrypting the user ID and password; the encryption involved here is strong enough that the average computer hacker cannot break it.

> The "S" at the end of HTTP (hypertext transfer protocol) simply designates it as a secure Web server. This type of server requires that a log-on with appropriate certificates be performed before any of the pages of the server can be accessed. It communicates by default on port 443, and requires an SSL, or secure socket layer to be successfully instantiated.

FTP: FILE TRANSFER PROTOCOL

Web servers commonly provide a file transfer protocol (FTP) service for uploading/downloading files, allowing remote users to modify the Web pages or share important files. FTP settings should be highly restricted, preferably allowing users to change the Web site only from within the local domain or IP address range. By requiring authentication (user IDs and password), the folders shared through FTP will be even more secure. This doesn't mean that a local computer within the domain can't be hacked and in turn used to access the Web server through FTP; it is at best an

> **FTP (file transfer protocol):** This server is a simple folder/file listing server for hosting files or capacity to authorized users. FTP clients can efficiently manage the upload and download of files—no Web browser is required, although they frequently will work well with an FTP server.

additional layer of protection. Ideally, the service should be turned off unless absolutely required.

SMTP SERVICE

SMTP, simple mail transfer protocol, is a valuable service for communication, both internal and external to the library network. If the library has a domain name, for example, Mylibrary.com, then an SMPT server can be constructed to provide personalized e-mail for employees of Mylibrary. This involves some time and effort devoted to the management and maintenance of a library's e-mail accounts.

A primary concern with SMTP service is a function known as "relay." This function allows an external entity to use the service as a way to hide its identity (spam is frequently sent via relay). Some organizations refuse to accept mail from servers known to support relaying; yours should not be among them.

> **SMTP (simple mail transfer protocol)**: The protocol on which e-mail servers run. Many server packages (Microsoft server 2003 as an example) have the capacity to act as an SMTP server, or there are vendors with stand-alone software packages.

MICROSOFT DOMAIN CONTROLLERS AND ACTIVE DIRECTORY

Whereas Web servers act as an interface to public data, Windows domain controllers and Active Directory act as gateways to your local network. They too can be compromised, leaving your entire network and all of the computers that authenticate against either the domain controller or Active Directory open to being compromised. These may actually be more useful, definitely more powerful, means of locking down and protecting data than the solutions offered by locally installed third-party applications.

Domain controllers offer ways to organize networked computers, and offer protection of computers on a network by requiring authentication at log-on/start up of a Microsoft operating system. This approach allows system administrators to grant highly customized types of authority to individual users, limiting the network assets to which a given user has access. Active Directory is the current generation of this model. Both domain controllers and Active Directory can offer additional control through preventing an unauthorized computer from obtaining a network-assigned IP address and routing information, thus preventing it from being able to use the Internet.

As Active Directory is both powerful and somewhat complicated, we start by looking at its predecessor, Windows domain controller. The following discussion seeks to lay a foundation on which a network administrator with limited experience might better understand the range of security options available to him or her.

Windows domain control is structured somewhat like a prison. A prison has an exterior fence, an interior fence, and guard posts and administrative offices, each having different levels of control and authority over prisoners. Prisoners will have different levels of freedom also, which include access to the exercise yard, library, work projects, or even excursions outside the prison for work details. Prisoners have restrictions on their cells—prisoners from cell block A aren't allowed to go into cell block B—designed to keep them out of trouble. Prisoners may also have privileges or restrictions, managed at the administrative level and enforced at the local level.

With a domain controller, the exterior fence is the log-on. If you don't log in, you can't get into the prison, whether you are an inmate, a guard, or the warden himself. Once you have logged into the domain, your credentials allow the system to consult your account and determine your preassigned authority level—warden (administrator), guard, (employees), or prisoner (public users).

The warden can go anywhere he or she wants to, and so can administrators of the domain. Guards have ranks, and depending on their rank, can be considered administrators with access to almost everything but the warden's office. A guard captain can assign guards responsibility for different areas, and can determine the authority those guards have over those areas.

Some guards will have very little authority, but they will still have more freedom than the prisoners in where they go and what they can do. Prisoners have very few privileges, and when they do go somewhere or do something, there are always restrictions and someone watching and recording what they do.

A warden might authorize a captain to be responsible for all the activities, access, and control of the recreation yards. Another captain would have authority of cells and dining facilities, and another captain would be responsible for communications (including reading at the library). These captains would in turn supply instructions and levels of authority for the guards and prisoners under their jurisdiction. Serious mistakes or rabble-rousing will result in the removal of the privileges, authority, or even the rank and status of anyone entering the prison.

DOMAIN CONTROLLERS

A domain controller offers different levels of access and authority to a network, from the domain administrator all the way down to simple user. These authority levels can be organized into workgroups, and privileges granted to specific users to allow them access and local levels of authority to specific areas of the domain or workgroup. Table 9-2 is a simplified visual of this explanation.

This arrangement can be as complex or simple as you need it to be. In Table 9-2 we see three workgroups, but these could also be created as domains, each having very high authority, and either trusting or not trusting

Table 9-2. How a Domain Uses Workgroups to Segment and Separate Computers and Users within the Domain

Domain Administrator Authority over every computer on the domain (Warden)					
Recreation (Workgroup) Administrator **(Captain)**		Housing (Workgroup) Administrator **(Captain)**		Communications (Workgroup) Administrator **(Captain)**	
Change	*Access/Use*	*Change*	*Access/Use*	*Change*	*Access/Use*
Power Users **(Guards)**	Users **(Prisoners)**	Power Users **(Guards)**	Users **(Prisoners)**	Power Users **(Guards)**	Users **(Prisoners)**

To bring the idea of domain control closer to home, consider dividing the library into two separate domains, Staff and Public. With this configuration, all public stations and any personal systems accessing the wireless access points would be required to log on the Public domain, using either a managed specific user account per public access station or a generic account in the case of wireless access. These two domains would be able to work together, the Staff domain having authority over the Public domain, but the Public domain not having "trusted" status with the Staff domain.

members of the other domains. This comes in handy when a user from one workgroup or domain needs to share or borrow files from a separate workgroup or domain.

The two domains must have a trust relationship before users from one can travel to or share with users on the other. This can also be a one-way trust relationship, where a user on domain A can reach files on domain B, but domain B users cannot see or reach files on domain A.

This approach to controlling and securing a network can be very powerful and efficient, or weak and destructive. It all depends on designing a domain or domains with appropriate levels of security for users and the groups they belong to, and understanding the work dynamics of all users as they exist within the library.

This approach can be applied to resources as well as to users. For example, a domain controller can restrict access to a networked printer in the way that a shared printer can be controlled by the computer to which it is attached. A shared printer can be instructed to grant printing privileges only to users who authenticate directly against the computer to which it is connected. A domain controller does the same thing, only on a larger level.

A further segregation of the domains can be accomplished by establishing workgroups within the separate domains. Table 9-3 is an example of how this approach might look.

Note the association directions and the terms "Trusted" and "Not Trusted." This is the one-way valve that allows the Staff domain to have authority over the Public domain. Should any system in the Public domain be compromised or attempt to access and change any setting on the Staff domain, it will be denied the right to do so, as the Staff domain does not "trust" the Public domain.

Table 9-3. Example of How to Use Two Domains to Separate Different Workgroups					
Public Domain	>>> Trusted >>>		**Staff Domain**		
	(Association)				
	<<< Not Trusted <<<				
Workgroups			Workgroups		
Wireless	**Workstations**	No Logical Network Path	**Staff**	**Admin**	
Generic **Log-in**	**Individual** **Log-in**		**Individual** **Log-in**	**Individual** **Log-in**	
Log-in not restricted to user and specific computer	**Log-in restricted to user and specific station**		**Log-in restricted to specific station**	**Log-in not restricted to specific station**	

The terms "physical" and "logical" in the network world can sometimes be a bit confusing. Construction zones in four-lane highways tend to use cement barriers or large orange cones and barrels to direct traffic flow. In and of itself, the pavement constitutes one large physical entity; the barriers create paths that allow the pavement safely and efficiently to be used by motorists. Taken together, the switches, patch cables, and data drops or wireless access points found in a library LAN form a single physical network. Just plugging all of the computers into the network would allow them all to see one another. That is, if there is no logical network in place. When we require workstations to log in to a domain or workgroup, we have created a logical network, where authority, access, and connectivity are controlled by software and not by physical cables: we have created a system of barriers that dictate the orderly use of what would otherwise be an undifferentiated network.

To demonstrate how a domain may be configured, we will now describe in further detail how the individual areas listed in Table 9-3 function together.

Naming Conventions

Everything that resides on a domain or in Active Directory will have a domain name. By right-clicking on "My Computer" on the desktop in Windows, choosing "Properties," you will obtain a new window. Under the "Computer Name" tab, you will find a number of specifications, as indicated in Table 9-4.

Computer Description. Use an intuitively graspable description, such as Public Workstation No. 1, or Circulation Desk Check In Station 1, for the

Table 9-4. List of the Different Components under the "Computer Name" Tab of "My Computer" Properties Window

Item Name	Item Description
Computer Description	Nonnetwork-related name, preferably a valid description of the computer and its purpose or job function
Computer Name	A valid network name that is recognizable by the network and other computers on the network, domain, or within that workgroup. If DNS is utilized locally, this name will have a suffix (e.g., Circulation1.Just-a-Library.Net).
Workgroup	This will be the individual workgroup, as mentioned in Table 9-3, with the examples of Wireless, Workstations, Staff, and Admin.
Domain	This will be the domain in which the workgroup resides, as mentioned in Table 9-3, with the examples of Staff and Public.

description. This will show up in the Active Directory and domain user groups for the workstations.

Full Computer Name. There are several ways to devise a good naming convention for computers on a network. You might name the computer for the user by their log-in ID, the user (log-in ID) and their room number, the room number and computer (207-CPU01, 207-CPU02, etc.), the computer purpose and number (Circ01, Circ02, Ref01, etc.), or another identifier that fits the needs of the library itself. Whichever approach you choose, apply it consistently. Lack of consistency in naming conventions will plague anyone troubleshooting the network and can cause problems when attempting to identify compromised computers.

Workgroup. The default name of a workgroup is "Workgroup." Although this tends to be fine for home or small office use, it should not be used in a public setting, as it is not considered a strong security design to use defaults.

Domain. There is no default name for a domain. It is best to choose names that can be easily identified by users and that are not terribly long (four to nine digits will suffice), though longer names are not unheard of.

Network Identification Wizard. We do not recommend using the wizard since all of the domain, workgroup, and log-in IDs will be controlled and set up at the domain level.

Rename. This will simply allow the computer to be renamed or to join a domain. To join a domain, the person logged in will need to have that privilege and authority assigned to their account. If not, a log-in screen should appear asking for a user ID and password of an authorized user to join to the domain.

Public Domain: Public Workstations

Public workstations used for research, Internet browsing, or productivity can be difficult to maintain, especially if inappropriate permissions are granted to public users. As discussed in Chapter 5, it is more common to find locally installed security solutions on individual public workstations than on staff machines. That being said, a centralized approach using domain control can ultimately provide a far more secure solution with less long-term overhead. The best solution is likely to involve a combination of centralized access control and individual adjustments to each public workstation.

Log-in. When choosing a domain/workgroup log-in name for public stations, it is best to keep it simple: the longer the user name, the greater the chance that patrons will mistype it.

It is possible to set a local computer to remember the user name at log-in. Where this is perfectly acceptable to a workstation that has a generic log-in ID assigned to it, and where staff members have locked offices, it is not recommended for publicly accessible stations on the staff or administrative logical network that share multiple users, such as a reference desk workstation.

It is also possible to set a workstation to automatically log in, password and all. This is probably the safest and easiest solution for public workstations, as it prevents patrons from even having the opportunity to change the log-in credentials. One problem might arise with this approach: if the pre-assigned domain or network is unavailable, the workstation will not be able to log in at all, and a local account will have to be used.

Domain Authentication. If the computer has been joined to a domain, a user ID and password must be authenticated at the domain level before the computer will even completely boot up. At the point of authentication, the user ID's privileges are made known to the local computer. The user account is created at the domain controller and grants the user whatever specific privileges are established for that account. For public stations, the "user" level is typical. This level allows users to run installed software but does not allow system-level changes or software installation.

A user can be assigned to use only a specific computer or series of computers. This is extremely helpful in stations that are used by the public. Table 9-5 gives examples of user names, passwords, the computers that they are allowed to log on, and even the hours during that each user can log on.

User Accounts and Groups. As mentioned in the previous section, control over user accounts is a highly effective management tool. User accounts are managed by the groups they are placed in. Within a domain there are numerous default groups, so many that any one or a combination of them

Table 9-5. Examples of Log-on Time Restrictions for Computers Joined to a Domain and the Users Who Can Log On

User ID	Computer Name(s)	Hours Can Log On
Public1	Public_No1	8am-9pm
Public2	Public_No2	8am-9pm
Public3	Public_No3	8am-9pm
Ref1	Ref_No1; Ref_No2	7am-10pm
Ref2	Ref_No2; Ref_No1	7am-10pm
NetAdmin	Public_No1; Public_No2; Public_No3; Ref_No1; Ref_No2	24 hrs

should suffice for most needs. Table 9-6 lists some of the most frequently used groups and offers a brief description of their properties on the local computer.

These groups exist almost identically on a local computer, with the exception of the domain-oriented groups such as domain administrator. Table 9-7 lists most of those additional groups.

After mapping out the library's conventions governing user names, authority levels, domain names, computer naming convention, and workgroups, the logical network can be created.

The first step is to build the domain controller(s). It is best to have two: a primary domain controller (PDC), and secondary or backup domain controller (BDC). These should be installed on separate networked computers. If something should happen to the PDC, the BDC would take over, allowing uninterrupted network services at the domain level.

After the domain has been created, create the workgroups. These will help build lines of demarcation within the created domains. It is possible

Table 9-6. Standard Groups and Their Definitions under Windows

Local Computer User Groups	
Administrator	Unrestricted access to the computer
Backup Operator	Authority to backup or restore files, otherwise denied other access
Guests	Limited authority, can run installed programs only
Network Configuration	Limited authority to manage network configuration
Power User	Limited authority, can do most administrative functions
Remote Desktop Users	Authority to log on a computer from a remote or another location
Users	Limited authority, can run installed programs only
Debugger Users	Limited authority, can run debugging processes on computer locally

Table 9-7. A List of Domain and Global Groups Defined by a Domain Controller	
Common Domain or Global Groups	
Domain Admins	Authority to modify any and all computers logged onto the domain
Domain Computers	List of computers joined to the domain
Domain Guests	List of all guests on the domain
Domain Controllers	Computers that are the actual domain controllers
Enterprise Admins	List of administrators over entire enterprise (if exists)

simply to create one domain populated with multiple workgroups; in some configurations, management may be rendered a bit easier this way.

Once the workgroups have been established, begin creating the user accounts in the domain controller. During the creation of these individual user accounts you can effectively build templates for different types of users by simply copying and renaming a given account and changing its description. These user IDs would then be associated with a specific workgroup or groups.

Once the users have been added, either add the computers (after being named appropriately) to the domain locally—while sitting at the computer itself—or at the domain after the computer has logged on. Much of this is accomplished through a simple drag-and-drop procedure.

You will then be able to associate user IDs with individual computers and may further isolate the log-on features and restrictions assigned to individual IDs or workgroups. As previously stated, the initial configuration requires extensive planning, and implementation takes some time. However, once implemented, the management and maintenance benefits of this approach will quickly become apparent. With this foundation you will be ready to begin the planning and eventual implementation of your library network's domain to improve the security of the network and servers.

ACTIVE DIRECTORY

Active Directory is the evolution of the system of shared folders, files, and printers made possible by domain controllers. Users, groups, and computers are no longer individually classed but are now known as objects. Objects can be grouped in a single container or in multiple containers (a container is essentially a much more precise and flexible way to group items than are workgroups or domains). The basic idea of authority is the same, but Active Directory's system of objects and containers causes the lines between computers and users blur just a bit.

Active Directory takes the power of a PDC and adds a higher level of descriptive detail and administrative control. In Windows server 2003, instead of offering every possible feature in one package, Microsoft established distinct editions of the software, each package tailored to a specific audience. These packages are Web Edition, Standard Edition, Enterprise Edition, and Datacenter Edition.

The Standard and Enterprise Editions deal primarily with domains. Server 2003 still allows administrators to establish a single domain model, created in much the same way as previously discussed in the earlier discussion of domains. Server 2003 can run in a mixed mode as well, taking over an existing domain controller and allowing smooth interaction between the older domain model and the newer server in a way not evident to local users.

We discussed logical networks before. Active Directory is a logical structure built on object attributes, associations, and classes. To some degree, these terms are almost identical in definition to terms in the older domain structure. However, the terminology had to be modified due to the inherently different definitions and capabilities assigned to those basic building blocks.

Before moving on, take another look at Table 9-3. Now let's look at a very simplified graphical view in Table 9-8 to get a comparison idea of the older domain architecture to Active Directory architecture.

Where groups and users were rather inclusive and not easily shared in respect to how they interacted, through Active Directory the logical structure and communication can be accomplished on a single object level with that objects' attributes shared with other objects and the same attributes. As detailed as it can become, the overall organizational features are not nearly as complicated as one would think to be able to deal with multiple objects that are all individual objects. The interaction between the different objects is all controlled through Active Directory based on the object attributes, not groups. Although in some form when multiple objects all

Table 9-8. Simplified Visual Depiction of Active Directory and How It Deals with Users, Computers, and All Aspects of Domain Control

OBJECTS			CONTAINERS	
(Name)	(Attributes)		(Name)	Contains
User1	Power User		Computer1	User1, Printer1
User2	Guest	**ACTIVE DIRECTORY**	Power User	User1 to User3
User3	User		Admin	User4
User4	Admin	**Sorts and Connects according to the attributes of each Object**	Computer2	User2, Printer1
Printer1	Printer		Computer3	User3, Printer1
Computer1	Computer		Printer1	User1 through User4
Computer2	Computer			
Computer3	Computer			

have an identical attribute (e.g., Power User) they could be considered to be in a "group," Active Directory isn't bound by that identification.

As an example, Object A and Object B both have the attribute of Power User. However, Object A has an attribute of Object C (a computer) and Object B has an attribute of Object D (a different computer). Object A can have Power User authority when combined with Object C, but not Object D. This is tremendously simplified to begin to open the door of how Active Directory associates objects and their attributes.

There are many books available on the market to give detailed upgrade step-by-step instructions, should you decide to upgrade or install server 2003 as a domain and Active Directory resource for your network. The same basic steps are required as discussed in the section on domain controllers in planning and implementing server 2003 as Active Directory, in any of its flavors. By using Active Directory as a form of security for any computers within the building that may be logging onto the network to perform office duties, productivity, research, or administrative duties, the remaining servers are much safer. Maintaining a secure Active Directory structure simply requires following recommendations offered within the book on passwords, user names, enforcing written policies, and reviewing the structure and nature of threats as they become apparent or reported.

NIS SERVERS

A network information server (NIS) is similar to the domain controller, except that it is directed toward Linux-based operating systems. It will work with Windows-based systems, but it does not have the tremendous capacity that Windows domain or Active Directory. An NIS server uses a small database to organize and authorize a user ID to log on a Linux computer system. This database will include the desktop settings, browsing history, bookmarks, and other associations to a particular user so that they are not stored locally on a computer.

To utilize an NIS server, each Linux flavor station must be administratively required to locate the specific NIS server and log on that server. The NIS must have a generated user ID and account before the Linux flavor system can log on. With the local computer being locked out, security is guaranteed to the degree that a user doesn't have the capacity/knowledge to be able to bypass the log-in through hacking.

Although the many flavors of Linux are becoming easier to use because of evolving graphical user interfaces, their dominance in the library field as standard public system, office systems, or servers, is yet to be realized. The susceptibility of NIS servers to hacking is no less than that of a Windows server. Maintaining patches, monitoring accounts and hard drive capacity (once a server is hacked, the drive space is commonly used for storage for questionable materials/items/data), and user accounts, is paramount to retaining the security of the server.

CONCLUSIONS

Should either of these two servers to be compromised, with the control they have over the network access and the individual computers accessing the network, the compromise would be catastrophic. As computers that log on an NIS, domain controller, or Active Directory, they are subject to control by that service. The importance of maintaining good security practice and controls with them becomes obvious.

These servers provide a different type of service and shouldn't be visible to anyone outside the local area network. This protection is best performed at the firewall level, but control over ports open at the server level is important as well. Even with the firewall protection, the servers are still accessible on the local area network. With proper access control placed on public stations within the building, an additional threat is reduced, if not entirely removed.

Due to the need for staff to have advanced levels of authority to perform their duties, all threats from the local area network cannot be removed. Even as recent as October 2007, a survey from Sophos, as reported in C-Net News.com by Marcus Browne, indicates that IT (information technology) personnel feel the biggest existing threat is the users—staff—of businesses. Although this survey was not specific to libraries, it can be safely assumed that most IT personnel have similar feelings.

Proper enforcement of both security policy and usage policy that is efficient, effective, and well balanced will help reduce the risk.

DOMAIN NAME SYSTEM

DNS poisoning: The falsification of a domain name and its IP address on an authoritative DNS server that causes other DNS servers to accept the new IP address. This is used by hackers in the acquisition of personal data by presenting an identical Web site or in blackmailing a legitimate Web site for money.

Domain Name System (DNS) is the directory of the Internet, and the directory of your local library LAN, if one is installed locally. Most libraries will not have a need to provide DNS services locally. Active Directory has an available DNS server component, but it is not the same as the DNS server provided by an Internet service provider (ISP).

DNS servers are prime targets for criminal attacks motivated by blackmail and fraud. Removing a DNS server from service brings a network down completely, and hackers have been known to threaten to do so unless payment is made. Another form of DNS attack is referred to as DNS poisoning. DNS poisoning occurs when a DNS server is fed invalid or incorrect information. If that DNS server is a "trusted" server—if it contains valid TCP information for many Web sites and is used constantly—then the bad information poisons all of the other DNS servers that refer to it.

As an example, a company that has a retail site is normally located at IP address 198.162.9.104. A criminal hacker locates the company that owns that IP address and the domain name service and is able to insert a different IP address that he controls to be associated with that company. As the new IP address is sent out to other DNS servers, the hacker already has an exact copy of the Web site and runs it during a peak business time, receiving multiple Visa or Mastercard numbers, names, expiration dates, and codes. It can take several days for a company to realize that they have been poisoned in this way, since not all DNS servers renew IP address information as often as others. Many buyers will actually end up at the legitimate retail site while others are routed to the criminal site.

When a DNS service is provided with a locally maintained computer server, such as Windows server 2003, it is as vulnerable as that server is. However, if the DNS server is maintained on its own computer, as long as it is patched to date, protected against viruses, and appropriate firewall settings are in place, it should be safe enough.

Due to their relative lack of vulnerability to attack, some libraries have maintained pre–OSX Macintosh computers for the sole purpose of providing DNS services. The computer in question need not be a top-of-the-line model, as DNS service is not terribly resource-intensive.

For security settings, when the DNS service is packaged with another service, such as Windows server 2003 or a Linux-based server, you should ensure that all unnecessary services are turned off. The security of the primary purpose of the server, Web server, FTP, Mail, etc., must be preserved to ensure that its secondary purpose (DNS) of the server is also secure.

> Although libraries are not thought of as profitable targets, they can be attacked for other reasons, such as revenge, as a political statement, or for practice/experience. A library must be secured against these threats to continue uninterrupted quality service for its patrons.

EXCHANGE SERVER; E-MAIL/CALENDAR SERVERS

Numerous companies offer support for e-mail, contact, and calendar services. Each one of these services has its own security concerns. The most common (and annoying) security concern for e-mail services is forwarding of spam. Spammers will locate e-mail servers that are not configured properly and use them to send out mass e-mails.

The most important e-mail server setting to check is whether the server is set to forward unauthenticated e-mail. This certainly needs to be turned off. In addition, you should require password authentication for accessing e-mail. Depending on the software versions being used—quite a few independent e-mail servers are intended for small business or organizations that do not require powerful servers—the default settings may or may not err on the side of greater security.

Once again, if the e-mail server offers use of a service that you do not use, be sure to explicitly turn that service off. In addition to being a drain on the server's resources, unused services can invite security threats if not configured properly.

Should you find that you have turned off too many services and that the e-mail server doesn't adequately fill your needs, it is a simple matter to locate the necessary services and restore their settings. E-mail servers by themselves are not excessively complicated. Throw in additional services such as a calendar program, notes, contact management, though, and connect a server to a domain controller, NIS, or Active Directory to coordinate user names, and the landscape can become somewhat complex.

MICROSOFT EXCHANGE SERVER

Microsoft Exchange Server provides productivity enhancement through a combined e-mail, calendar, contact management, and project sharing through file-sharing in public folders.

Setting up the Exchange server requires preplanning to determine how it will incorporate into your existing server infrastructure. Licensing and cost are a key issue, as those are determined by the number of users to be supported within the Exchange environment.

During preplanning phase, review the security settings within Exchange to see how they mesh with the broader policies developed for your library network's security. Should Exchange already be incorporated and implemented prior to the security policies, review the settings available that will strengthen the security of the Exchange server.

TERMINAL SERVERS

Terminal servers provide a way to reduce end-user ability to damage a desktop computer through software settings and unnecessary and possibly unauthorized software additions. A terminal server provides a unique desktop with the array of productivity software (as determined by the server) to a remote workstation that does not have its own operating system. In simpler terms, this workstation consists of a computer monitor, keyboard, and mouse, with a basically hollow computer shell that uses a server to provide the same desktop and software it would have if it were a full computer. Table 9-9 outlines a typical terminal server setup.

Depending on a library's budget, this approach may be considered for public access stations. As they have no locally controllable or modifiable software, the local system security is not a factor.

These systems typically cost no less than individual desktop computers—the software license cost for productivity software packages and the license-per-user cost of the terminal server software are comparable. The benefit to this particular consideration is the time and energy spent on dealing with software and hardware issues on the individual public stations or office stations, as the case may be. No individual hard drives going out, no

Table 9-9. Terminal Server Control of Workstations and How They Interact

Terminal Server				
User 1	**User 2**	**User 3**	**User 4**	**User 5**
Internet access, productivity software	Internet access only	Internet access only	Internet access, productivity software	Internet access, productivity software
Library Local Area Network				
Station One	**Station Two**	**Station Three**	**Station Four**	**Station Five**
Terminal with monitor, keyboard, and mouse, looks like regular computer with Internet access and productivity software	Terminal with monitor, keyboard, and mouse, looks like regular computer with Internet access only	Terminal with monitor, keyboard, and mouse, looks like regular computer with Internet access only	Terminal with monitor, keyboard, and mouse, looks like regular computer with Internet access and productivity software	Terminal with monitor, keyboard, and mouse, looks like regular computer with Internet access and productivity software

operating system failures or security bypasses, and no "guess what they installed today" surprises. Everything that the end user sees and has access to is controlled by the terminal server.

It is recommended that the particular network backbone or structure supporting these computers be segmented from the rest of the network. This isn't as much a security issue as it is a network-efficiency issue. Each desktop that a particular user sees can be modified at the terminal to fit the needs of that user. As seen in Table 9-9, not all users need productivity software available. This is accomplished by the creation of individual "virtual computers" within the server itself. Where each virtual computer is able to act as a real desktop computer, the reality is that when the user logs off, all of it goes away. The only thing saved related to that user is their documents and desktop look—if the terminal server is set to keep that information. If not, then the next time that user logs on at a terminal, they get a brand new desktop. The benefits to using a terminal server for public stations and possibly even for office stations such as the circulation desk stations are clear.

The terminal server is not frequently a target for attack, other than to simply cause a denial of service or disruption. However, taking strong precautions and looking at all possible settings is always recommended to help keep the server stable and reliable. The location should be in a secure room, with a strong uplink to the network. Ideally it would be on a separate subnet from the rest of the network, preferably behind its own firewall. As all Internet traffic will be channeled through the server for the terminals in use, its connectivity to the network should be as fast as possible, preferably on a separate Ethernet connection than the Ethernet that would be used to route the virtual desktops to the terminals themselves. As the terminal

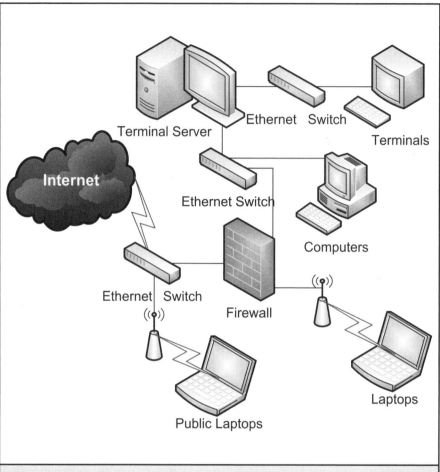

Figure 9-2. The Location of a Terminal Server within a Library Network

Note that the wireless access is directly ported to the Internet, on the other side of the firewall in both Figures 9-2 and 9-3. This allows patrons Internet access without policing the software, antivirus software, and patches or viruses of the users' laptop.

server is inherently secure, keeping it behind the firewall is not a security concern, as shown in Figure 9-2.

The network can further be segmented to improve the LAN traffic by isolating the switch or switches from terminals to the terminal server as shown in Figure 9-2.

Again, depending on the terminal server software brand, certain settings can be made that will help secure the terminal server itself. One setting in particular is to restrict administrative access to the actual server itself. In other words, do not remote connect as an administrator from a desktop or terminal. Although this may seem an inconvenience, the only real inconvenience is having to walk to the terminal server itself and log on there to make adjustments or troubleshoot any problems. As the remote terminals themselves are relatively inexpensive, retain one to sit next to the terminal server for testing of user IDs and log-on configurations and views.

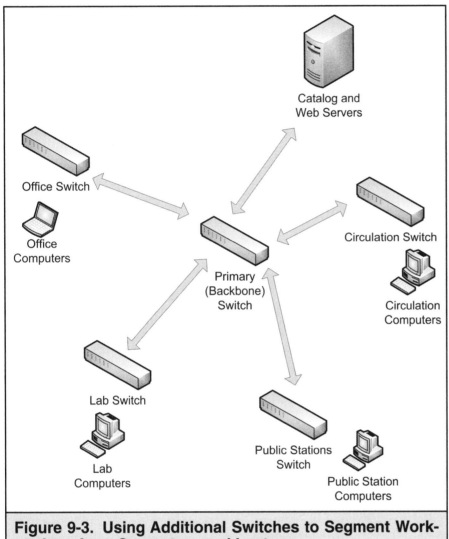

Figure 9-3. Using Additional Switches to Segment Workstations from Computers and Laptops

Logging on the terminal server from a terminal may be acceptable, as long as the terminal isn't sitting next to a patron that is logged on as a user. The possibility—although you may believe it to be remote—that the patron could see the user ID and password is definitely a possibility. Keep in mind that if someone knows the administrative user name (keeping the default name "Administrator" is not recommended) and sees even a portion of the password, it becomes a simple matter of trial and error over time to guess the actual password. Patience is a hacker's best friend. This may become a policy addition should staff neglect to maintain a security mind-set.

Restrict log-on access to the designated subnet or to the MAC (media access control) addresses if that is a feature of the terminal server (it should be). On some terminal servers, it is also possible to restrict a particular log-on ID to a particular terminal. In keeping track of who may be sitting where, should someone be found to be conducting questionable activity, having User1 being able to log on only at Terminal 1 is helpful in both tracking logs and in court testimony.

REVIEW QUESTIONS

Use these questions as a guideline to evaluate the knowledge gained from this chapter.

- What is a server?
- What do servers actually do?
- What is a mainframe computer?
- What are the hardware requirements for a server?
- What are ports and how do servers use them?
- What is a Web server?
- What port does a Web server use?
- How does one secure a Web server?
- What is a Domain Name System?
- How can a Web server be compromised?
- What is a secure Web server?
- What is a simple mail transfer protocol?
- What is file transfer protocol?
- What is Active Directory?
- What are domains?
- What are the naming conventions for a domain?
- How does one authenticate to a domain?
- What is a network information server?
- What is an Exchange server?
- What is a terminal server?

KEY POINTS AND CONCLUSION

- Servers play an important role in any library and require that close attention be maintained when implementing security practices and monitoring their functionality.

- Although servers exist in most flavors of operating systems, from Windows to Linux, how they interact with one another over networks and the Internet is based on very specific protocols that are common to all platforms.
- Best security practices in applying stringent password requirements, controlling who has authority to access, their level of access, and what they can access, is key in protecting servers from intentional or accidental damage or unexpected outages.
- Balance functionality, accessibility, and productivity through settings and software that are part of the server operating system. These, and all server settings, should be reviewed on a regular basis.

With the multitude of software platforms and services provided and the varying individual needs of the library, installing and maintaining any server that is not turnkey or contracted requires considerable time, energy, dedication, and skill in implementation and continued support. With the basic elements of the most common servers and their security considerations explained, a library administrator should now have the foundation to make appropriate decisions concerning purchase and risk pertaining to all such services and servers.

A librarian with some basic understanding and relative expertise that has been assigned the responsibility of implementing such services should now have the foundation in which to research the individual software or platforms, choose the best for the library's mission, and implement same in a secure environment and fashion.

Always use resources available, such as technical forums and security oriented Web sites, to maintain a working knowledge of current security concerns with the server platforms in use by your library.

READINGS AND RESOURCES

Allen, R. 2005. *Windows Server 2003 Security Cookbook.* Sebastopol, CA: O'Reilly Media.

Bautts, T., Dawson, T., and Purdy, G. N. 2005. *Linux Network Administrators Guide.* Sebastopol, CA: O'Reilly Media.

Browne, Marcus. 2007. "Survey: Office Workers Still the Greatest Security Threat." Available: http://news.cnet.com/Survey-Office-workers-still-the-greatest-security-threat/2100-7355_3-6213227.html.

Danseglio, M. 2004. *Securing Windows Server 2003.* Sebastopol, CA: O'Reilly Media.

Hassell, J. 2006. *Learning Windows Server 2003.* Sebastopol, CA: O'Reilly Media.

Hassell, J. 2008. *Windows Server 2008, The Definitive Guide.* Sebastopol, CA: O'Reilly Media.

Hunt, C., and Bragg, R. 2005. *Windows Server 2003 Network Administration.* Sebastopol, CA: O'Reilly Media.

Schroder, C. 2007. *Linux Networking Cookbook.* Sebastopol, CA: O'Reilly Media.

Stern, H., Labiaga, R., and Eisler, M. 2001. *Managing NFS and NIS.* Sebastopol, CA: O'Reilly Media.

Tulloch, M. 2003. *Windows Server 2003 in a Nutshell.* Sebastopol, CA: O'Reilly Media.

10 SECURING THE LIBRARY NETWORK FROM EXTERNAL THREATS

The base requirements for any network include an Internet service provider (ISP), a router, and network connectivity devices such as Ethernet switches or hubs. A firewall or similar device is not strictly mandatory, but should be included in any network configuration. These devices must be installed, configured, and adjusted to meet your library's specific needs. In this chapter, we discuss ways in which network configuration can be secured against external threats.

ACCESS TO THE INTERNET: A BRIEF REVIEW

Computers, laptops, printers, cell phones, wireless PDAs, bar code readers, and a multitude of devices rely on network access, through either wireless or wired connections. Wireless access is an excellent way to offer connectivity through personal devices brought into the library, and wired access is a safer way to connect office and public stations to the library's network.

A network device uses a specific hardware component (called a network interface card, or NIC, which can be wireless or require a cable) to connect to the LAN. Each NIC has a unique identifier known as a MAC (media access control) address. This MAC address is a series of 12 alphanumeric hexadecimal numbers, hexadecimal being 0 thru 9 and A to F. Table 10-1 shows the standard numeric value on the first line and the hexadecimal equivalent value on the second line.

Characters A–F are considered numeric values by the devices on the network. Later in this book, we demonstrate how these MAC addresses can be used to secure network access, and to locate and identify disruptive devices on the network.

Table 10-1. Numerical Value of Hexadecimal Characters															
0	1	2	3	4	5	6	7	8	9	10	11	12	13	14	15
0	1	2	3	4	5	6	7	8	9	A	B	C	D	E	F

Domain names are easily identified according to their suffix. The most common of these suffixes are *edu* for education; *com* and *biz* for businesses; *gov* for government; and *org* for nonbusiness organizations. Countries also have specific suffixes, such as *uk* for United Kingdom or *ca* for Canada.

The LAN (local area network) is designed to identify and respond to the presence of network-ready devices (computers, laptops, printers, and so forth) either through an Ethernet cable or a wireless access point and assign each a specific identification number (using the TCP/IP, transmission-control protocol/Internet protocol), which allows communication between a given device and others on the LAN, the Internet, or both. This ID assignment can be accomplished in a number of ways, but most common is through a dynamic host configuration protocol (DHCP) server, a service that is commonly incorporated into both firewalls and routers.

Even after receiving this combination of a MAC address and a TCP/IP address, a networked device still needs a way to locate other devices on the LAN and the Internet. On a library's LAN, computers have a third means of identification—a network name, usually the name of the workstation. These workstation names are grouped together by a common group name or workgroup. Unless configured otherwise, the default network group name is "Workgroup." For a visual layout of a normal network with Internet access, look at Figure 10-1.

For access to Internet sites, a networked device will need a way to cross-reference a location (for instance, a URL such as www.neal-schuman.com) in order to obtain the site's TCP/IP address, which is the fundamental means by which networked computers identify one another over the Internet. This cross-referencing is performed by Domain Name System (DNS) servers. A local DNS server is typically provided and managed by the Internet service provider (ISP); some libraries, however, choose to host their own DNS servers.

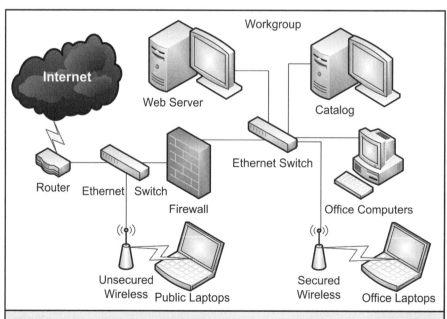

Figure 10-1. Visual of Both Logical and Physical Network Designs for a Library

Domain names are registered by private companies (e.g., Network Solutions and GoDaddy) and are propagated across several primary DNS servers in protected locations throughout the world. These primary DNS servers are simply tables that link a friendly name such as an URL to a TCP/IP address. They do not store every name that exists on the Internet, but they do store all of the addresses represented by all domains.

A library computer will typically know the address of the DNS server by virtue of information stored in the router to which it is connected. This ISP-provided DNS server will be the first one that a computer contacts when, for instance, a user requests a URL through a Web browser. If no appropriate entry exists on that DNS server for the URL requested, it will relay the request to a larger DNS server containing more entries, and so on if need be until the primary DNS servers are consulted. The TCP/IP address corresponding with the requested URL is then used to contact the appropriate Web site.

USING FIREWALLS FOR EXTERNAL PROTECTION

Firewalls are gateways that allow traffic to originate outward from a network, but which allow only authorized traffic to flow back into the LAN. Firewalls can be as tightly secure or as porous as desired. In a library setting, the firewall should be invisible to clients within the LAN who are using the network for legitimate purposes and a solid barrier for those attempting to perform questionable activity. For any questionable activity taking place outside the LAN, the firewall should be impenetrable.

Firewalls come in many different varieties. A firewall is not a router, although a top-of-the-line firewall typically comes with a DHCP (dynamic host configuration protocol) server, network address translation (NAT), and virtual private network (VPN) capabilities built in.

FIREWALLS AND DATA TRANSMISSION

The basic function of a firewall is to police the flow of traffic to and from the Internet into the LAN. It may help to think of this flow of Internet traffic as occurring along a series of multilane roadways, as in Figure 10-2.

These lanes are called "ports," and the traffic that travels along them is the data requested or sent by library computers. This includes all types of computers, including servers, printer/copier devices, and anything that can connect to the Internet. Figure 10-3 offers a brief refresher on the kinds of traffic that typically travel along these ports.

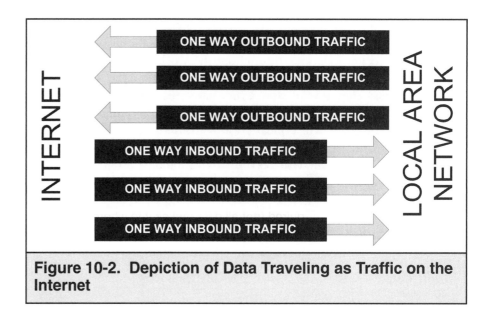

Figure 10-2. Depiction of Data Traveling as Traffic on the Internet

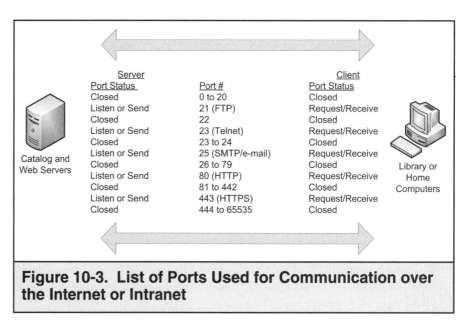

Figure 10-3. List of Ports Used for Communication over the Internet or Intranet

All of these ports will travel through the firewall when it is installed in-line with the router and the ISP. A firewall by default will allow any port to be opened by any computer or device on its "inside," within the LAN that it is protecting. We will cover port configuration in greater detail later on. For now, be aware that by default a firewall will not interfere with any traffic originating from within the network to which it is assigned: this can have significant implications for staff-side security strategy.

To better understand firewalls, let's focus on the composition of the data they control. The protocols describing and governing data traveling on

Table 10-2. List of the OSI Model with Simplified Definitions	
Layer	**Definition**
Physical	The actual hardware components that create the signal—in most cases the Ethernet card or onboard Ethernet, but by definition can also be a modem
Data Link	This layer is for controlling that signal, when the device sends and receives transmission (and thus data). This also can be the Ethernet card.
Network	This is the routing of the data, where it travels and how it gets there. This is controlled by software typically.
Transport	The movement of the actual data from one place to another, retransmitted as required (not all data makes it to where it is going in one piece).
Session	The logical connection—two components (an example would be peer to peer) talking specifically to each other for a specific transaction.
Presentation Services	This layer is responsible for the actual data format, or the syntax of data.
Application	User application—the interaction of the user and the application of network access.

library networks are organized within a common standard, open system interconnection (OSI). OSI describes various levels, or "layers," of data transmission, each governed by specific protocols. These are defined briefly in Table 10-2.

The physical and data link layers are considered lower-layer protocols, and the remaining five are considered upper-layer protocols. This information is not centrally important when dealing with firewalls, but is a basic understanding of OSI will help make sense of how firewalls operate.

Lower-layer protocols govern common communication paths. Some of the following may sound familiar: ATM (asynchronous transfer mode), Ethernet, FDDI (fiber distributed data interface), frame relay, SDLC (Synchronous Data Link Control), token ring, and X.25. Because most people are familiar with Ethernet, we use it to illustrate our discussion of lower-layer protocols.

ETHERNET

Ethernet transmits data between computers within your network along a single pair of wires. A separate pair of wires is devoted to controlling the data flow, to keeping various packets of transmitted data from being conflated. Imagine a loud party in which everyone talks at once: an outside observer would have a difficult time picking out individual conversations from the jumble of words being uttered. Along its data-transmission wire pair, without its data-control wire pair, Ethernet is such a jumble.

To lend some order to the babble, the partygoers must take turns conversing, so that no more than a single sentence is spoken at a time by anyone in the room. John says to Jane, "Have you heard the gossip?" and Jane replies, "No, I haven't." They must then wait for their turn as the couple next to them speaks, each in turn. And so on throughout the room. This approach obviously slows down the individual conversations a bit in exchange for the benefits of structure and intelligibility. Occasionally two people will speak at once, with neither hearing the other. Realizing what happened, one will defer to the other, offsetting the timing of their responses so that their individual sentences are spoken sequentially.

That, in a nutshell, is Ethernet—somewhat slow, cumbersome, and tedious, with potential for confusion. However, great strides have been made in speeding up the conversations and shortening the number of words required to get a point across so that Ethernet now works fairly well and speedily. Ethernet transmissions are composed of very specific components. At the lowest level, there is a preamble, a destination address, source address, type, data, and frame-check sequence. This is depicted and defined in Table 10-3.

The lower-layer protocol is the network's packhorse: it simply carries the load. The MAC addresses contained in Ethernet's source address component are very important later on; for one thing, they allow system administrators to control internal LAN access at the Ethernet-switch level. Firewalls do much of their work by referencing information carried through low-level protocols.

Lower-layer protocols transmit data along with basic identifying information. They describe the data being transmitted but do not describe the route along which the data travel. Routing information is described by upper-layer protocols. All upper-layer protocols are in a basic sense the format and design that data take on when traveling over that particular network

Table 10-3. List of the Lower-layer Protocol with Simplified Definitions of Each Component

Function	Definition
Preamble	Allows synchronization between the two communicating Ethernet devices.
Destination Address	This is the physical address, hardwired onto the Ethernet board, known as the MAC address, of the device receiving the data. A computer or printer will not know all of the actual MAC addresses on the network; it will keep track of only those it deals with most frequently.
Source Address	The physical MAC address of the computer or device sending the information.
Type	An identifier of the protocol that is used when multiple upper-layer protocols are on the same physical medium—not something to worry about in understanding this chapter.
Data	The actual data, which can vary in length/size within certain parameters.
Frame-Check Sequence	This segment of information is used to test and confirm that the data contained is valid and hasn't deteriorated or been lost. It is performed through a cyclic redundancy check (CRC) on the receiving device.

Table 10-4. List of Upper-layer Protocols and Simplified Definition of Each Component	
Protocol	**Brief Description**
Systems Network Architecture (SNA)	IBM designed protocol specifically for IBM hardware and network architecture. Very robust, and very complicated.
Transmission Control Protocol / Internet Protocol (TCP/IP)	Shared protocol used as for client/server applications, e.g., the Internet, where a client (computer) requests something from a server.
Netware	Novell designed protocol specifically for print and file sharing services within a LAN.
AppleTalk	Apple designed protocol specifically for print and file-sharing services using Apple Macintosh computers and printers.

architecture. They were designed by manufacturers such as IBM to deal with specific circumstances and needs of clients. Table 10-4 lists a few of the more well-known upper-layer protocols and very brief descriptions.

Firewalls work on all levels of a network, both upper and lower layers. Most important to the average library is the TCP/IP (referred to from here on as IP) protocol in the upper layer, as both the Internet and most LANs rely heavily on that protocol. As explained in previous chapters, IP assigns a specific address for a server or computer, allowing direct communication among devices.

A typical firewall setup allows traffic initiated from an internal LAN computer to flow both ways. In addition, it functions as a DHCP server, assigning internal LAN IP addresses, and performs NAT. When a computer on your network requests an Internet resource, NAT takes the internally assigned IP address of that local computer and erases it from the data packet it sends outside of your library, replacing it with a global IP address. This global address is a single IP address that anyone looking at the traffic on the Internet would see. This prevents external attacks from trying to steal and use a networked computer's internal IP address, which would allow hackers to penetrate the firewall and access the internal workings of your LAN.

Servers behind the firewall are normally assigned specific, static IP addresses. This address may be the original IP address assigned by the ISP vendor, but it needn't be. The firewall deals with these static addresses by referring to settings that exclude specific addresses from being translated via NAT. In addition to being excluded from translation, these IP addresses must be specified in a table that allows external inquiries or requests from outside computers via the Internet, thus allowing a library Web server to communicate and serve Web pages to the Internet.

Catalog services provided by a server will require specific ports to be available, or open for communications, to work properly. This may include the Web services port 80. These ports will be identified by the vendor and must be kept in mind when adding or modifying a firewall.

> This exclusion is sometimes called a tunnel. Opening a tunnel to a Web server by default opens only the default port 80, but this can be widened to all ports if required. Obviously, it isn't recommended that you have all ports open to the Web server; leave open only the ones required for the specific services being offered by that server.

SPECIFICATIONS FOR FIREWALL LOCATION

The firewall should be placed physically in a secure location, preferably within the same room as the primary switches and if possible with the router. Refer to Figure 10-1 for the typical placement of the firewall. Physical and administrative access to the router should be strictly limited. Passwords should be very secure, and should contain capital letters, numbers, and a minimum of eight characters, and should in no way resemble any common word, phrase, name, or acronym. It should be changed at least every year, preferably every six months, ideally every 90 days.

The room in which the firewall is located should be always locked and closed when not attended. Keys and access should be limited to those with appropriate authority to make changes or who have valid reasons to access other items within the room. If the location appears to be insufficiently secure, consider purchasing a well-ventilated wall mount enclosure with a locking door.

The firewall's physical security is paramount. If anyone can gain access to it, they could easily reboot the firewall, connect physically to its serial port, bypass the setup routine, reset the firewall's password, and reconfigure it to allow remote access. Once this is accomplished, a hacker can gain LAN network connectivity from any location outside of the library and modify the firewall at their leisure.

OBTAINING AND CONFIGURING THE FIREWALL

Every firewall manufacturer provides its own preinstalled software, and thus there is no standard firewall-configuration interface. The same as operating system, application, and productivity software, firewall software is updated periodically, and the changes are sometimes subtle. As with other software, detailed universal instructions are impossible due to the multitude of brands and individual versions of the interfaces.

Configuring a firewall is best done directly, connecting the firewall and server via their serial ports. Avoid using Web interfaces to interact with firewall settings unless the computer and firewall are in a secure and encrypted connection.

Most of the major network device vendors offer different levels of training and certification on how to configure their devices. While such training is certainly helpful, unless a library has a support contract that prevents local control of network devices (a turnkey contract), it is not impossible for a technologically oriented and intelligent librarian to research the proper guidelines, follow them, and successfully configure a firewall.

The following sections will cover three steps toward obtaining and configuring a firewall. The first involves gathering information required for the installation of a new firewall. The second describes configuring a new or existing firewall. The third focuses on replacing or upgrading an existing firewall.

Obtaining a New Firewall

Determine the need. The following areas must be taken into consideration before determining which firewall will best fit library needs:

- *The sheer number of computers and network devices.* This includes the maximum number of wireless devices per wireless access point (WAP), printers, bar code scanners, and other devices that use the network.
- *Network backbone speed.* Typically this will be 100mbs, but could be as low as 10mbs or as high as 10gbs. Most newer computers have 10/100/1000mbs ranges, but not all network switches will have that range. The backbone is the connectivity between switches, closets, and routers (includes firewall if applicable).
- *Review the network section of your technology plan.* If the network is due to be upgraded to a higher backbone speed or more available nodes, be sure to take this into consideration when choosing the firewall.
- *Create a report in the following format* (or something similar—just ensure that all needed information is present in one document):

Just So library is currently looking to purchase (or upgrade) a firewall.

The current network configuration consists of four server rooms with a fiber backbone of 1 gb, and a total of 14 switches that have a capacity of approximately 300 nodes. All switches are currently able to handle only 10/100mbs. In addition, there are 6 wireless access points with a maximum capacity of 10 nodes each, for an additional 60 nodes.

The current computer and networked device population is 260, with 80 percent having 10/100/1000mbs capabilities; 14 of the devices are portable, and feature both wired and wireless access.

The technology plan calls for an expected backbone upgrade to 4gbs on existing fiber, with the four primary switches having 10/100/1000mbs capacity within the next year. The router will be upgraded to handle the higher capacity as well. Over the following three years, the remaining switches will be upgraded to 10/100/1000mbs. There are no plans at this time to upgrade wireless access points.

The firewall will be placed immediately behind the router, and should have the network capacity of at least

1000mbs, and initially a set amount of RAM (random access memory) to adequately handle existing network bandwidth; it has the capacity add enough RAM to adequately handle future planned bandwidth improvements.

Seek out vendor information. With the previous information, vendors can be contacted and will be able to offer informed price quotes based on the library's needs and expectations. At this point the library must decide if its technology personnel have the background to configure and maintain the firewall or if the vendor has a turnkey and maintenance program available to assist in setting it up, changing as needed, and troubleshooting when required. It is also possible to modify most contracts to allow local control and modification with technical assistance over the phone should problems arise.

Research the vendor suggestions and equipment offers. This can easily be accomplished by joining technical support forums and searching the archives for items concerning the products under consideration. Forums can be wonderful research tools in which participants are quite honest about the problems encountered and typically aren't showcases for vendors.

Programming the Firewall

Before bringing the firewall on-line, it should be tested in a safe, nonimpacting way. A small switch, a couple of computers, a network connection, and the firewall is all you need to build a test base.

Programming firewalls does require some technical background, especially when dealing with higher-end firewalls featuring greater flexibility and wider ranges of features. Generally speaking, the smaller the firewall, the less expensive it should be, the fewer features it will have, and the less bandwidth capacity it will provide. The information obtained previously in this chapter should help in determining the needs of your network.

First, the firewall should not become a bottleneck for Internet traffic. Valid Internet traffic should flow virtually unrestricted by the firewall. Although this depends on the vendor's default settings, a firewall is typically set to allow internally initiated requests to outside Web sites through HTTP (hypertext transfer protocol), FTP (file transfer protocol), SMTP (simple mail transfer protocol), and so on, and the return of the requested information. For everything else, before traffic is allowed through the firewall, it must first be identified and approved.

An inventory of network assets will provide a summary of software packages, database subscriptions, servers, printers, vendor agreements, and turnkey products that may require unfettered communications. It is extremely important to obtain this information before bringing the firewall online and setting out to ensure that the firewall has the appropriate ports open. Create a list as in Table 10-5. Use this list to determine what ports need to be opened. In some cases, the ports can be restricted to IP ranges and specific computers that have static IP addresses within the LAN. This should be considered if specific personnel have discrete tasks that require secure logins to servers or services outside the LAN. An example of this would be an administrative business position that must log in a county

Table 10-5. Sample List of Software, Subscriptions, etc., That Require Specific Ports to Function Properly

Vendors

Company	Product	Service	TCP	UDP
MyCatalog Inc.	Online catalog system	Turnkey	140	140
" "	" "	" "	141	141
" "	" "	" "	80	80
" "	" "	" "	21	21
" "	" "	" "	20	20

Staff Required Access

User	Reason	Static IP address	TCP	UDP
Director	MVS/3270 Access	168.192.1.212	443	443
" "	" "	" "	23	23
Assoc. Director	MVS/3270 Access	168.192.1.143	443	443
" "	" "	" "	23	23
Collection Dev	MVS/3270 Access	168.192.1.14	443	443
" "	" "	" "	23	23
Copy Cataloger	National Copy Catalog	168.192.1.76	443	443
" "	" "	" "	23	23

Software Licenses

Company	Product	Service	TCP	UDP
MyScience Inc.	Molecular Simulator	License key server	80	
" "	" "	" "		2001

Subscriptions

Company	Product	Service	TCP	UDP
MyD-base Inc.	Statewide journal db	Proxy required	80	80
My-Books Inc.	New Book Reviews	Web site	80	80
" "	" "	Secure sign-in	443	443
" "	" "	FTP downloads	21	21

MVS (Multiple Virtual Storage) system through a 3270 emulation to manage financial transactions. For those computers, if a static IP has not been assigned to that employee's computer, for best security practices one may need to be assigned.

If you look closely, you'll see that some of the ports listed here are repeated. This is not a problem, and these ports need only be opened once, unless they are tied specifically to a static IP address within the LAN. Keep this document and update it as required, as frequently as the firewall needs to be modified for new or canceled services and subscriptions. If the port evaluation is maintained digitally, encrypt the file, as it will reveal weaknesses to anyone desiring to attack the LAN from without. Knowing what standard ports are not blocked (standard being HTTP port 80 or FTP port 21), is a goldmine of information for hackers.

Next, review the firewall vendor's manual. Often, information must be programmed into the firewall in a specific order for it to work properly. It may be helpful to map out the instructions: there is nothing wrong with typing out the instructions in step-by-step detail, using your own words and adding your own notes. This can make it easier to review the sequence of steps involved.

Save work frequently, in an encrypted folder on the computer used to configure the firewall. Firewall devices allow saving of the configuration file through a program called TFTP (trivial file transfer protocol). This is a simplified FTP service that is not encrypted and is predominately used for firewall configuration, storage, and restoration. A version of this software can be easily found as shareware on the Internet.

Saving the configuration file typically involves typing a single command, which will include the specific IP address identifying the computer to which the file will be sent. The computer with that IP address must have the TFTP software turned on and ready to receive data. Saving the configuration file every few steps can be a tremendous help when troubleshooting setup problems. Of course, once the configuration is working completely, the configuration file should be stored somewhere safe, in an encrypted form, and the supporting documentation deleted and stored off of the computer as well.

When the entire programming/configuration is complete, and the configuration file resides safely on the TFTP server, it is time to test the firewall. If all goes as planned, it will of course work smoothly. If not, document which features work and which don't. Refer to the manual to determine where something might have gone wrong. Then restore the configuration file that was saved prior to the suspected incorrectly completed step, reboot the firewall, and see if a different approach works. Refer frequently to the manual and do not be afraid of looking through any online forums that might exist that discuss the particular firewall being installed.

It can be a bit challenging and even frustrating at times, but these are the steps necessary to properly configure a firewall. The last thing to remember is to change the IP information for the internal and external sides of the firewall, as they will change when it is placed into the production side of the LAN. The tools and suggestions offered here should assist in the installation and configuration of a new firewall. They are referred to in the next section.

Replacing or Upgrading a Firewall

The most important point to remember if the library has a firewall in place is that the current configuration obviously works. The configuration file will contain all of the appropriate ports, IP addresses, and settings for that particular firewall to function in your library LAN environment. Save that file, and print it out.

Complete the previously discussed tasks of inventorying LAN devices and users and listing software subscriptions and licenses. An upgraded firewall should be chosen in the same fashion that a first-time purchase of a firewall is chosen. Attention to the technology plan and consideration of future growth must be taken into consideration when making the purchase.

Follow the same procedures for reviewing the upgrade or replacement purchase. Be forewarned: the upgrade could be just as difficult as an original installation, especially if the firewall is of a different brand. There will also be differences between firewall operating system versions, even for firewalls manufactured by the same company.

During the upgrade or replacement, take time to update the inventory of IP addresses, TCP and UDP (user datagram protocol) ports, and other settings that were in the original firewall configuration. It is almost certain that the configuration file will not translate perfectly to the new hardware. The firewall's vendor may provide a conversion software package or import feature, but more likely you won't have such recourse. Be prepared to start from scratch.

With the current firewall in place, you can test the new firewall (attached to a minimal test configuration running beside the main network) at your leisure. As with a new installation, you should take pains to ensure that all information describing the replacement firewall is updated and current. Failure to perform this evaluation might lead you to leave ports unnecessarily open, such as peer-to-peer networking ports.

Just remember to save your configuration file frequently, and to save it in an encrypted form. Follow the same procedures laid out in the previous section, and the upgrade should proceed smoothly.

LOCAL COMPUTER-LEVEL PROTECTIONS FROM INTERNET THREATS

Local computers and devices within the library LAN are subject to external threats from the Internet. Even a networked copier that is improperly configured can be attacked if it has been assigned a specific IP address, as is likely.

While stories abound about students hacking into school mainframes and changing their grades, there are those who hack into libraries—networks notoriously weak on security—to obtain personal patron information, enough to steal patrons' identities. Away from the server, staff will often maintain mailing addresses and other personal information on local workstations simply

To see hidden files, simply open up My Documents, go to the Tools drop-down menu, and select Folder Options. Under the second tab in the Folder Options window, deselect Do Not Show Hidden Files under the Hidden Files and Folders section, and deselect Hide Protected Operating System Files. When the second one is deselected, a warning box will pop up—simply select "yes I understand and know what I want to do." This will allow you to view the hidden directory named "Default."

out of convenience. The threat may be mitigated somewhat in these cases, but unencrypted data on staff computers still constitutes a security risk.

Building a disk image with preset restrictions may be the most straightforward way to manage both office and public computer systems. A disk image represents a complete copy of a computer's hard drive; this allows administrators to completely erase all data on a given machine's hard drive and replace it with a clean, known version of its operating system, user account information, and file structure.

When building an image, it is wisest to begin by creating a user profile and granting it limited authority and access. Once this profile has been adjusted to your satisfaction, log on using an administrator's account and copy the entire user profile into the default profile. This requires that you override Windows' default settings and view hidden files.

In addition to these steps, if a smaller image is desired, while in the Explore view, delete temporary Internet files, caches, cookies, and in the Windows directory delete the files in the "Prefetch" folder. This is easier done while logged in as an administrator. If any error messages appear, such as "File In Use" when performing the cleanup or copy, the solution is to restart the computer.

Default settings generally represent security risks. The administrative account, named Administrator by default, is an obvious target for hackers and viruses programmed to run under the Administrator account and should be changed to something less obvious. Administrative account names that follow your library's general user-name conventions add a simple but effective element of protection against intruders.

FIREWALL SOFTWARE

WINDOWS XP

Windows XP's built-in firewall is a reliable performer that provides a helpful degree of local protection for individual computers. More sophisticated software firewalls are available for a price, but be careful about relying on firewalls offered free of charge. They may work just fine, but the updates may not be as readily available as those offered in support of commercial software.

Microsoft's firewall utility can be managed through the control panel. The control panel interface does not have terribly many selections available for adjustment; the firewall is configured to respond automatically to various contingencies. For example, a JavaScript-enhanced Web site might require data to be transmitted on a port other than the default Web port 80. When that request is made, the Windows firewall will notify you that a nonstandard transmission is being attempted and will ask for approval before proceeding. It will then remember your decision and the setting authorized for that port.

If you intend to use a disk image as the foundation for all office or public computers, you should open all important Web sites, including subscription sites, and all programs intended for use by the image's eventual users. This allows the computer from which you will derive the disk image to establish all appropriate Active X, Java, and communication port assignments and associate them with the appropriate user account.

To review the Windows firewall and its available settings, use an available computer while logged on as the administrator to follow along while reading this segment. The firewall administration screen's three tabs are reviewed here in turn.

The General Tab

There are only three available options on the General Tab: On, With Exceptions; On, Without Exceptions; and Off, as seen in Figure 10-4.

When the firewall is on, it will block everything not approved by the user. Configuration, including an option to manually identify trusted services, is available in another tab.

When the firewall is on and the "without exceptions" option is selected, any exceptions that may be listed on the next tab will be blocked. This setting is infrequently used and in a library setting is very impractical.

When the firewall is off, the firewall blocks no ports and undertakes no monitoring of user activity. This setting should be turned off when a third-party firewall is installed or as needed when troubleshooting connectivity issues related to Web sites or network devices such as printers or shared drives.

Exceptions Tab

The Windows firewall will automatically block all nonstandard traffic unless it is listed as an exception. All exceptions that have been added are listed under the Exceptions tab. The initial view of this list is shown in Figure 10-5. Some items are preinstalled: File and Printer Sharing, Remote Assistance, and Remote Desktop. Most public workstations will have no need for options like File and Printer Sharing, Remote Assistance, or Remote Desktop. If an office computer does not share files or a printer over the network, there is no need for it to have the File and Printer Sharing listed as exceptions. The computer will be able to access a remote network drive or shared folder successfully without that service turned on locally.

When the Add Program option is selected, a new window is opened listing default software installations. If the software you wish to authorize is not listed, the Browse button will allow you to manually choose the correct program.

> It is easier to allow Windows to add the software name than to manually add it through the Exceptions tab. Simply starting an applicable program or visiting an applicable Web site will cause the firewall to prompt for permission to proceed. If use of a particular resource is authorized, it will be added to the Exceptions list.

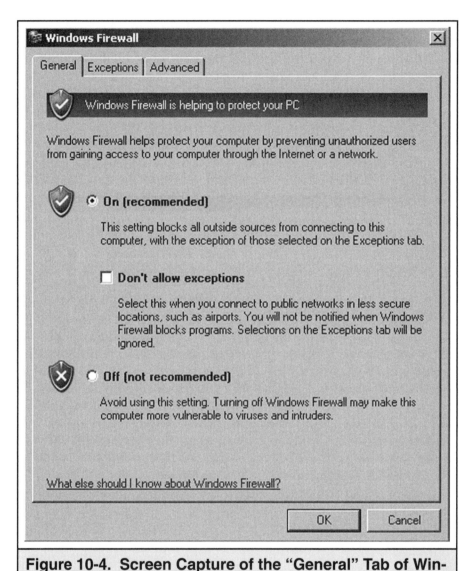

Figure 10-4. Screen Capture of the "General" Tab of Windows Firewall Control Panel

After the program is added, identify the appropriate scope—which computers on the Internet or LAN need access to this program on this computer—and choose one of the three options presented. The default scope is the most generous: "Any computer." The second selection limits access to only those on the local subnet (computers sharing a specific range of IP addresses within the library LAN). The third selection allows you to specify precise IP addresses and subnets.

The second option under this tab is to open specific ports. Notice the TCP and UDP radio buttons; only one of these options can be selected at a time. If the same port number must have both UDP and TCP access, then the port will have to be added twice. Scope is a simple question when

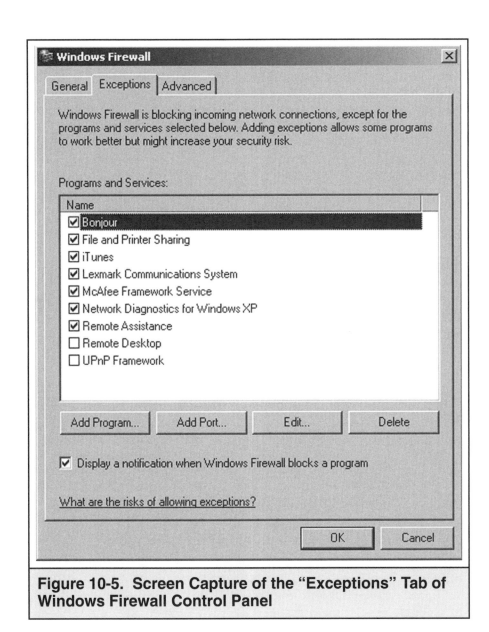

Figure 10-5. Screen Capture of the "Exceptions" Tab of Windows Firewall Control Panel

opening specific ports, as the IP address can reflect a single location or group of locations. Again, Windows will configure this option automatically when an appropriate Web site or program is accessed, as long as the "Display a notification" is checked on the Exceptions tab. For public computers, you may want to leave the notification option unchecked.

Highlighting a particular program allows access to the Edit button. This enables you to change the scope assigned to the program in question. If for some reason a Web site modifies its server's IP address, it is possible that Windows may not identify the new address as valid, and will block access. This window will allow you to change the scope by adding the new IP address.

The Advanced Tab

The Advanced Settings dialog (Figure 10-6) allows control over similar settings, but with more options and a finer degree of control. Specific IP addresses can be indicated for specific services. As an example, if the only FTP server that the system needs to access belongs to a vendor providing downloads of PDF files, then this is where that vendor's FTP IP address would be identified.

The ICMP (Internet control message protocol) tab is seldom used, except when troubleshooting network issues. Leaving this unchecked is a good security practice. Starting these services creates a vulnerability, in

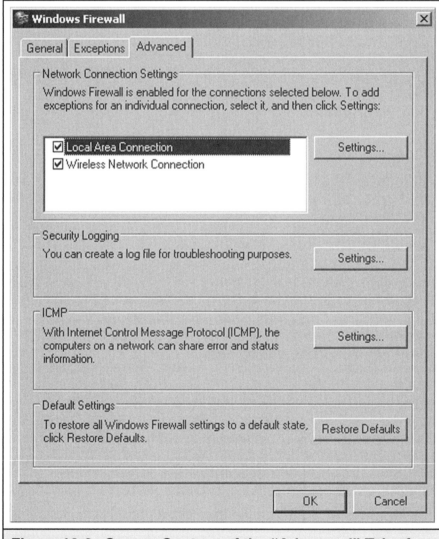

Figure 10-6. Screen Capture of the "Advanced" Tab of Windows Firewall Control Panel

that a person armed with no special software except the Windows command prompt can locate and map actual IP addresses on the network. With one computer's IP address at hand, a hacker can go on to target other specific computers from behind the firewall, bypassing an important network security measure. Once a hacker has gained control, it is a simple process to install a program that makes requests for resources located outside of the library. Since the infected computer is initiating the outbound traffic from within the library's network, the firewall will allow the traffic unless it is on ports that are specifically closed.

To continue with the settings, do not turn on logging unless the computer is experiencing difficulties. The log may help isolate problems in troubleshooting, but as an everyday activity, it represents another drain, albeit a modest one, on the computer's resources.

Even though the Network Connection Settings option provides an ICMP tab, even more features can be controlled under the ICMP Settings button. Enabling any of these options for normal use is not recommended. Firewall settings are seldom taken into consideration on most desktops, but many features can be used to assist in overall network security within a LAN.

Updates Settings

Regular maintenance of the network computers, including patching and updating the software they run, is a fundamental aspect of your security strategy. Our previous discussions of routine maintenance have focused on what can be done directly on individual computers; in this section, we turn our attention to network-wide approaches to the same issue.

As mentioned, a desktop computer is a liability to the network if it is not adequately protected. Mapping the IP addresses within a LAN over a period of time, say, a month, will show a hacker what IP ranges are set as DHCP, and which IP addresses always match or are in use. Network administrators tend to assign static IP addresses in groups; this allows them to maintain specific IP address ranges for different types of equipment (switches, printers, print servers, and so on). It also allows hackers to readily identify valuable targets.

For computer workstations, every popular operating system created within the past few years includes an update-management system that allows patches to be installed unobtrusively during scheduled times.

Each library computer should be set to automatically download and install OS patches at a scheduled time. By default, Windows Update runs every day at 3:00 a.m. This is fine if you choose to leave your library's computers running throughout the night (and if your library can afford the electricity bill), but the default time for automatic updates can be freely changed. Because the process of checking for, downloading, and installing patches consumes some system resources, it is preferable that you schedule such updates to run during times of light workstation use.

> After hackers determine which IP addresses are assigned to the switches, router, and firewall, they can begin to target known weaknesses and suspected configuration flaws of each device. Taking over a switch or groups of switches, for instance, will allow a denial of service attack, simply by shutting off all the switch's ports and changing its password. Hijacking the firewall and router gives hackers the ability to move around within the network freely and undetected, using network devices as they choose.

Running an SMS or other software installation server is also a valid way to control patches for computers on the network. This allows a centralized control of updates, patches, and related matters, which can be extremely helpful when patching non-OS (operating system) software. Some programs can become liabilities if they are not kept up to date. Most of these programs allow for manual update checks, which tends to be a cumbersome approach in library settings; a few provide automatic updates, typically with little control and limited settings available to the customer.

For network devices such as printers, routers, and switches, which do not have robust user interfaces, the task of keeping BIOS (Basic Input/Output System), EPROM (erasable programmable read-only memory), and operating systems (on routers and switches) can be a challenge. An experienced, resourceful technician can install these updates without much difficulty. However, if not done properly, BIOS and hardware updates can impair equipment such as printers, switches, routers, and firewalls.

While some vendors make patches and updates freely available, others charge money for the privilege, often by requiring that users enter into service contracts. Given the high stakes involved, it may be wise to obtain a service contract that guarantees access to all patches and updates appropriate to your network hardware.

LINUX, RED HAT, AND OTHER FLAVORS OF OPERATING SYSTEMS

The principles described previously apply equally to Unix-based computers and to Windows-based systems. With Unix-style operating systems, including Apple OS X, the same policy should be in effect for patching and updates; software installation servers exist for all popular operating systems.

Linux is an open-source operating system built along the lines of Unix; most Linux implementations are freely available (commercial Linux vendors monetize the product by providing paid-for technical support). Because Linux is an open-source OS, meaning that its source code is freely available for people to study and adapt, updates to any given flavor of Linux tend to be made available frequently and to be released irregularly.

REVIEW QUESTIONS

Use this checklist as a guideline to evaluate the knowledge gained from this chapter.

- What is a local area network?
- What is a network device?

- What is a network interface card?
- What is a domain name?
- What is a firewall?
- What is open systems interconnection?
- What is Ethernet?
- Where should a firewall be located?
- How do you configure a firewall?
- How does one obtain a new firewall?
- How do you upgrade a firewall?
- How do you protect local desktop computers from Internet threats?
- How do you build an image of a computer?
- What types of firewall software are available?
- What are some other external threats for networks?
- What are some external threats for non-Windows operating systems?

KEY POINTS AND CONCLUSION

- Securing network technology while ensuring network availability and capacity requires understanding of the basics of how networks function. Networks simply provide paths for data to move from one location to another, with controls on how that data travels.
- Firewalls offer powerful ways to protect a library network by preventing unsolicited incoming traffic from hackers attempting to assess weaknesses of the technology connected to the library network. They are also able to mask how many components are actually online in a library by using NAT to show a single TCP/IP address to the WWW for the numerous computers and other devices within the library.

Protecting the LAN from external threats is a serious task. The wide array of network devices within the library LAN can present a challenge to network administrators hoping to keep each piece of equipment up to date and well defended. A properly programmed and configured network firewall, in combination with an aggressive patch-management and update plan for computers and other network devices, can greatly reduce your network's susceptibility to risk.

READINGS AND RESOURCES

Dhanjani, N., and Clarke, J. 2005. *Network Security Tool.* Sebastopol, CA: O'Reilly Media.

Donahue, G. A. 2007. *Network Warrior.* Sebastopol, CA: O'Reilly Media.

Dooley, K., and Brown, I. J. 2006. *Cisco IOS Cookbook: Field-tested Solutions to Cisco Router Problems.* Sebastopol, CA: O'Reilly Media.

Gast, M. 2005. *802.11 Wireless Networks: The Definitive Guide.* Sebastopol, CA: O'Reilly Media.

Harris, J. 2002. *Cisco Network Security Little Black Book.* Sebastopol, CA: Paraglyph Press.

Hunt, C. 2002. *TCP/IP Network Administration.* Sebastopol, CA: O'Reilly Media.

Kozierok, C. 2005. *The TCP/IP Guide: A Comprehensive, Illustrated Internet Protocols Reference.* San Francisco, CA: No Starch Press.

Lucas, M. W. 2004. *Cisco Routers for the Desperate: Router Management, The Easy Way.* San Francisco, CA: No Starch Press.

McNab, C. 2007. *Network Security Assessment.* Sebastopol, CA: O'Reilly Media.

Peikari, C., and Chuvakin, A. 2004. *Security Warrior.* Sebastopol, CA: O'Reilly Media.

Pogue, D., and Biersdorfer, J. D. 2006. *The Internet: The Missing Manual.* Sebastopol, CA: O'Reilly Media.

Potter, B., and Fleck, R. 2002. *802.11 Security.* Sebastopol, CA: O'Reilly Media.

Sloan, J. D. 2001. *Network Troubleshooting Tools.* Sebastopol, CA: O'Reilly Media.

Zwicky, E. D., Chapman, D. B., and Cooper, S. 2000. *Building Internet Firewalls.* Sebastopol, CA: O'Reilly Media.

11

SECURING THE LIBRARY NETWORK FROM INTERNAL THREATS

In the previous chapter, we looked at ways of protecting library networks from myriad external threats. In this chapter we point out that the aforementioned policy of aggressively patching and updating is a major component of this chapter, which is devoted to protecting the LAN (local area network) from internal threats.

In this chapter, we make recommendations on network layouts, routing, and network-specific firewalls within a library's LAN. We then discuss desktop security settings for public and staff systems. Once again, there are so many ways to protect the LAN from internal threats that we cannot presume to cover specific software or hardware in a step-by-step manner.

LAN DESIGN AND CONFIGURATION

The average LAN will consist of a router, a firewall, switches, cabling, and computers or network nodes (any other network device, e.g., printers, PDAs, etc.) as shown in Figure 11-1. It may also contain a wireless access point.

This basic setup is inherently unsecure, leaving library staff computers on the same network as the public computers and wireless access point. You may have placed restrictions on the public computers that prevent most hacking attempts, but there are other ways to obtain network access than via the computers you make available to the public.

It is not unusual to discover that a patron has, out of malice or ignorance of the risks involved, disconnected an Ethernet cable from a public workstation and inserted it into his or her private laptop. If a library uses the standard DHCP (dynamic host configuration protocol) setup, which is generally recommended, the rogue user will have no difficulty in accessing the network via a computer possibly carrying viruses, hacker software, peer-to-peer software, and myriad other problems. If a person is discrete enough, it is possible to remain plugged in to a library's network this way for hours without being noticed.

One solution to this problem is to not have a DHCP server at all (not a recommended approach). A second is to host a DHCP server that assigns

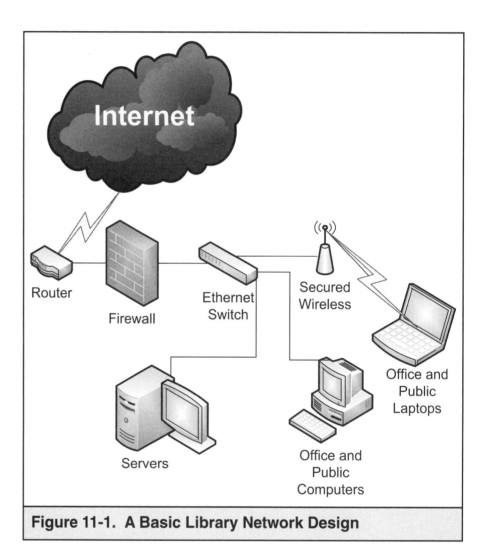

Figure 11-1. A Basic Library Network Design

IP addresses to specific MAC (media access control) addresses. This approach involves a fair amount of time and effort to originally configure, and it requires due diligent maintenance. A third is to locate data drops to discourage access. However, this causes difficulty for technicians performing network maintenance and does not offer anything resembling a guarantee of increased security.

Finally, the most practical and easiest-to-maintain approach for most libraries is to lock the port at the Ethernet switch to the specific MAC address of the computer assigned to that port. MAC-based port locking is a standard feature in most Ethernet switches. This approach is aided by a well-organized wiring rack in the closet, which is properly labeled to correlate with the identifier on each data drop.

The design and layout of a LAN can be just as effective at protecting important equipment and data as software-based protection schemes.

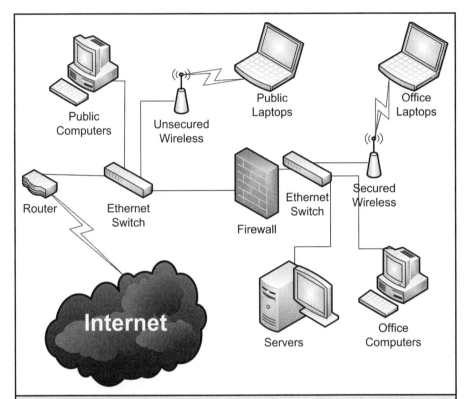

Figure 11-2. A Library Network Design Incorporating Security by Placing Firewall between Public Stations and Office/Administrative Network

Creating a hardware-based barrier, either with the addition of a firewall or a router, is an effective design to protect staff and office equipment. A firewall will create a one-way gate allowing valid traffic to go out, but preventing unrequested traffic from entering, as displayed in Figure 11-2. A router, although a little more difficult to set up, will effectively create a barrier by placing one side of the network on a different level, as displayed in Figure 11-3.

The following point, while unrelated to securing a network, is extremely important when designing a network. A computer or Ethernet switch can only see up to five hops away. Anything beyond five hops is invisible and completely inaccessible. This includes the Internet.

A hop is the connection between two separate network devices, primarily switches and firewalls, that are not logically one device (two switches physically connected to each other and acting for all practical purposes as a single device); it can include other devices as well if data passes through them. This connection must be on a non-Ethernet connection to work, typically through a serial or parallel port that is specifically designed for this

A better way to describe the router effect is to compare it to putting a keyboard on a keyboard tray underneath the desk. It is an extension of the desk, allows effective work flow, but is on a different level. It is impossible to roll a ball from the lower level to the desktop without a hop, and vice versa from the desktop to the tray. It acts in some ways as an invisible wall.

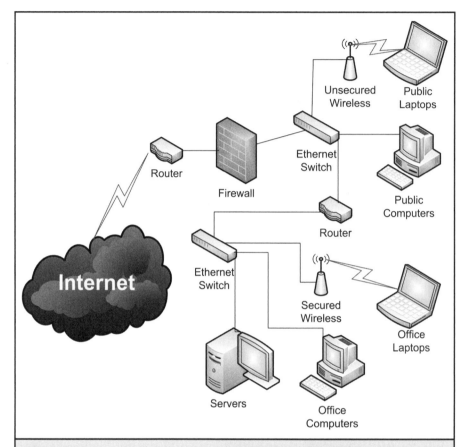

Figure 11-3. A Library Network Using a Router to Separate Public Stations from the Office and Administration Network While Keeping All Components behind a Firewall

purpose, as displayed in Figure 11-4. Data is routed through the serial port between the devices to get to the Internet.

When the devices or switches cannot be connected to one another to form a single logical device, care must be taken to not have excessive hops. Figure 11-5 shows what a network would look like in this regard, and is labeled to show that the computers connected to Ethernet switch G will not access the Internet because they are farther away than five hops.

As we count the hops, A to B is 1, B to C is 2, C to D is 3, D to E is 4, E to F is 5, and F to G is 6, we see that Ethernet switch G is more than five hops away. Therefore, any computer connected to Ethernet switch G will not have access to the Internet. The recommended way of dealing with this issue is to have all switches that cannot serially connect to one another connect to the primary backbone switch.

Segmenting the network to divide staff and administrative computers and devices from the public workstations is a relatively simple and

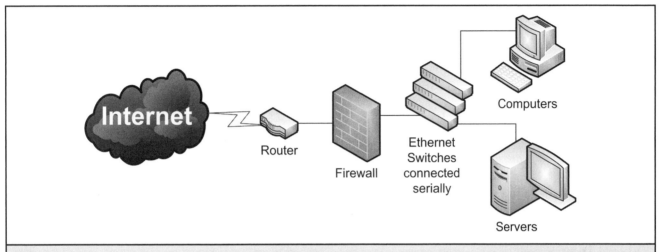

Figure 11-4. Two or More Ethernet Switches Can Connect through a Serial Port to Act as a Single Switch

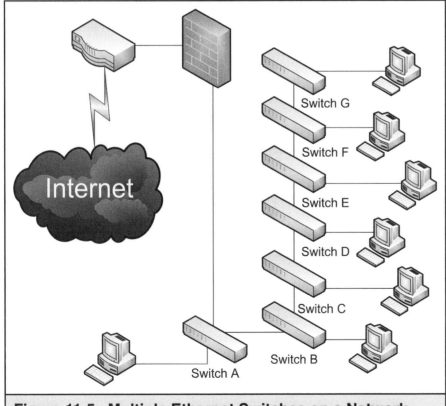

Figure 11-5. Multiple Ethernet Switches on a Network That Exceed the Maximum Number of Hops

effective way to add security. Security derives in this sense from the nature of the network's design in conjunction with the basic functionality of the network itself.

WIRELESS ACCESS POINTS AND WIRELESS SECURITY

Wireless access is a prominent feature of most libraries. Most patrons with laptops are not terribly proficient with technology and may have difficulty simply connecting to a library's wireless network; to remove undue burdens from public services staff, many libraries configure their wirelesss networks as freely and openly as possible, allowing anyone within network range to connect.

In most applications, this would be a serious flaw in network security. In the library this approach is fine, as long as additional network and LAN security is in place to protect library property. Leave the security off—just be sure a notice to patrons explains that any information they send over the wireless network is not secure and that they should avoid doing personal business that involves credit card information, user names and passwords, and so on.

> Wireless access points for staff and administrative use should have encryption enabled, using WEP (wired equivalent privacy), and staff computers should be preconfigured to log on the library's network. Figure 11-3 depicts this design.

In the network design, wireless access points used for public access should be located in such a way that they are not on the same logical network as the staff and administrative network, as described in the section on design and configuration. The separate logical networks provide an effective barrier to widespread infiltration.

Even if the staff wireless access point is behind a firewall or router, traffic to and from it should be secured and encrypted. Although a person could not log on the network without its WEP key, if the transmission between the laptop and WAP (wireless access point) is not encrypted, it can be monitored. In this sense, a wireless network is a bit like a police-band radio scanner. Just as a scanner allows people to listen in on certain transmissions without sending messages of their own, computer-to-WAP transmissions can be observed. In a wireless network environment, this is a serious breach of security.

A brief explanation of wireless security is required to allow appropriate decision making concerning which of the several types of security to use for staff and administrative wireless access.

WIRED EQUIVALENT PRIVACY

Wired equivalent privacy (WEP), also referred to as wireless encryption protocol, is built into most wireless access points and wireless routers.

It is available in either 64-bit or 128-bit encryption; the higher the number, the stronger the encryption. Each wireless network can be assigned a specific "passkey" or can generate one from a chosen word or passphrase.

When the key is generated by using a passphrase, a specific mathematical formula is applied to the word to generate a string of numbers. This string of numbers must be identical on both the client laptop and the wireless access point for the client to successfully log on. Keep the passphrase safe by storing it in a secure area or simply by memorizing it. Do not store it in a text file on any computer.

The resulting string of numbers is the code that the wireless access point will look for when any other wireless device attempts to use it as a portal to the Internet or LAN. This string must be entered into any computer's wireless configuration setup before the computer can gain access to the network.

Encryption, then, employs a mathematical formula to chop up data and send them over the wireless network. Anyone seeing it—recall that people can listen in on wireless transmissions—won't be able to make sense of the encrypted data. At the other end, the receiving computer or wireless access point uses the same identical code to put all the pieces back together in their original form.

Standard functions check to ensure that encrypted data made a safe transition to its destination. These are called checksums: simple mechanisms that look at specific locations along the binary data stream, pulling out the 1 or 0 from each of those locations and comparing them to the numbers found in the same position prior to sending. The digits should match. If not, then the data did not make it through successfully, and will need to be resent.

Encryption should be mandatory for all staff and administrative wireless devices and should be a part of library network policy. Encryption for patron laptops and wireless devices does not need to be implemented, especially if the burden of extra patron-support work outweighs the benefits of enhanced security. As patrons become more and more comfortable with technology—an increasing number of people have WEP–protected wireless networks at home—it may be reasonable to require encryption with personal laptops in the future.

Although encryption may not currently be required for public access to a library network, additional safety measures should be made, as described previously, to protect office and staff computers.

> Having worked on military-grade encryption equipment many, many, years ago, my understanding of encryption is more advanced than that of most technicians. The easiest way to understand encryption is to consider it as a food processor that can "unchop" anything that it has processed. Throw in a handful of pecans, walnuts, and peanuts, turn it on and empty it out—there are millions of little pieces of the different nuts. Just looking at them will not really tell you which piece is a pecan, and trying to piece them back together is impossible. However, this particular food processor can run in "reverse" and will undo all that it has done. Throw all of the pieces back in, use the reverse button, and when it's done, all the pecans, walnuts, and peanuts are back to their original forms.
>
> —*Paul W. Earp*

USING ROUTERS FOR INTERNAL PROTECTION

Routers can act as barriers to malicious traffic if installed within a network. Previously, devices called bridges were used in this role, but their functionality and flexibility were very limited. Technicians have since moved

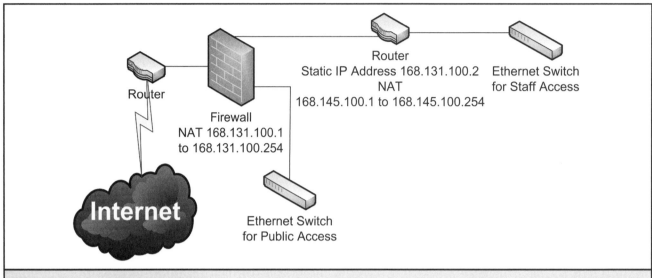

Figure 11-6. Network Address Translation (NAT) Being Used within a Library Network

Previously we discussed ARP (address resolution protocol) tables, used in routers and firewalls. These tables list the IP address (as assigned by DHCP) and the physical address, or MAC. This is how the router knows where to send data to a specific computer within its domain.

toward utilizing routers carefully within a LAN to improve security because of their low cost, inherent strengths, and flexibility.

As previously mentioned, most routers have the ability to provide network address translation (NAT) and DHCP (handing out IP addresses) in the same way a firewall can. A router, if placed as a barrier to the rest of the network, must comply with the hop rule, remaining within three hops of the primary router for the entire LAN, preferably within two hops. If NAT is utilized, it will create two separate logical networks, quite possibly on two separate IP subnets. Although this can be a difficult configuration, it does offer some security gains. (See Figure 11-6.)

See the difference in the NAT? The first NAT at the firewall gives a Class C Subnet of 168.131.100.* (0 to 255, 1 and 255 being reserved, which leaves the 1 to 254 shown). Of this NAT, the IP address 168.131.100.2 is statically assigned to the router. When a computer from the public side of the LAN does actually communicate (for whatever reason) to a staff computer, the only address that will be seen associated with the staff computer will be 168.131.100.2. The router uses its own NAT and DHCP to translate the appropriate data stream to the appropriate computer behind its "barrier."

In this figure, all computers behind the router have a different Class C subnet, 168.145.100.*. This creates the separate "level" discussed earlier. Keep in mind that this is a greatly simplified illustration designed to give you a basic understanding of how this configuration can be created. Implementing this router configuration requires a considerable amount of forethought and research.

USING FIREWALLS FOR INTERNAL PROTECTION

As discussed previously, a second approach is to separate the staff and public networks with a firewall. Although a quality firewall device will have a DHCP and NAT as part of its features, just as a router will, the actual design is a little different. Among the differences is that a firewall, by design, will actually lock out any incoming queries from outside the LAN that it protects. This omnibus approach to protection can be modified by creating tunnels for an interior IP address that is statically assigned, say, as a server. Tunnels might be used to ensure that patrons outside the LAN can reach the Web site or catalog.

Due to their design, setting up a firewall within a LAN to protect a series of computers is actually much easier than configuring a router for the same purpose. With a firewall there is no need to use NAT or to create a separate subnet of IP addresses. This greatly simplifies the network's design, setup, and implementation. Computers on the protected side of the firewall would simply use the network's LAN DHCP server to obtain an IP address. All computers on the inside of the firewall would be, by default, allowed to begin sessions with computers on the outside, and computers on the outside would be prevented from initiating a query with a computer on the inside. (See Figure 11-7.)

As the firewall would also block ICMP traffic and nonapproved TCP (transmission-control protocol) and UDP (user datagram protocol) ports, the computers and devices internal to the firewall would be well protected from the spread of any viruses, worms, or other forms of attack from a rogue computer or a laptop that gains access to the LAN through wireless access.

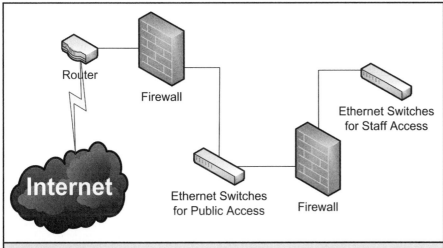

Figure 11-7. Firewall Separating the Publicly Accessible Network from the Staff and Administration Network

It is possible to have multiple firewall devices within a LAN. It is not unheard of to separate a library's office computers from its public computers with a firewall, and to have a third firewall device (the first being at the Internet gateway) protecting the servers. The most important thing to remember here is that network connectivity drops if too many hops occur in the network between computer and gateway.

Servers typically would not be located on the inside of this firewall. Such a configuration is possible, but when a server is configured properly and secured properly against threats, including the software firewall being utilized, it should be safe on the LAN. The reason behind this logic is that most servers, especially those hosting turnkey ILS (integrated library system) software, require that specific ports remain unblocked for maintenance purposes. Although these ports can be tied to a specific IP address, this is not always a workable solution due to shortcomings in the firewall itself; in some cases, for the ports to work properly, they cannot be tied to specific IP addresses. This effectively leaves those ports open to all devices on the inside of the firewall. A port-scanning utility brought into the library on a laptop with access either physically or through wireless will quickly locate those ports.

Another complicating factor concerns establishing tunnels through a firewall. When NAT is disabled and a firewall is configured to allow a separate device on its external side to assign via DHCP all IP (Internet protocol) addresses, specifying a tunnel to a particular static IP address of a server can be a challenge. Although theoretically possible, in practice it can often be inordinately difficult.

PUBLIC ACCESS SYSTEMS: SECURING WORKSTATIONS

Having an aggressive patch and software update policy and practice is extremely important in protecting the LAN from patron-side threats. These threats often take the form of denial of service attacks and attempts to hack into servers or staff computer systems.

Moving away from devices such as firewalls and routers, we now look at the computers that provide end-user access to library networks. We will first look at public workstations.

Our primary focus here is on the methods to mitigate threats from viruses, worms, and hackers, specifically the settings that can be managed either through a domain controller, Active Directory, NIS (network information server), or on the local system itself. Our recommendation is to utilize those devices (if they are available in your particular network configuration) to secure workstation access via log-in accounts. Patrons and staff alike generally do not need very generous access to a workstation's administrative settings. In Windows environments, for example, the most powerful account type a patron should have on a computer is Power User, but User is the best choice. This limits the authority of the patron using the computer.

In addition to domain controls, software packages are available that have the ability to disable specific tasks, menus, and commands. Using one of these applications, it is recommended that the areas listed in Table 11-1 be locked out from the user.

Table 11-1. List of Recommended Restrictions to Be Applied to Public Computers

Feature	Description
Desktop	Desktop Properties should be disabled
Menu Bar	Menu Bar Properties should be disabled
Menu Bar	Administrative folders through Programs should be disabled
Menu Bar	Settings (Control Panel, Printers, etc.) should be disabled
My Computer	System Properties, all Tabs except General disabled
Local Disk	Properties under Right Click should be disabled
Local Disk	Format under Right Click should be disabled
Local Disk	Rename under Right Click should be disabled
Network Places	not available on Desktop
All Folder Views	Tools menu should not offer Map Network Drive
All Folder Views	Tools menu should not offer Disconnect Network Drive
All Folder Views	Tools menu should not offer Synchronize
All Folder Views	View menu should lock out toolbar selection

Note: These are the minimum suggestions in securing the desktop settings, specific programs installed may require review and discussion on what menus should be locked out or disabled.

PROTECTING THE INTERNAL NETWORK FROM PATRON LAPTOPS

Laptops brought into the library by patrons to access the Internet through the wireless access points present a challenge in preventing the spread of viruses and thwarting the use of patron machines to attack and hack the LAN. A strong policy and unbiased enforcement is a key factor, but other steps are required as well.

Home computers, whether desktops or laptops, are notorious to service technicians for being unkempt. Too few users, for example, bother to install antivirus software, and fewer update their virus protection regularly. On a similar note, many computer owners fail to update and patch their operating system and browser software appropriately.

Applications are available that are designed to prevent LAN access for computers and laptops that are not patched to date, have outdated operating systems, or that do not have acceptable virus protection, all within guidelines established by a system administrator. Virus protection is commonly the most contentious topic. Many free virus protection applications are on the market, and many are not very good. Sometimes users will confuse their spyware-protection software for virus-protection software.

Expect patrons to be upset if the library already offers wireless access without these restrictions in place and places restrictions on such access without warning. Long before any such restrictions are instituted, libraries should decide how to publicize the new rules and what type of support will be offered to patrons whose computers do not meet the new criteria for network access. At least three months notice, with publication in a local newspaper or library newsletter, will greatly reduce the stress on employees when the change takes place.

Before deploying an application that can enforce wireless compliance, be sure that the existing LAN infrastructure and design will work with the chosen approach. Prior to purchasing, ask questions of the application's vendor about library servers, firewalls, routers, the types of wireless access points, and switches that are currently installed. If the vendor can guarantee that the current LAN with all its equipment and devices will work, then by all means implement it.

A direct, less expensive option is to not have an open wireless network at all, instead requiring that all laptop users connect using the library's WEP credentials. This approach requires more intensive patron support by the library's public services staff and should involve weekly modification of the wireless access point's passcode and key. Patrons wishing to access to the wireless LAN would need to check out the key from a public service desk. Prior to the laptop being approved for access, the system must be started and checked for current antivirus software and OS (operating system) patches.

Among the incidental costs involved with this approach are time and effort spent on training staff to adequately inspect patron computers. The time taken to change the codes weekly on the wireless access point would not be excessive, but would need to be accomplished at the same time each week. The person changing the key would need to test the code each week and ensure the validity of the key given to public services staff.

> Personal laptops whose operating systems are not adequately patched and whose virus detection software is not up to date represent a risk that can be managed, but at a cost of both money and staff time. Before committing to an ambitious plan to protect against such risk, be sure to conduct a study of laptop usage in the library. If findings indicate that the level of usage warrants investment in a resource-intensive plan of action, the information gathered from the usage study will help make a case to library administrators.

SECURING STAFF SYSTEMS FROM INTERNAL THREATS

Staff workstations are primarily used to support each employee's contribution to the library. Just as a library's organization chart reflects different types and levels of responsibility and authority, library employees should be granted authority over their workstations and network presence in accordance with their specific responsibilities. Employees who require little other than e-mail access and productivity applications such as a word processor and spreadsheet program may safely be granted very basic levels of authority. Systems staff and others who may need to save, use, and modify a wide array of files may require extra degrees of flexibility over their workstations and should be granted accounts that convey more authority.

Although some library staff need access to administrative accounts that grant them complete authority over all workstations, it is best that they use these administrative accounts sparingly. One little mistake—a public workstation, for instance, left unattended after a full administrative account has been used to log in—can spell disaster. The library may want to grant everyone, even senior systems personnel, accounts with limited authority, and share full administrative accounts with those who need them, to be used only when necessary.

Granting staff members limited authority over their workstations also reduces their ability to install, however unintentionally, software that may have spyware or tracking capabilities; at best, these may compromise the performance of both the workstation and the network. Under this scenario, when software must be installed on an employee's computer, someone with access to a full administrative account must personally conduct the installation.

As previously mentioned, authority can be controlled locally, via the user accounts represented on each computer, or centrally, via a user's login when a workstation is joined to a domain; in this case the privileges are set by either a domain controller, Active Directory, or NIS.

It is a simple fact of life that most library staff will make extracurricular use of their workstations. Therefore, policies must be written and enforced to prevent the most dangerous types of recreational computer use. Peer-to-peer networking should be considered a threat to the local LAN, and prohibited. Passive measures can be taken, such as using the firewall to lock out the standard ports used for peer-to-peer software, but more aggressive measures may need to be pursued. Newer versions of peer-to-peer clients allow the user to change the ports used and to receive data to typically open ports such as 80 (http, hypertext transfer protocol) and 21 (ftp, file transfer protocol). If an already busy port such as port 80, used for regular Web traffic, is now also used for file sharing of music, video, and games, network performance could suffer dramatically. If after locking down standard peer-to-peer ports such traffic is still suspected of affecting network performance, an audit of staff workstations may be necessary.

Policies such as logging off or locking the computer when away from the desk, requiring strong passwords, and enforcing a 90-day life span for user passwords will all help protect the LAN from being compromised by staff computers. A simple way to mitigate the effects of network contamination is to insist that all workstations be turned off at the end of each work day. This basic daily quarantine provides some protection against hackers and ensures that, even if a given workstation is compromised, the effects of its contamination will not spread unchecked throughout the entire day. Conventional wisdom once held that turning off computers at the end of each day placed an unnecessary and untenable strain on their most delicate

> The LAN can be negatively affected by staff computers, which are traditionally not locked down or monitored closely at all. Whether intentionally or by ignorance, staff computers pose a risk when the user has administrative authority to install software.

physical components, especially their hard drives. Concerns over energy efficiency, however, have driven technology to match the expectations of computer users. As a result, more robust hard drives and power supplies have been developed that are not as negatively impacted when workstations are turned off.

Most hacking takes place at night; computers left on overnight are more susceptible to attack. Should a computer be compromised during the day (through a hijacked Web site or user-installed application), the security breach merely opens the door for a hacker to gain access to the network. Since a hacker's exploitation of a compromised machine is likely to occur at night, turning off a contaminated computer provides a basic safeguard against this type of threat.

When computer policy has been adjusted to enforce power management, automatically downloaded patches and updates are at risk of falling behind. For instance, the default download time for Microsoft's patches and updates check is 3:00 a.m. each morning. This is also the preferred time for general downloading from Microsoft, as its servers are in relatively light use. Most antivirus applications also provide for scheduled update downloads. Should a decision be made to adjust the computers' automatic updating schedules, take into account the overall use of the LAN, the schedule on which staff and patrons use library workstations, and the restrictions, if any, imposed by each Web site providing updates. Because a flurry of simultaneous downloads may require a good deal of LAN bandwidth, it is a good idea to schedule updates away from peak usage times. A quick review of library network usage patterns may reveal that lunchtime is the best time to schedule updates; at many libraries, the start of the business day is best.

Staff computers are less likely than public workstations to be the launching grounds for network attacks, yet the possibility does exist. Well-written policies and thorough training of users will help secure the LAN from internal threats.

SECURITY CONSIDERATIONS FOR STAFF LAPTOPS

Library staff, especially those who frequently travel, are often issued laptops; some libraries have replaced staff desktop computers with portable workstations. The precautions mentioned earlier in this chapter apply to desktop and laptop computers alike, but laptops require further considerations.

Staff laptops should log on a separate wireless network, preferably one set to a different frequency than the public wireless network. Wireless access points for staff laptops should be located in such a way as to provide coverage throughout all appropriate parts of the library while minimizing network availability outside the library's walls.

WEP should be used to secure staff-side wireless transmissions. The key controlling access to this network does not need to be changed once a week, but a schedule of quarterly or biannual changes is a recommended security precaution. Written records of this key should be kept in extremely secure locations, and electronic copies should be maintained only if encrypted.

Staff with library-issued laptops may be assigned two sets of log-in credentials, one set allowing access to a limited-authority account, used for everyday tasks, and another with full administrative privileges. The administrative account assigned to laptop users should be different from the administrative account used throughout the library itself; its purpose is simply to empower remote users to perform needed maintenance on their machines. All other work should be done under the limited-authority account.

REVIEW QUESTIONS

Use this checklist as a guideline to evaluate knowledge gained from this chapter.

- What are some internal threats for a network?
- What is a typical LAN design and configuration?
- What is a way to prevent rogue computers attached to a network?
- What is a typical LAN layout?
- What is a hop?
- What is a wireless access point?
- What are some security concerns regarding wireless technology?
- What is a good configuration for wireless network?
- What is wireless encryption?
- What are checksums?
- What is the purpose of a router?
- What is the most effective way to configure a firewall?
- What are some measures that can be taken to protect computers from internal threat?
- What are some ways to protect the library's network from patrons' laptops?
- How does one secure staff workstations from internal threats?
- What are some ways to use power management to secure technology?
- What are some ways to protect against threats posed by staff laptops wireless connections?

KEY POINTS AND CONCLUSION

- Whereas a router and firewall are common in protecting library technology from external threats, they can also be used within the library network to protect it from internal threats.
- Segmenting a network within the library by the use of domain controllers, routers, and firewalls, are excellent ways to protect public stations from staff stations.
- Ensure that all devices connected to the network are protected from viruses through working virus software and operating system patch management.
- Using access control through a domain controller to prevent persons without log-on credentials from even accessing the network will protect the network from unauthorized use at a station that has higher authority than the user normally has.

Given the status of technology today, security is beginning to seep into the conscious level of thought for the average computer user. This is primarily due to events such as thousands of people having their identity stolen, losing their data from viruses, or having their computers crashed from having been hacked.

Businesses have been placed in the position of being held accountable for poor security practices at the state level through laws and also by stockholders, clients who have been compromised, and the public in general. Universities and colleges, the last remaining entities to be held accountable for security, are finally facing pressure at the state and federal levels to continue receiving support funds.

Libraries, as part of public, county, city, business, or educational entities, are often the last to consider true security for their technology due to lack of funding and direct oversight by authorities. Implementing secure library technology before being mandated to do so will allow libraries to implement security procedures gradually and affordably, with consideration for the needs of patrons and the mission of the libraries.

APPENDIX

LINKS TO STATE LAWS ON CYBER CRIME OR COMPUTER CRIME

Links are provided to primary state Web sites that have indexes or quick search engines that allow the searcher to locate the particular article or law. Typically these links change or are often dynamic, so placing them here as text would be bulky and unwieldy. Instead we offer the title and section number of each related section per state.

STATE LINKS

Alabama
http://alisdb.legislature.state.al.us/acas/alisonstart.asp
Criminal Code. Title 13

Alaska
www.legis.state.ak.us/default.htm
Criminal Code. Title 11

Arizona
www.azleg.state.az.us/ArizonaRevisedStatutes.asp
Criminal Code. Title 32

Arkansas
www.arkleg.state.ar.us/
Title 5. Criminal Offenses
Title 13. Libraries, Archives

California
www.legislature.ca.gov/
California has a search engine to locate specific laws, but not a directory listing of the Codes and Statutes.
www.leginfo.ca.gov/calaw.html

Colorado
www2.michie.com/colorado/lpext.dll?f=templates&fn=fs-main.htm&2.0
Title 18. Criminal Code

Connecticut
www.cga.ct.gov/
Title 11. Libraries
Title 53. Crimes
Title 53a. Penal Code

Delaware
http://delcode.delaware.gov/
Title 11. Crimes and Criminal Procedures

Florida
www.leg.state.fl.us/Welcome/index.cfm
Title 46. Crimes

Georgia
www.lexis-nexis.com/hottopics/gacode/default.asp
Title 16. Crimes and Offenses

Hawaii
www.capitol.hawaii.gov/hrscurrent/ (directory listing)
Volume 14: Title 7. Penal Code

Idaho
www3.state.id.us/idstat/TOC/idstTOC.html
Title 18. Crimes and Punishments

Illinois
www.obre.state.il.us/LAWS/Laws.htm
Chapter 720. Criminal Offenses

Indiana
www.state.in.us/legislative/ic/code/
Title 35. Criminal Law and Procedure

Iowa
www.legis.state.ia.us/IowaLaw.html
Title 16. Criminal Law and Procedure

Kansas
www.kslegislature.org/legsrv-legisportal/index.do
Chapter 21. Crimes and Punishments.

Kentucky
www.lrc.state.ky.us/statrev/frontpg.htm
Title 14. Libraries and Archives
Title 40. Crimes and Punishments

Louisiana
www.legis.state.la.us/lss/toc.htm
Title 15. Criminal Law
Title 25. Libraries and Museums

Maine
http://janus.state.me.us/legis/statutes/
Title 17. Crimes
Title 17A. Maine Criminal Code
Title 27. Libraries, History, Culture, and Art

Maryland
http://mlis.state.md.us/#stat
Maryland Code: Criminal Law

Massachusetts
www.mass.gov/legis/laws/mgl/
General Laws of Massachusetts
Section 4. Crimes, Punishments, and General Procedures in Criminal Cases

Michigan
www.legislature.mi.gov
Chapter 397. Libraries
Chapter 750. Michigan Penal Code
Chapter 752. Crimes and Offenses

Minnesota
www.leg.state.mn.us
Chapters 134–135. Libraries
Chapters 609–624. Crimes, Criminals

Mississippi
www.sos.state.ms.us/ed_pubs/MSCode/
Title 39. Libraries, Archives, Arts, and History
Title 97. Crimes

Missouri
www.moga.state.mo.us
Title 11. Education and Libraries
Title 38. Crimes and Punishments

Montana
http://data.opi.state.mt.us/bills/mca_toc/index.htm
Title 22. Libraries, Arts, and History
Title 45. Crimes

Nebraska
www.unicam.state.ne.us/web/public/home
Chapter 28. Crimes and Punishments
Chapter 51. Libraries and Museums

Nevada
www.leg.state.nv.us/Law1.cfm
Title 15. Crimes and Punishments
Title 33. Libraries and Museums

New Hampshire
www.gencourt.state.nh.us/rsa/html/nhtoc.htm
Title 16. Libraries
Title 57. Criminal Code

New Jersey
www.njleg.state.nj.us/
Title 2C. The New Jersey Code of Criminal Justice

New Mexico
http://legis.state.nm.us/lcs/
Chapter 18. Libraries, Museums, and Cultural Properties
Chapter 30. Criminal Offenses

New York
http://assembly.state.ny.us/
Consolidated Laws: PEN Penal

North Carolina
www.ncga.state.nc.us/gascripts/statutes/Statutes.asp
Chapter 14. Criminal Law
Chapter 19. Offenses Against Public Morals
Chapter 125. Libraries

North Dakota
www.legis.nd.gov/
Title 12.1. Criminal Code

Ohio
http://codes.ohio.gov/orc
Ohio Revised Codes
Title 29. Crimes and Procedures
Title 33. Education and Libraries

Oklahoma
www.lsb.state.ok.us/osStatuesTitle.html
Title 21. Crimes and Punishments
Title 65. Public Libraries

Oregon
www.leg.state.or.us/ors/
Title 16. Crimes and Punishments
Title 30. Chapter 357 Libraries

Pennsylvania
www.legis.state.pa.us
Consolidated Statutes
Title 18. Crimes and Offenses

Rhode Island
www.rilin.state.ri.us/Statutes/
Title 11. Criminal Offenses
Title 29. Libraries

South Carolina
www.sc.gov/Portal/Category/GOVERNMENT
Title 16. Crimes and Punishments
Title 60. Libraries

South Dakota
http://legis.state.sd.us/statutes/StatutesTitleList.aspx
Title 14. Libraries
Title 22. Crimes

Tennessee
www.legislature.state.tn.us
Title 10. Libraries
Title 39. Criminal Offenses

Texas
www.legis.state.tx.us
Texas Statutes
Penal Code

Utah
www.le.state.ut.us
Title 9. Chapter 7 Libraries
Title 76. Criminal Code

Vermont
www.leg.state.vt.us/statutes/statutes2.htm
Title 13. Crimes and Criminal Procedures
Title 22. Libraries

Virginia
http://leg1.state.va.us/lis.htm
Title 18.2. Crimes and Offenses Generally
Title 42.1. Libraries

Washington
www.state.wa.us
Revised Code of Washington
Title 9. Crimes and Punishments
Title 9A. Washington Criminal Code
Title 27. Libraries

West Virginia
www.legis.state.wv.us/
Chapter 61. Crimes and Their Punishment

Wisconsin
www.legis.state.wi.us/
Cultural and Memorial Institutions
Chapter 43. Libraries
Criminal Code
Chapters 938 to 951
Also visit http://dpi.state.wi.us/pld/librarytech.html

Wyoming
http://legisweb.state.wy.us/
Title 6. Crimes and Offenses

FEDERAL LINKS

The U.S. DOJ Computer Crime/Intellectual Property Web site
www.usdoj.gov/criminal/cybercrime/index.html
Very helpful in obtaining information and trends of prosecuted cases, with many manuals, links, and guides.

Cyber Security Enhancement Act of 2002
(TOC) www.usdoj.gov/criminal/cybercrime/homeland_225.htm
www.usdoj.gov/criminal/cybercrime/homeland_CSEA.htm

Text of USA PATRIOT Act
http://thomas.loc.gov/cgi-bin/bdquery/z?d107:HR03162:%5D
www.lifeandliberty.gov/

APPENDIX

REFERENCED VENDOR OR SOFTWARE WEB SITES

The Web site www.download.com offers a direct pipeline to many of these Web sites for downloading demo software, freeware, and shareware. Its biggest benefit is the search engine when looking for software for specific purposes.

Antivirus Software
McAfee: Antivirus www.McAfee.com
Symantec: www.Symantec.com
AVG: www.avg-antivirus.net
BitDefender: www.BitDefender.com
Alwil: www.Avast.com
AntiVir: www.Free-AV.com

Operating Systems Software
Windows XP or Vista: www.microsoft.com
Apple OS X: www.Apple.com
Unix: www.unix.org
CentOS: www.centos.org
Red Hat: www.redhat.com
Fedora: www.fedoraproject.org
Ubuntu: www.Ubuntu.com
Linux: www.Linux.org
Solaris: www.Sun.com/software/solaris

Network Mapping, Scanning, and Inventory Software
NMap: www.nmap.com
Nessus: www.nessus.org
Core Impact: www.coresecurity.com
QualysGuard: www.qualys.com
IBM Internet Security Systems: www.iss.net
AppScan: www.www-01.ibm.com/software/awdtools/appscan/
WebInspect: www.spydynamics.com
Spiceworks IT: www.spiceworks.com

TheOne Computer Inventory: www.theonesoftware.com
zCI Computer Inventory System: http://zci.sourceforge.net
Numara Track-It: www.numarasoftware.com
E-Z Audit: www.ezaudit.com

Desktop Security and Maintenance, Web Site Security Software
Ad-Aware: www.lavasoft.com
Prevx: www.prevx.com
Spybot: www.safer-networking.org
Spyware Doctor: www.pctools.com
IClean: www.moosoft.com
Window Washer: www.webroot.com
Internet Privacy Pro: www.sofotex.com
WebWatcher: www.webwatcherkids.com
SteadyState: www.microsoft.com
Retina Network Security Scanner: www.eeye.com
Deep Freeze: www.faronics.com/html/deepfreeze.asp
Centurion Guard: www.centuriontech.com
eBlaster: www.spectorsoft.com
Spector Pro: www.spectorsoft.com
SpyAgent: www.spytech-web.com
TweakUI: www.microsoft.com

Miscellaneous Software
Ghost Imaging Software: www.symantec.com
True Image: www.acronis.com
Exact Image: www.paragon-software.com
LoJack: www.lojackforlaptops.com
Inspice Trace: www.inspice.com
PC Phone Home: www.pcphonehome.com
XTool: www.xtool.com

Network Hardware (Switches, Routers, Firewalls, Wireless Access)
Cisco Networking: www.cisco.com (you will have to use their vendor
listing, you cannot easily buy directly from Cisco)
3Com: www.3com.com
D-Link: www.dlink.com
Linksys: www.linksys.com
Sun Microsystems: www.sun.com
Barracuda Networks: www.barracudanetworks.com

GLOSSARY

Having become frustrated on several occasions with technical book glossaries, it is our hope that this glossary won't result in endless loops of looking up words to understand just one technical term or word. The definitions of terminology in this glossary avoid this by using the simplified explanations that we have used throughout the book. Because the terms defined are not tech specific, some minor discrepancies can occur between the actual technical definition and ours. Please keep this in mind when using this glossary and visiting with technicians, as the glossary, like the rest of this book, is a foundation for understanding and the tool for achieving the goal of securing library technology.

10/100/1000Base T Ethernet:
> **10Base T:** This Ethernet works on Category 3, 4, or 5 cabling, with a maximum speed of 10 megabits per seconds (mps). Maximum cable distance is 100 meters.
> **100Base T:** This Ethernet works on Category 5 or 5e cabling, with a maximum speed of 100 mps. Maximum cable distance is 100 meters, cabling must be run according to IEEE 802.3 standards to maximize speed and minimize interference.
> **1000Base T:** This Ethernet works on Category 5e or 6 cabling, with a maximum speed of 1,000 mps, also referred to as gigabit Ethernet. Maximum cable distance is 100 meters on copper and must be run according to IEEE 802.3 standards to maximize speed and minimize interference.

Active Directory: Active Directory is Microsoft's most recent incarnation of network management for Windows-based computers. It does work with non-Windows-based systems as well. This is the evolution from Domain Controllers and carries with it backward compatibility. Active Directory views every item on the network, all of the users, and policies as "objects," which can be grouped dynamically by placing the objects into containers. This creates a very powerful and sometimes complicated network management system, depending on the experience of the administrator.

Active Directory container: Part of the Microsoft Active Directory system, a container is a grouping of objects that give them identical properties, restrictions, permissions, or descriptions, to name only a few, and offers a way to manage the different components of a Windows-based network.

Active Directory forests: Active Directory forests are Microsoft's most current implementation of a domain, with trees instead of workgroups, and leaves instead of users/computers. The relationships between the different logical segments and devices are very similar to those of a domain and workgroup but have a considerably more powerful management structure.

Active Directory object: Also part of the Active Directory, an object is any individual item such as a user, a privilege, authority, computer, printer, or restriction, to name only a few. Objects can be grouped into almost any configuration by placing them in Active Directory containers.

Active Directory trees: Trees are part of the logical network within Active Directory that effectively replace workgroups in a Microsoft Domain. Where there were numerous workgroups within a domain, there are numerous trees in a forest, which is also a Microsoft term that effectively replaces domains.

Active X: Active X is a programming tool within Internet Explorer, similar to Java, that allows a greater level of interactivity with a Web site and the user. Microsoft uses Active X to assist in validating an operating system, add features through Internet Explorer, and download and update different patches and software updates.

address resolution protocol (ARP): This protocol is referred to frequently in routers and firewalls, typically in association with a table of IP addresses and MAC addresses. It is defined in RFC 826 as the protocol that traces out IP addresses to their MAC addresses. This is not directly related to a DHCP server, which simply assigns IP addresses to network devices.

Apache: Apache is a server software that is typically associated with Linux-flavored systems, primarily used in a Web server application, but can be adjusted to serve additional Web services.

AppleTalk: Apple's operating systems prior to OS X used this protocol for networking different Apple Macintosh computers over their own serial cable design. Prior to OS 7, when Ethernet started to become dominant in networking, AppleTalk was the only way Macintoshes could communicate to share files. AppleTalk is still used as a protocol for Macintosh computers but is no longer tied directly to a serial cable and works with most network protocols such as Ethernet or Token Ring.

ARP: *See* ADDRESS RESOLUTION PROTOCOL.

asynchronous transfer mode (ATM): This method of data transmission works beyond the typical LAN, at the ISP side. It is designed for high speed transmissions with particular strength in voice, video, and data. It is not something a LAN manager will deal with, unless it is the transmission provided by the ISP to the router. ATM cannot communicate directly with Ethernet, so it must be translated.

asynchronous transmission: These are digital transmission signals over wires that are not tied to timing. Without timing, the information is carried by different frequencies and phases with standardized signals to indicate the beginning and end of a length of data. As an example, a tone that lasts exactly 1.75 seconds (a great exaggeration) would tell the receiving device that data that is exactly 32 bits of data is coming immediately afterward, and would be completed when the same tone arrives.

ATM: *See* ASYNCHRONOUS TRANSFER MODE.

backbone: The segment of the LAN that is specifically designated for traffic between network closets/switches and routers. This segment should typically run at a greater speed than the speed from the switches to the desktop or laptops is set at. As an example, a LAN backbone might run at 4 GB Ethernet between closets and the router, but offer from the closet to a computer or other network device only 1 GB Ethernet.

backdoor: This is a term used by hackers to signify an access to computer or server that is set up by the hacker to let him or her have complete access to the computer/server without being observed. Backdoors can be found only by specific software designed for the search, or by someone well versed in computer forensics. Once a backdoor has been installed on a computer through an unpatched or unreported flaw, even when a patch is applied the backdoor will typically still exist.

backup, CDRW: This refers to the use of a writable CD-ROM drive to create backups of data on a computer. It should be noted that this is a much cheaper way to do a backup, but that the possibilities of data being corrupt, the CD being damaged, and that the life of the CD itself is an issue, places it in the low position of reliable backup mechanisms.

backup, off-site: Off-site backup is the use of the Internet with encrypted data streams to backup a computer to a computer storage facility not within the building that a database is housed in. This is an excellent way of ensuring a database is available after a cataclysmic event such as fire, theft, or earthquake in which the computers are completely inoperable or missing.

backup, tape: The oldest mechanism still in use for backup up data on a server or highly important computer. This is the most reliable backup format available to the average library, when all standard procedures are followed, including storing a weekly backup tape out of the building.

bandwidth: The term used to describe the capacity of an Internet connection, the connections between computers on a network, and the frequency of wireless transceivers. Bandwidth on the physical layer— the copper wires—is the difference or distance between the highest and lowest frequencies used by network signals. Bandwidth on the wireless layer is the specific frequency (such as 2.4 Ghz) a wireless router or wireless access point uses for data transmission and reception.

BDC: *See* DOMAIN CONTROLLER, BDC.

binary: The most basic language a computer uses to process data or function. It consists of two values, "0" or "1." A "0" represents negative or no voltage, and a "1" represents a positive voltage. Binary is the building block of all computers and digital devices.

bit: A single binary digit, either a "1" or a "0." When placed in a sequence, they are considered to be binary language. Each bit, as seen by a digital device, is a specific length in time. As an example, if this time was 1 second, a digital device receives a positive voltage at a point in its chip for 2 seconds, no voltage for 2 seconds, and then voltage for 2 seconds, it would be read as "110011."

bottleneck: A term used in Ethernet or within the network to signify a location that is greatly reducing the capacity of data flow through a specific point. Frequently a bottleneck will be a single device, such as a router or firewall, that does not have appropriate throughput of data for an increase in network traffic.

bridge: Infrequently used devices that connect, or bridge, two separate networks of identical protocols, such as Ethernet to Ethernet or Token Ring to Token Ring.

broadband: Also known as wideband. A single cable that carries multiple independent signals that are multiplexed. *Multiplexed* can be defined in a base manner as location assignment within a signal, kind of like a seating arrangement in a car. It is also a term used to identify coaxial cable that uses an analog signal to transmit digital data.

broadcast, broadcast domain: A specific signal or data segment that is transmitted to every device on the network. It is a tool used in requesting information, but when a system is malfunctioning it can bog down the network and disrupt valid data transmission on the LAN. Also known as a broadcast storm. A broadcast does not travel through routers, so the network between two routers is known as a broadcast domain.

byte: Byte is eight bits, or an octet. The standard is "B" for byte, and "b" for bit. This is not always held to, and can create confusion when trying to understand a capacity, since ten bytes is 80 bits and so on.

cable, cat 3, 5, 6: A category of cable defined by the number of times each pair of wires twists within a specific distance (e.g., 1 inch), and the number of times the four pairs twist around one another in a longer specified distance (e.g., 10 inches). These formulas are used as a way to decrease the signal interference that a pair may receive from another pair of wires within the cable.

cat 3: Fewer number of twists in both pair and combined pairs, used only for analog telephone.

cat 5: A much more rigid requirement of twist in both pair and combined pairs, can be used for analog telephone and for 10/100 MBs Ethernet. It can be used for 1,000 MBs Ethernet, but interference will degrade the signal and reduce the speed.

cat 6: An even more rigid requirement as mentioned previously, which, when standards are followed in the placement of the cable between closets or closet and computer, will allow full use of 10/100/1,000 MBs Ethernet.

cable, crossover patch: A specifically wired cable that is used to connect a switch to a switch, host to host, hub to hub, or a switch to a hub. As the name indicates, certain pairs of wires are crossed/swapped as opposed to a standard Ethernet cable. This arrangement is a standard that switches, routers, and hubs are designed to recognize so that they understand another network device (switch, router, hub) that are connected to it.

cable, standard: A cat 3, 5, or 6 cable with RJ45 connectors that connect to the Ethernet port on a computer or laptop or other network device and the wall jack that connects to the network closet. It is important to use the correct category cable appropriate to the correct speed of the Ethernet network.

cable modem: A modem that uses television cable instead of a phone cable to receive and transmit data. A phone cable is dedicated to the computer when in use, and due to restrictions on phone lines has a maximum speed of 56 kb/second. These restrictions do not exist on television cable, which has a thicker wire than a phone for transmission, and so the speeds are greater and able to be shared with television programming signals.

cache: Cache is the term used to define a storage location, either physically or logically, within a digital device. Example: Physical cache would be files actually stored on a hard drive in specific folders to allow quick recall of the file, where logical would be memory set aside for temporarily storing files or programs used frequently to increase access to them when needed.

Cent OS: A linux-based operating system.

channel service unit/data service unit (CSU/DSU): This device is a connection point and type for connection with T-1 capacity or greater Internet connection. May be associated the with ATM protocol.

checksum: This is a test used to ensure the integrity of data passed from one device to another. Most frequently seen in dealing with compressed files or transmission of files (which is usually compressed), checksum is a simple mechanism that compares specific bits at specific locations within a data stream against a segment of bits at the end of the stream. These should match up exactly, and when they do not, it indicates that the data was corrupted at some point during the compression, decompression, or transmission.

class A, B, and C networks: These are the three classifications of networks in dealing with IP addresses. Looking at an IP address that contains four sets of numbers, it is easiest to see the different segments as the classes. This is not technically or specifically correct, but for a general understanding it is effective. The first segment is class A, the second segment is class B, and the third segment is class C. An IP address looks like this: 168.131.100.10. The 168 is the class A, the 131 is the class B, and the 100 is the class C. As each segment is between 1 and 254 (for all practical purposes), a class A segment—someone assigned the 168 address—would have every class B (1 through 255) and class C (1 through 255) section of addresses between 1 and 255 for each (255 × 255 = app 65,000 × 255 = 1,660,000 possible individual IP addresses). Thus the largest quantity of addresses available is a class A, then the class B, and last is the class C, which has only 254 addresses. The fourth segment is the actual final identifier and is unique to the particular device that it is assigned to. This is IP version 4. As the Internet is running out of these addresses, IP version 6 is ready to be implemented, which has more than the four addressing segments mentioned as a way to increase the available IP addresses.

collision, collisions, collision domains: A collision occurs when two devices on a network send out data at the same time, effectively canceling each other out. Collisions occur on only networks that use hubs instead of switches. Hubs do not regulate traffic and subsequently cannot hold or buffer data to help prevent collisions. Collisions will slow down a network or even stop the network from functioning. The collision domain is the group of devices connected to a particular network that utilizes hubs. As switches buffer and regulate the flow of data traffic, they are not impacted by collisions and cannot be part of a collision domain.

computer:

  desktop: Any computer that has the capacity to run its own operating system, store files locally, but is not readily portable and is set on top of the desk (either flat or as a small tower). Internet or network access is not required.

  dummy station: A station that does not have the capacity to run its own operating system or store files locally. This unit requires network access to communicate with a mainframe or terminal server to function.

  laptop: Small profile computer that is easily portable and can run off of either a battery or external electricity. Has the capacity to run its own operating system and store files locally. May or may not have Internet or network access.

  mainframe: A specific type of computer with multiple processors and multiple hard drives that cannot run standard operating systems such as Windows operating system (any version), Apple, and most flavors of Linux. A high end operating system is required. A mainframe is not easily portable.

  server: Any computer that can run its own operating system and store files locally; that is, running a server software as its operating system or as a software package running on the desktop operating system (e.g., Windows XP).

thin client: A computer that has no local hard drive or capacity to run its own operating system or store files locally. It loads a virtual instance of an operating system on a terminal server that creates the look and feel of a desktop computer for the user.

tower: The same as a desktop computer except that it stands vertical and typically has more space and capacity for additional components such as hard drives, CD-ROM drives, or other similar devices.

workstation: A desktop computer that has a limited operating system that requires network access to load a virtual instance such as a thin client or to load the actual operating system over the network from a terminal server or similar server. Typically it will not have a large hard drive if any, and may actually run off a floppy diskette or CD-ROM.

zombie: A desktop or laptop computer with Internet access that has been taken over by a hacker and is used to propagate illegal activity without the knowledge of the user or owner.

computer, data terminal: Used in conjunction with mainframe computers or terminal servers, these simply act as a means for a user to access data through a provided interface. Previously common as the green-only screens with text, they are now more complicated, with graphic user interfaces available in some instances. A data terminal can also be software that is run on a desktop computer that emulates the functions of a data terminal to allow interaction with a mainframe.

congestion: Congestion occurs when the traffic on a network exceeds the network's designed sustainability and negatively impacts the speed of the network. It can be caused by multiple problems, such as infected computers, damaged operating systems, or network cards.

cookies: Small text files set by Web sites that are written to by the Web browser on a user's computer. It stores data that a Web site requests the browser keep track of and uploads that data to its own database. It can also be used to signify that a computer has logged on a Web site so that each time a page is accessed on that Web site the user does not have to log on again.

crossover patch cable: *See* CABLE, CROSSOVER PATCH.

CSU/DSU: *See* CHANNEL SERVICE UNIT/DATA SERVICE UNIT.

date-time stamps: Each and every file that is created, accessed, or copied has a date-time stamp attached to it to identify when it was created and, if modified, when this occurred. These are excellent in determining from a backup file set which file is the most recent. They are also important in determining when a computer may have been compromised, if the computer has new files/folders created as a part of the hack.

defragmentation: A status or description of the file system of any computer operating system when it has become fragmented. Fragmentation occurs when a file is written in a specific location on a hard drive in which it is "penned in" by other files and does not have room to increase. Instead of moving the file to another location, the operating system segments the file and annotates where the rest of the file is. This can occur so frequently that the hard drive becomes slow (slowing down the operating system) as it tries to get all the pieces of the fragmented files from all the different locations on the hard drive.

denial of service (DoS): A form of attack by a hacker that has the end result of causing network or Internet access to fail. Typically accomplished by flooding a server with so much traffic that it stops responding to any requests at all, whether valid or not. It can also be accomplished by attacking supporting servers (such as a DNS server) to effectively make the Internet inaccessible.

DHCP server: *See* SERVER, DHCP.

DIMM: *See* MEMORY.

disaster recovery plan: A comprehensive plan that implements daily activities and specific steps to allow quick recovery of data, services, and productivity after a major disaster that completely or partially reduces services offered by an organization.

DNS: *See* SERVER, DNS

DNS poisoning: The falsification of a domain name and its IP address on an authoritative DNS server that causes other DNS servers to accept the new IP address. This is used by hackers in the acquisition of personal data by presenting an identical Web site or in blackmailing a legitimate Web site for money.

domain controller: A Microsoft logical network management system that allows the control and administration of a LAN that utilizes the Windows operating system. The use of workgroups and user profiles allows an administrator to secure a network and computers from a central location and manage user accounts and privileges.

 BDC (backup domain controller): A server that acts as a backup to the primary domain controller, imaging the management files and profiles so that if the PDC fails for some reason, the BDC will step in and take over the role of the PDC to provide uninterrupted service.

 PDC (primary domain controller): The domain controller that is the lead computer in a network. Can be a stand alone or have multiple BDCs to ensure uninterrupted services should a hardware or software failure occur.

domain groups: When more than one Microsoft domain exists on a LAN, they create a domain group. This group can share files, not share files, trust one another or not trust one another, depending on the needs of the network and organization.

Domain Name System (DNS): *See* SERVER, DNS.

DoS: *See* DENIAL OF SERVICE.

DRAMM: *See* MEMORY.

encryption: The process by which data is plugged into a mathematical formula based on a specific key that causes the data to be unreadable unless it is reverted to its original format through the same mathematical formula and specific key. The key, 32 bit or 64 bit, is required to decrypt the data. The larger the number of bits, the more complicated the encryption, so 64 bit keys would be better than 32 bit. However, using a standard formula means that with time, the key can be discovered, since there is a finite number of combinations of bits.

Ethernet: This is a network protocol that has become widely accepted, even though there are more stable (albeit more expensive) protocols available such as Token Ring. The IEEE standard for Ethernet continues to expand and build on the foundation laid out years ago. It is important to recognize that even when there are only two devices on an Ethernet network, neither computer will actually run at the maximum speed (10, 100, or 1,000 MBs). The more devices on a network, the slower the network will run, unless properly segmented and configured with proper equipment.

extensible markup language (XML): A language used in conjunction with Web browsers that allows the designer to create a common or typical layout/format for all viewers and not be dependent on the Web browser or operating system a user may be utilizing.

FDDI: *See* FIBER DISTRIBUTED DATA INTERFACE.

Fedora: A popular Linux-based operating system.

fiber distributed data interface (FDDI): a protocol used for fiber-optic cable. This is different from Ethernet—although data is transmitted in a serial format on both—in that there are only two fiber-optic fibers used in FDDI, where there are four pairs of wires in Ethernet protocol. This difference requires a different format to transfer data. Fiber ports on an Ethernet switch simply convert it into a fiber-optic format for transfer and back to Ethernet on the other side.

fiber optic: The physical format of a glass fiber that allows light to travel over long distances with deterioration at a high speed of travel (speed of light). This can be used to transmit data within a LAN when the distances between network closets is too far for standard copper cabling or in which copper cabling would be severely interfered with by outside sources of electricity (large fans or other utilities).

file system: The organization of files on a computer or server, dependant and specific to a particular operating system. Microsoft uses FAT, FAT32, and NTFS. Linux-based operating systems typically use "ext3."

firewall: A physical device or software program that creates a barrier by allowing or denying data to be transferred via any port used by a computer over a network.

frame relay: A network protocol that is used for high-speed transmittal of network data. Not typically used within a LAN, usually it is used as a communication protocol between an organization and their Internet service provider (ISP).

gateway: Term used to identify the specific point in a network where all devices on that network can access the Internet. This is typically the IP address of a router or firewall, depending on the LAN design/configuration.

graphic user interface (GUI): This is the layer of an operating system or software program that is used to interact with a user. Prior to Apple Macintosh and Windows, all interaction with computers was done through a text and command line, where specific instructions had to be understood and known. With GUI, the use of a pointing device such as a mouse or ball tab were incorporated to allow a user to simply point to a graphic (icon) to select and run its program or function.

GUI: *See* GRAPHIC USER INTERFACE.

hacker: Term or name used to identify a person who understands programming languages and uses that knowledge to access networks, computers, and mainframes without proper authority.

hard drive: A device based on the design of a floppy diskette, using metal platters instead of the floppy material within a diskette, that is treated to be sensitive to magnetic adjustment. These platters are used to store files, programs, and software, and continue to increase in capacity as the read/write heads and quality of the platters improve. Hard drives come in several different physical sizes and with different quantities of platters. The two common are 3.5 inch hard drives (used in desktops and servers) and 2.5 inch drives used in laptops. Hard drives have different interfaces to communicate within a computer, SCSI, IDE, and ATA/SATA.

hard drive capacity: The capacity of a hard drive is determined by the number of platters, read/write heads, and the quality of the magnetic properties of the platters. High quality platters allow data to be packed closer together, allowing a higher capacity.

hexadecimal: A basic of machine language that is binary at a more manageable level, based on a radix (base) of 16. There are 16 possible combinations of the four binary digits, including "0." Rather than using "10," which is also a binary code, programmers started with "A" after reaching "9" to signify the quantity of "10." This continues to "15," which is the letter "F." Remember that "0" counts as a number, which is why the count stops at "F" (15), for a total of 16. MAC addresses are in hexadecimal.

hops, network: *See* NETWORK, JUMPS.

HTM/HTML: *See* HYPERTEXT MARKUP/HYPERTEXT MARKUP LANGUAGE.

HTTP: *See* HYPERTEXT TRANSFER PROTOCOL.

HTTPS: The "S" at the end of HTTP simply designates it as a secure Web server. This type of server requires that a log-on with appropriate certificates be performed before any of the pages of the server can be accessed. It communicates by default on port 443, and requires an SSL, or secure socket layer, be started successfully.

hub: This is an Ethernet device that allows multiple Ethernet connections at a time to occur. Although still a valid Ethernet device, it has been replaced primarily with Ethernet switches. An Ethernet hub does not have the ability to manage traffic; in simple terms, it just throws the dog bones into the dog pen and whoever gets one, gets one. It is not effective in high-traffic conditions, as there will be collisions of Ethernet communication packets that degrade the speed of the network.

hypertext markup/hypertext markup language (HTM/HTML): A suffix typically used as a Web page served from a Web server. This is the most common form of Web page, based on a text/common word association language. All of the command lines are standard so that any Web browser may interpret them the same.

hypertext transfer protocol (HTTP): This is the protocol of the Internet, the WWW (World Wide Web). It is designated to use port 80 of a networked computer and is the designated and default "listening" port for all Web servers (unless specifically set otherwise).

ICMP: *See* INTERNET CONTROL MESSAGE PROTOCOL.

instant message (IM): This is a service provided by a server that allows a text message (and sometimes attached files) to be sent immediately to a specified recipient that is participating as a user of that same service. There are numerous IM servers out there, the most common belonging to Microsoft and AOL.

integrated services digital network (ISDN): A service provided by most phone companies in which voice (analog) and data (digital) are combined and translated to be transmitted over existing phone lines. This is the phone companies' answer to cable, and is a considerable step up from a telephone modem. It requires specialty equipment (an ISDN modem) to function.

Internet control message protocol (ICMP): ICMP is the protocol used by network technicians to troubleshoot the network. The most common tool or command is "ping," used at a DOS prompt in Windows. Ping will send a test packet to the specified IP address and receive a return confirmation of the data received, which will include any errors or losses that may have occurred in transmission to the receiving device.

ISDN: *See* INTEGRATED SERVICES DIGITAL NETWORK.

Java: A simple programming language that will function across all platforms of operating systems, created by SUN Systems. Most commonly used in Web-based applications and pages.

jump drive: Also known as a USB key, USB drive, and similar names as coined by different manufacturers. The term "drive" is deceptive since there is no actual "drive" in the sense of a floppy, CD-ROM, or hard drive. It shows up logically as a "drive," but it is actually a small self-contained memory chip that uses the power (electricity) of the USB port to manage itself. As microchip capacity increases, so will jump drive capacity.

jumps: A network term that describes the number of connections between logical devices on an Ethernet network and the gateway. If there are too many connections, or "jumps," the devices beyond the last connection will not have access to the gateway to see the Internet or other computers. The maximum number of logical devices (switches, hubs, and firewalls) between a gateway or router and the remotest network node is five.

key logger: A software program that runs in a stealth or hidden mode and creates a text file of all the keystrokes of a keyboard. Commonly used as a way to obtain user names and passwords, it can also be used to log the text of an e-mail that is intended to be sent encrypted. The logger has all the key strokes prior to actual encryption.

LAN: *See* LOCAL AREA NETWORK.

local area network (LAN): A local area network is simply a logical grouping of switches, computers, servers, printers, and other network devices that share a common location or logical network (domain). Normally this would be all of the computers on the same network within a library that reach the Internet through a single router.

log files: These are files used by numerous programs and operating systems as a way to troubleshoot, track, and protect a computer. Log files are created by operating systems when installing, so in case something doesn't install correctly, there is a log to see the error messages. Log files are also used by the operating system to protect a computer by keeping track of working configurations, so that if a change occurs and the system no longer functions normally, the log is used to return to a working configuration.

MAC address: *See* MEDIA ACCESS CONTROL ADDRESS.

malware: Software that is specifically designed to be destructive or to obtain information on a user or organizational network infrastructure to be used for malicious intent.

media access control (MAC) address: The MAC address is a specific 16 bit identifier that is viewed in hexadecimal format to identify a specific device on a network. This is true for any network protocol, Ethernet or Token Ring. In the remote chance that there are two identical MAC addresses on a single network, each network interface card (NIC) has an alternate that it can revert to.

memory: Memory is the physical chips within a computer or digital device that allow it to store working data and programs so that it doesn't have to access the storage device constantly. Hard drives are sometimes (and incorrectly) referred to as memory, since they are measured in a similar standard, for example, a 20 GB hard drive, and memory is referred to in MB and in GB. Hard drives have capacity that can permanently retain data, where memory loses all data when power is no longer applied to the computer. Memory comes in many forms and sizes, and speeds. A few of their common names are: DIMM, DRAM, SDRAM, and RAM.

mirror image: A term referring to the use of an RAID array configuration in which the entire logical hard drive is constantly being mirrored and copied to other hard drives within a server configuration. This is most common in large database and file storage servers.

modem: A device that converts the digital information of a computer into a more suitable format for travel over a phone line. Phone lines work best with a person's voice, which is an analog signal. Digital signals do not travel well over phone lines; modems were created to turn digital data into an analog signal so that they could be easily reconstituted at the receiving end.

names: There are many different types of names in the computer world, from domain names to user names to computer names. Identification of a computer or network device depends on there being only one unique name for a computer on the operating system level. This is not the same as a MAC address, which is a unique identifier at the physical level of the computer or network device.

naming convention: The policy of naming computers and network devices with specific types of names and numbers to signify the location, purpose, or actual item.

NAT: *See* NETWORK ADDRESS TRANSLATION.

NetBIOS: A network protocol used in earlier versions of Windows and some other operating systems, but not as prevalent or common as it used to be.

NetWare: A brand of software that is specifically designed to act as a foundation for all network devices to communicate, much in the way that Microsoft domain controllers and Active Directory perform.

network:

> **Bluetooth:** A network protocol that utilizes wireless connectivity. This is *not* Ethernet, but a separate network protocol.
>
> **logical:** A logical network is a grouping of devices that share a common theme or purpose that may or may not be on the same LAN.
>
> **physical:** The actual physical layout and design of the network, including a LAN that is divided by logical design and use. It could be referred to as the nuts and bolts of the network.
>
> **VPN (virtual private network):** This is a logical network that is not based on or dependant on any physical design. It requires that a secure socket layer or similar protocol of communication be established before any real communications may begin. Theoretically this VPN creates a private tunnel of encryption between the two points that none of the equipment or transmission devices can listen in to.
>
> **wireless:** The use of radio waves to transmit digital data over both secure and unsecure airwaves, which allows mobile devices to have network and Internet connectivity.

network address translation (NAT): NAT is used by routers, firewalls, or other Internet gateway devices to protect the IP identity of computers on a LAN. A router will present one IP address to the rest of the Internet, even though there may be hundreds of IP addresses assigned within its LAN.

network information server (NIS): *See* SERVER, NIS.

network infrastructure: All of the hardware and cabling that provides the actual connectivity of a LAN. This includes the network closets and their switches, the router and firewall, and the cabling between network closets and office computers and nodes and between the actual network closets.

network interface card (NIC): This is the Ethernet, Token Ring, or other network protocol card that allows communication over a network media such as wireless, copper cabling, or fiber-optic cabling. The NIC can be built into a computer or be a card that is installed into a slot on the main/mother board.

network jumps: Also known as "hops," each jump or hop is an individual network device that uses Ethernet to communicate and not a serial or other non-Ethernet connection. Network devices include managed switches, routers, and firewalls. Connectivity is limited to a maximum of five jumps or hops.

network node: Any device, whether a computer, printer, wireless PDA, or laptop (to name a few) that has network connectivity and is physically connected to a network.

network protocols: Any of the protocols that can be used by an operating system to effectively communicate over a LAN or the Internet.

network security: The process by which a network is secured from threat by policy, practice, design, and hardware. This can include location of hardware equipment and access to that equipment.

NFS: Network file structure. *See* FILE SYSTEM.

NIC: *See* NETWORK INTERFACE CARD.

Node: *See* NETWORK, NODE.

Novell: A specific brand of network protocol and software that manages network connectivity over a LAN similar to Microsoft domain controllers.

NTFS: New Technology File System, for Microsoft Windows. *See* FILE SYSTEM.

octal: A base computer language, one step up from binary. Based on three digits, the values of which when added up will equal 7, that when the 0 is included is actually 8 possible values, thus the term octal for eight.

operating system (OS): The software foundation that is required for a computer to be functional. This foundation creates an interface in which users may use additional productivity software that works on top of the operating system to enhance their job performance. Operating systems are sometimes proprietary, such as Apple Macintosh, or may be functional on a wide variety of hardware, such as Microsoft Windows or a Linux-based operating system such as Red Hat or Cent OS.

OS: *See* OPERATING SYSTEM.

passkey: The series of alphanumeric (when in hexadecimal) values provided by a wireless router for a mobile device or wireless device to access securely a wireless network. The mobile device must use the passkey in its setup to join the wireless network.

passwords: User chosen words or a selection of alphanumerics that are required to access a computer BIOS, load an operating system, access shared network devices, or access and administer servers, to name only a few of the applications. A good password will be alphanumerics that include a symbol (such as # or $) and is at least eight characters long.

patch cable: *See* CABLE, STANDARD; CABLE, CROSSOVER PATCH.

PDC: *See* DOMAIN CONTROLLER, PDC.

peer to peer: A term used to identify two or more computers or network devices that are communicating without the control of a domain controller or NIS server or similar device. The communication is mutually controlled by the devices on the network. Home networks that have two or three personal computers are considered peer to peer. Peer to peer also refers to a group of computers that through the use of a software package share server style services to delegate the load of sharing files, which often include video or music and sometimes copyrighted material.

permissions: The term used by any software program or hardware device that sets limits on a user's authority within that program or hardware.

phishing: This is the falsification of a Web site address within an e-mail or other communication format that will lead receiving persons to believe that they have received a legitimate e-mail from the original Web site. This is typically used as a way to steal user log-in and password to access the account illegally and without permission.

PHP: Hypertext preprocessor (the first "P" has no definition or word association, the acronym originally stood for "personal home page"), a programming language similar to HTML, except that it allows a more dynamic interaction with the Web page recipient. PHP allows a Web developer to build a Web page "on the fly" so to speak, specific to the user receiving the page. Most frequently it is used in accessing simple a database such as MySQL.

ping: A DOS command line instruction used to test network connectivity between two devices on a network. It would look like this at the command prompt: "C:\PING 168.123.1.1," and would then show how well the data was received, whether any of the packets were lost, and how long it took to receive the entire data packet. It would also indicate if the receiving device even acknowledged or participated in the request. The ICMP protocol must be turned on at the receiving device and must be one of the allowed protocols through the switches, routers, and firewalls.

pop-ups: When Java is activated, Web sites can include in their HTML a request to run a Java command that can open a new Web page or tab within the browser that the user did not request. This is known as a pop-up, and usually contains extra advertisement. It can also contain viruses or rogue Java commands that can seek to compromise the user's computer system.

port: This term has two uses in this book. The first is in relation to a network device and the line of communication it chooses, called a port. This port is standardized throughout the industry for the few specific functions of networking, such as Web browsing, e-mail, and FTP. The second reference is in the physical term for the actual jack in a switch, hub, router, or firewall that is used to connect the Ethernet cable.

printer:

color laser: A laser printer that uses the three primary colors along with black in a superfine toner to create color printouts on paper or other medium, then fused with heat onto the medium.

dot matrix: The use of a series of pins that are forced to hit a ribbon of ink, pressing the ink onto the paper. These are used only for multipart form printing anymore.

inkjet or bubble-jet: The use of nozzles to shoot liquid ink onto a piece of paper, using either the three primary colors and black, or just black, to print.

laser: The use of a laser onto a light-sensitive drum to change the electrical charge where the light hits. This as it turns is exposed to toner that sticks to the drum where the electrical charge has been changed, and is then transferred onto the paper as it presses onto the drum while it turns. This is then fused onto the paper by heat.

multifunction: The term for a printer that also has the ability to scan and copy and may also be able to act as a fax machine. This includes the large and expensive copy printer systems often made available to the public for a fee.

processor: A chip containing the primary source of processing power for any digital device, from printers to computers to switches. Almost all digital devices have some form of a processor. Specifically to computers, it is the primary chip needed to perform the control and execution of software, and it handles all of the serious number crunching for any actual hardware or software process being performed by the computer.

proxies, proxy, proxy server: *See* SERVER, PROXY.

RAID array: RAID (redundant array of inexpensive disks) is a protocol that allows multiple hard drives to be seen as a single hard drive. This is commonly used in database servers, and allows a server to create a mirror image so that when a hard drive fails it can be "hot swapped" (if the computer has that capability) with a working blank drive and continue with its functionality without degradation.

Red Hat: A popular Linux-based operating system.

remote access: The use of software (often included in an operating system such as Windows XP) that allows other users or computers to access a computer from somewhere else on the network. This is not restricted to a LAN; it can be performed over the Internet if the computer being accessed is set up to do so. Typically the remote access location will see the screen that is currently up on the computer being accessed and may have actual power to move the mouse, start or stop programs, and use their own keyboard to type or run command line instructions.

remote procedure call (RPC): This is a subroutine built into much of the operating systems out there that brings up a specific program to execute a specific function. RPC is often intensely scrutinized by hackers to see if they can use it to bring up functions that it shouldn't, that would allow them to take over or create a backdoor of access to a computer.

router: Succinctly put, this device routes information between two locations. Within the network world, it frequently is used for translations of different network protocols, such as Ethernet to ATM or ISDN. It can also be used to physically segment or separate a single physical LAN into two.

RPC: *See* REMOTE PROCEDURE CALL.

scripts: Scripts are typically written within a programming language, such as Visual Basic (VB), and are used by programmers and technical support personnel to speed up repetitive processes. As an example, a technician may write a VB script to add a specific printer to all of the computers on a LAN. The script would simply be "run" at each computer and would save the technician the time of using the mouse and GUI to go through all of the different steps required to add the printer to the computer.

security audit: The close examination of all user and administrative practices and policies in relationship to the use, access, and purpose of the network, all computers and nodes on the network, and data shared or secured on the network or any device connected to the network.

security plan: The written policy that designates what levels of security and procedures are in place to ensure that the network, network nodes, and information that may reside on devices connected to the network are safe from intrusion or abuse.

server: A server is a device (not always a computer) that offers a service or serves in a management/administrative or support capacity to the network and other devices connected to the network.

catalog: Specific to libraries, this server houses the database of books, periodicals, etc., of the library, and often maintains related fields of responsibility such as circulation, collection searching, collection development, and fiscal management.

DHCP: Dynamic host configuration protocol. Frequently included in routers and firewalls, and also a part of most network administration software packages (Microsoft domain controllers, etc.), this server simply assigns an IP address to any requesting network device that comes online to the network. The IP address range is set by the network administrator or manager.

DNS: Domain Name System. Unless the library has multiple Web services and servers, the DNS is provided by the Internet service provider

(ISP). All computers on the LAN with Internet privileges/access will need to know these IP addresses as provided by the ISP. Normally this information is included (if programmed) with the IP address assignment by the DHCP server.

Exchange: A Microsoft product that is used to serve e-mail and provide calendar services and day planner type services for individual account holders.

FTP: File transfer protocol. This server is a simple folder/file listing server for hosting files or capacity to authorized users. FTP clients can efficiently manage the upload and download of files. No Web browser is required, although they frequently will work well with an FTP server.

license key: Some vendors use a license key server to allow a specific quantity of software they offer to run within a LAN. Typically the software itself can be installed on any or all computers, but will function completely only when authenticated with the license key server. This allows a site to have the software available at any public station so as to not tie it down to just one but pay for only a select quantity of users to be able to utilize the full version at any given time.

NIS: A server using a Linux-based operating system that acts as a controlling device on an internal network for Linux-based operating system computers. It provides basic security by controlling the authority of any user in its database that logs onto a Linux computer, where that computer is set to allow only users in the NIS database to log in.

printer: A printer server can be attached to a printer or simply control the interface of all users on a network to a networked printer device. The first is simple, and is normally available with the standard operating system without any additional software. The second requires a management software like Microsoft Active Directory, where users send the print request to the actual server, that in turn sends the print request to the printer. This helps keep the printer from being overrun with print jobs.

proxy: A proxy server performs the function of making a computer appear to be on a different network or have a different IP address than it actually has. It simply relays the requests/communications to a destination and uses its own IP address instead of the originating computer. Frequently used in the library world for "out of the building" or remote users to legally access database subscriptions.

SMS: SMS has two definitions: storage management system, where user data is backed up and stored, or Systems Management Server (a Microsoft product) that is used to maintain the patches and updates for Microsoft products. It can also be used to "push" new software, patches, policies, and related fixes that are not products of Microsoft.

SMTP: Simple mail transfer protocol. This is the e-mail server. Many server packages (Microsoft Server 2003 as an example) have the capacity to act as an SMTP server, or there are vendors with stand-alone software packages.

SQL: This is a database server, and there are multiple versions available ranging in price from free to expensive, depending on the features needed.

terminal: A server software that creates individual sessions of a virtual operating system on its own computer as a host to a dummy terminal that does not have the ability to run its own operating system.

TFTP: Trivial file transfer protocol. This particular server is used predominantly to back up or restore the configuration for network devices (routers, firewalls, and switches). The configuration files for these devices are a simple text file, seldom more than 12 KB. TFTP servers seldom have any log-in or security features and are kept in a "turned off" status.

Web: Used for serving any type of WWW or Web page, regardless of the complexity or simplicity of the page or Web site. This includes software packages like Apache and Microsoft IIS (Internet Information Server).

service packs: A package of all of the combined patches and updates vendors may offer for a software they sell. Most vendors will offer a service pack as a single download when the combined patches and updates could possibly become or have become a bandwidth hog to both the client and the vendor.

shared drive: A logical folder on a networked computer that allows access to a hard drive located on that computer from other users on that network. The owner of the computer has the capability of requiring passwords for access and may control the level of access to the drive and subsequent files and folders.

shared files and folders: *See* SHARED DRIVE.

SMTP: *See* SERVER, SMTP.

SNA: *See* SYSTEMS NETWORK ARCHITECTURE.

spam: Spam is defined as mass mailed e-mail to accounts that have been obtained through questionable or less than appropriate means. Spam accounts for a noticeable amount of Internet traffic and causes without intent frequent slow downs in Internet access for users.

spoofing: A technique used by hackers to display the expected Web address in a client's browser, when in fact the Web page the client is viewing is being hosted on a different Web server at a different Web address. Used for identity theft and as a means to hijack computers.

spyware: Depending on the viewpoint, either benign or malicious software that is used to accumulate data and habits of the user on whose computer the spyware has been installed. Many free software packages come with spyware as part of the license agreement to use the software without charge. The provider then sells the users data/habits information to vendors for future client targeting for sales.

subnet, class A: *See* CLASS A, B, AND C NETWORKS.

subnet, class B: *See* CLASS A, B, AND C NETWORKS.

subnet, class C: *See* CLASS A, B, AND C NETWORKS.

subnet/subnet mask: A subnet is a particular segment of related IP addresses located on a physical network. As an example, 15 computers may have an IP range of 168.1.100.1 to 168.1.100.15, and another set of computers may have an IP range of 168.1.200.1 to 168.1.200.15. These would be considered separate subnets because one is on the 100 subnet of 168.1, and the second is on the 200 subnet of 168.1. A subnet mask, the 255.255.255.0, defines the range of a subnet. It is best to let the computer automatically assign the subnet mask, as it would require a whole chapter to explain how it is calculated.

switch: Short for Ethernet switch. An Ethernet switch differs from a hub in that it can manage the traffic on the individual ports. It has the capacity to maintain its own ARP table of which MAC address is on which port. This allows it to send a request from one computer to another computer without stopping the traffic on all of the other ports. Ethernet is a community network language in which all of the computers or nodes can speak at once (thus no one hearing any of the others) if they so choose. Switches offer control to allow the orderly flow of communication, improving the performance of the network.

systems network architecture (SNA): The standard for designing and managing the layout of a LAN.

TCP/IP: *See* TRANSMISSION CONTROL PROTOCOL/INTERNET PROTOCOL.

technology plan: The technology plan is a tool for ensuring that the network, computers, and related peripheral devices are viable for their life span and that they can be replaced in a timely and monetarily responsible manner. It allows for fiscal planning when proper research is done on current equipment purchases. When properly designed, it also allows for prioritization of purchases, new equipment assignments, and the cascade use of viable but older equipment.

telnet: A method of communication to a server in which the client computer emulates a data terminal. This creates a text-only interface that is adapted for communication with a mainframe through the network connection.

temporary Internet files: Small files that are stored in hidden folders within a user's profile. These are small graphics or HTML that are downloaded to the computer, and then for each subsequent need for the file or graphic it is readily available and does not have to be redownloaded from the Web site the user is visiting. The one drawback is that most operating systems do not clear out these files to any satisfactory degree, and they tend to cause fragmentation of the hard drive. The smaller the space set for these files to be saved (we recommend 50mb) the less frequently they need to be deleted and the defragmentation program needs to be run.

terminal server: *See* SERVER, TERMINAL.

Token Ring: The IBM designed equivalent of Ethernet. It is a communication protocol that travels on a single pair of wires, using a token system of determining whose turn it is to pass data on the single pair of wires. The ring design is connected to other rings through a bridge device that performs similar duties to that of a router. An actual router is then attached for Internet access to any one of the rings. Token Ring offers a true speed as advertised (e.g., 100 MBs) since there is no cross-talk or other computer jumping in unannounced. The computer that has the token gets to send the data, and then it passes the token onto the next computer.

transmission control protocol/Internet protocol (TCP/IP): This is the primary addressing system of the Internet. Every device that connects to the Internet has in some shape or form an IP address to represent itself. Organizations that have a single IP address can use internal devices with DHCP to allow more than one computer to access the Internet through that single IP address.

tunnel/tunneling (firewall): A term used to describe the specific communication between two network devices on either side of a firewall that are specifically identified and authorized to communicate to each other. The opening cannot be used for any other purpose or by any other set of network devices.

Ubango: A Linux-based GUI operating system.

UDP: *See* USER DATAGRAM PROTOCOL.

Universal Serial Bus (USB): This is a simple form of communication, similar in functionality to Ethernet, only not a true network protocol. When a device or devices are connected to the USB port of a computer, they all share the same access point and communication line. Each device connected takes its turn in communication and transferring of data.

USB: *See* UNIVERSAL SERIAL BUS.

USB key: *See* JUMP DRIVE.

user accounts: The actual account that allows a user to log on a local computer, or if designated, via the network domain controller on any computer the account is authorized for. The account can exist locally on a computer with no domain connection, or it can exist on the domain and be tied to a specific computer or group of computers.

user datagram protocol (UDP): This is the control side of port management. Only control signals are sent through this protocol by the router, server, or firewall device.

user profile: A user profile shows the authority, group associations, and specific information about a particular user. The profile can be stored locally on a computer where the user has an account, or it can be stored on the domain and be temporarily transferred to a computer that the user logs on, if they have the authority to do so.

virus: A small stealth program designed to perform malicious activity on a computer. A virus can be hidden as a Trojan horse, as part of a legitimate program or file, or it can act as its own carrier, where it tries to copy itself to other computers any way it can. Recently some viruses have included their own SMTP server and use the infected computer and any e-mail addresses that are stored there to send itself as an attachment via e-mail.

voice-over Internet protocol (VoIP): Network quality and speed improvements have recently made the conversion of an analog signal (voice, video, music) into a digital signal for transmission over the Internet into a reliable method of transportation. Previously the transfer of the digital packages containing the converted analog voice signal would lose too many bits to be successfully converted back to voice with any quality. Having created compression techniques to handle the capacity and quality, this method has become quite popular. VoIP can be a bandwidth hog, and with software programs like Skype, which are virtually undetectable by network monitoring devices, an aged network would be negatively affected. Some organizations are using VoIP on a physically separate network to avoid the conflict, with a separate Internet connection from their data.

VoIP: *See* VOICE-OVER INTERNET PROTOCOL.

VPN: *See* NETWORK, VIRTUAL PRIVATE.

WAN: *See* WIDE AREA NETWORK.

WAP: *See* WIRELESS ACCESS POINTS.

WEP: *See* WIRED EQUIVALENT PRIVACY.

WEP key: A WEP key is a key that is created by the wireless router. It is *not* transmitted over any airwave, but must be manually set up on any wireless access device that wishes to use the WAP.

wide area network (WAN): A wide area network is defined for the purpose of this book as an organization's physical network that may include several different buildings over a space but geographically local to an area. Transmissions between buildings could be in any form—copper, fiber optic, radio, or infrared. It is not, for the purpose of this book, to include distant sites that are connected via the Internet through a virtual private network.

Windows Internet Naming System (WINS): This is the Microsoft version of Domain Name System (DNS), specifically designed to work well with Windows and its network design. It is strong in features, but does not seem to be a popular addition to traditionally designed LANs.

Windows Registry: Caution: the Windows Registry is the backbone of the Windows operating system, and is very sensitive to modifications. The registry is a simple database of what the computer is physically, the software and operating system installed, the security and management of the software, user profiles, and network features and security, to name a few. Every software installed onto a Windows computer is in some shape or form recorded and categorized in the Windows Registry. Changes or modifications to the registry could impact software or functionality in unforeseen and incomprehensible ways, so be very cautious when dealing with the Windows Registry.

WINS: *See* WINDOWS INTERNET NAMING SYSTEM.

wired equivalent privacy (WEP): As radio waves are open to listening in on where a physical network is not (with any ease, that is), some type of protection is needed to protect the user and the network. (Access to a wireless access point within an organizations network is access to that network without going through the firewall.) Most wireless routers and access points have the ability to enforce the use of WEP as a method to protect wireless communication while it is in the airwaves. Once the communication has been established and authenticated, all further transmissions are encrypted. Also sometimes referred to as wireless encryption protocol.

wireless access points (WAPs): WAPs are normally not routers; they act more like switches. Instead of requiring a physical connection to obtain Internet or LAN access, the connection is via the radio waves. WAPs have limited capacity and can slow down or drop users if they reach their threshold. They are controlled remotely via standard IP access from within the LAN or via a serial connection (depending on the brand).

workgroup: A Microsoft logical network device that allows Windows operating system to use group associations to limit network traffic via Windows OS to other Windows systems. Computers joined to a single workgroup are joined logically and are capable of easily sharing files, folders, and printers. Workgroups do not require a Windows domain controller to be managed. Each individual computer within the workgroup still retains authority privileges over its own files and folders and determines what is shared and who has access.

worms: Worms are a form of virus, named for their activity and form of infection. It is considered a form of a virus, but does not require user interaction, such as opening an e-mail attachment. A worm will spread via a specific software flaw and seek that flaw out on other computers within its reach on a LAN. They are sometimes discovered not because of their activity on a computer but because of their activity over a LAN.

XML: *See* EXTENSIBLE MARKUP LANGUAGE.

INDEX

*Page numbers followed by "i" indicate an illustration; those in **bold** indicate a sample policy.*

A

Academic libraries and technology use, 53–57, **58i**
Active Directory, 155–157, 213–214
Active X programming, 214
Ad-Aware, 139
Address resolution protocol (ARP), 81, 196, 214
Administrative accounts, protection of, 200–203
Administrator responsibilities, 37–40, 43, **45i**, **47i**, 62, **65i**
Alwil, 138
Antispyware software, 139–141, 212. *See also* Spyware
AntiVir, 138
Antivirus software, 137–138, 211. *See also* Viruses
Apache software, 214
Apple computers, 23i, 173i, 214
Application scanners, 109–110
Appropriate use policies, 55, 57, **58i**
ARP (address resolution protocol), 81, 196, 214
Assessment proxies, 110
Asynchronous transfer mode (ATM), 214
Asynchronous transmission, 215
ATM (asynchronous transfer mode), 214
AVG, 137

B

Backbones, 215
Backdoors, 215
Backup domain controller (BDC), 220
Backups
    for administrators, 43–44, **47i**
    definition, 215
    office computers, 133–134
    policies, 40–43, **46i**

Bandwidth, 215
Banner grabbing, 82, 83i
Base systems, ILS, 1
Basic input/output system (BIOS), 116
BBS (electronic bulletin board systems), 75
BDC (backup domain controller), 220
Binary, 216
BIOS (basic input/output system), 116
Bit, 216
BitDefender, 137
Bluetooth networks, 225
Bottlenecks, 216
Bridges, 216
Broadband, 216
Broadcast, 216
Browser history and patron privacy, 122
Bubble-jet printers, 228
Buffer overflow and hackers, 86, 88
Byte, 216

C

Cable categories, 216–217
Cable modems, 217
Cache, 8, 217
Catalog servers, 40–41, **46i**, 229
CDRW backups, 215
Cent OS, 217
Centurion Guard, 7
Channel service unit/data service unit (CSU/DSU), 217
Checksums, 195, 217
Classification of information, 32–34, **34i**
Collisions, 218
Color laser printers, 228
Computer Fraud and Abuse Act of 1986, 76
Computer languages, 216, 221, 222, 223, 226

Computer patches. *See* Patches, operating system
Computers. *See also* Office systems, library; Public access computers
access categories, 7i
inventory form, 25i
security factors, 7–8
staff abuse of, 131–132
threats to, 179–180
types of, 218–219
use restrictions, 55, **58i**
Confidential information, 32–33, **34i**
Congestion, network, 219
Containers, Active Directory, 155–157, 213
Cookies, 122, 219
Corporate libraries and technology, 53–57, **58i**
Criminal activity
laws on, 205–210
policies, 56–57, **58i,** 67–68, **69i**
Crossover patch cables, 217
CSU/DSU (channel service unit/data service unit), 217
Cybercrime. *See* Criminal activity

D

Data terminal computers, 219
Data transmission
data packets, 61
and firewalls, 169–173
integrity of, 217
overview, 57, 59–62
and ports, 169–173
Date-time stamps, 219
Deep Freeze, 124–126
Defragmentation, 219–220
Deleted file restoration, 8
Denial of service (DoS)
definition, 220
examples of, 77
hacker use of, 82, 83, 220
and Web servers, 147
Desktop computers, 218
Desktop settings restoration, 7–8
DHCP (dynamic host configuration protocol), 195–196, 229
Directory browsing and hackers, 88
Disaster recovery plans, 220
Disk Cleanup, 8
Disk image, 180

DNS. *See* Domain Name System (DNS)
Domain controllers
definition, 220
functions of, 148–155
naming conventions, 151–155
policies, 41–42, **46i**
Domain groups, 220
Domain Name System (DNS)
attacks on, 158–159
definition, 146, 229–230
poisoning of, 220
servers, 168–169
DoS (denial of service). *See* Denial of service (DoS)
Dot matrix printers, 228
Dummy stations, 218
Dynamic host configuration protocol (DHCP), 195–196, 229

E

E-mail
hacker use of, 86–87
servers, 159–160, 230
Eavesdropping and hackers, 84
Electronic bulletin board systems (BBS), 75
Encryption, 195, 220–221
Equipment location and access policies, 34–37, **45i**
Ethernet
bottlenecks, 216
and cable categories, 213
definition, 213, 221
functions of, 8–9
and local area network security, 191–194
and lower-level protocols, 171–172
media access control (MAC) address, 172
switches, 191–194, 232
Exchange servers, 230
Extensible markup language (XML), 221
External hard drives, 134

F

FDDI (fiber distributed data interface), 221
Fedora, 221
Fiber distributed data interface (FDDI), 221

Fiber optic, 221
File systems, 85–86, 221
File transfer protocol (FTP)
    definition, 105, 230
    functions of, 147–148
    hacker use of, 85
Files, restoring, 8
Filters and phishing protection,
    120–121
Firefox 2.0 and phishing
    protection, 121
Firewalls. *See also* Servers and server
    security
    access to, 174
    and data transmission, 169–173
    definition, 221
    as internal security device,
        197–198
    and local area networks, 169–173,
        191–194
    location of, 174
    operation of, 174–179
    policies, 63, **68i–69i**
    programming of, 176–178
    replacing, 178–179
    security of, 174
    selection of, 174–176
    and servers, 198
    software, 180–186
    and technology inventory, 176–179
    upgrading, 178–179
    and Windows XP, 180–186
Flash drives, 134, 223
Forests, Active Directory, 214
Form memory and patron privacy, 122
Frame relay, 221
FTP. *See* File transfer protocol (FTP)

G

Game playing policies, 55, **58i**
Gateways, 221
Google Toolbar and phishing, 121
Gralicwrap and phishing, 121
Graphic user interface (GUI), 222

H

Hackers. *See also* Firewalls; Viruses
    application attacks, 86–87
    backdoor attacks, 215
    definition, 73, 222
    denial of service, 82, 83, 220

examples of, 73–74, 77–78, 82
history of, 74–77
malware, 224
motivations of, 77–78
network attacks, 81–88
operating system attacks, 84–86
overview, 78–80, 96–97
phishing, 227
spoofing, 231
Web server attacks, 87–88
wireless network attacks, 83–84
worms, 235
Hard drives, 134, 222
Hardware suppliers, 212
Hexadecimals, 222
Hidden field information and
    hackers, 88
Hops, 191–194, 223–224, 226
HTM/HTML (hypertext markup/
    hypertext markup language), 223
HTTP (hypertext transfer protocol),
    105, 223
HTTPS, 147, 222
Hubs, 222–223
Hypertext markup/hypertext markup
    language (HTM/HTML), 223
Hypertext preprocessor (PHP), 227
Hypertext transfer protocol (HTTP),
    105, 223

I

ICMP (Internet control message
    protocol), 223
ILS (integrated library systems), 1–3
IM (instant messaging), 87, 223
Imaging, 180, 212, 224
Inappropriate use policies, 66–67, **69i**
Information classification, 32–34, **34i**
Inkjet printers, 228
Instant messaging (IM), 87, 223
Integrated library systems (ILS), 1–3
Integrated services digital network
    (ISDN), 10, 223
Internet
    bandwidth, 215
    connecting to, 167–169
    staff use, 133
    temporary files, 122
    threats from, 179–180
Internet control message protocol
    (ICMP), 223

IP addresses
  network classifications, 217–218
  policies for, 63
  sample forms, 64i–65i
ISDN (integrated services digital
    network), 10, 223

J
Java, 223
Jump drives, 134, 223
Jumps, 191–194, 223–224, 226

K
Key loggers, 224

L
LAN. *See* Local area network (LAN)
Laptop computers
  definition, 218
  security for, 118
  security threats from, 199–200
  for staff, 202–203
  use in library restrictions, 56, **58i**
Laser printers, 228
Lava Ad-Aware, 139
Law enforcement investigation policies,
    67–68, **69i**
Laws and computer crime, 205–210
Library staff. *See also* Office systems,
    library
  computer use, 129–135
  security training, 129–131
  technology policies, 49–51, **52i,** 66,
    69i, 200–203
License key servers, 230
Link manipulation and phishing, 119
Linux-based systems
  Apache software, 214
  Cent OS, 217
  Fedora, 221
  hacker attacks on, 85–86
  and network information servers,
    157, 230
  operating systems, 217
  patches for, 186
  Red Hat, 228
  server software, 214
  Ubango, 233
Local area network (LAN)
  connecting to, 167–169
  definition, 224

  and domain controllers, 148–155
  and firewalls, 169–173, 191–194
  security design factors, 189–194
  and terminal servers, 160–164
Log files, 224
Logical networks, 225
Log-in spoofing and hackers, 88
LoJack for Laptops, 118

M
MAC address. *See* Media access control
    (MAC) address
MacAfee Antivirus, 137
Mainframe computers, 218
Malware, 224
Man-in-the-middle attacks and hackers, 84
Media access control (MAC) address
  definition, 16, 224
  and Ethernet, 172
  functions of, 61, 167
  hacker use of, 81
  how to find and use, 22–23, 24i
Memory, 224
Microsoft. *See also* Windows
  Active Directory, 155–157, 213–214
  Active X, 214
  antispyware, 140
  domain controllers, 220
  Exchange Server, 160
  firewalls, 180–186
  hacker attacks on, 84–85
  SteadyState, 123–124
  workgroups, 235
Mirror image, 224
Mission-critical information, 33, **34i**
Modems
  cable, 217
  definition, 225
  functions of, 9
  rouge, 79
Modules, ILS, 1–2
Morse code and data transmission, 57,
    59–60
Multifunction printers, 228
Multiplexed signals, 216

N
Names and naming conventions,
    151–155, 225
NAT. *See* Network address translation
    (NAT)

Nessus and security audits, 108–109
NetBIOS, 225
NetWare, 86, 173i, 225
Network address translation (NAT)
    definition, 225
    policies for, 63, **68i**
    and routers, 195–196
Network analyzers and hackers, 82
Network classifications, 217–218
Network information server (NIS), 157,
    230
Network interface card (NIC), 22–23,
    167, 226
Network management. *See also*
    Backups
    administrator responsibilities, 37–40,
        43, **45i, 47i,** 62, **65i**
    inventory forms, 26i, 27i
    jumps, 191–194, 223–224, 226
    overview, 8–11, 57, 59–62
    software for, 211–212
    types of, 225
Network security. *See also* Servers and
    server security
    and Active Directory, 155–157
    criminal activity, 67–68, **69i**
    definition, 226
    DNS attacks, 158–159
    and domain controllers, 148–155
    external threats, 167–187
    features of, 62–68, 70–71
    firewalls, 63, **68i–69i,** 167–187
    health tools, 62, **68i**
    inappropriate actions toward, 66–67,
        69i
    internal threats, 189–204
    law enforcement investigation,
        67–68, **69i**
    routers, 62, **68i**
    switches, 63, **69i**
NIC (network interface card), 22–23,
    167, 226
NIS (network information server),
    157, 230
NMap and security audits, 105–108
Nodes, 226
Novell, 226

O

Objects, Active Directory, 155–157, 214
Octal, 226

Off-site backups, 215
Offensive materials policies, 55, **58i**
Office systems, library. *See also* Library
    staff
    appropriate use, 49
    backups, 133–134
    computer patches, 134–135
    laptops, 50–51
    policies, 3–4, 47–51, **52i**
    printers, 50–51
    security checklist, 130i
    security training, 129–131
    virus protection, 135–138
Open system interconnection (OSI), 171
Operating system (OS), 211, 226. *See*
    also Apple computers; Linux-based
    systems; Windows
OSI (open system interconnection), 171

P

Paros Proxy, 110
Passkeys, 226
Passwords
    and computer security, 132–133
    definition, 227
    and hackers, 80
    policies, 39, **45i**
Patches, operating system
    functions of, 185–186
    keeping up to date, 85, 134–135
    Linux-based systems, 186
    policies, 43, **47i**
Patrons. *See also* Public access
    computers
    descriptions of, 53–54
    inappropriate technology use,
        66–67, **69i**
    privacy for, 122
    rights of, 54
    and technology security, 115–116,
        121–122
    updating information on, 44
    user agreements, 54–56, **58i**
PDC (primary domain controller), 220
Peer to peer, 87, 227
Permissions, 227
Personal computer use restrictions,
    56, **58i**
Personnel changes and server policies,
    44, **47i**
Phishing, 119–121, 227

PHP (hypertext preprocessor), 227
Physical abuse of technology, 55, **58i**
Physical networks, 225
Ping, 81–82, 227
Poisoning, DNS, 158–159
Pop-ups, 227
Port scanners and security, 81,
    105–108
Ports, 169–173, 228
PrevX 2.0, 140
Primary domain controller (PDC), 220
Printers
    policies, 51, **52i**, 56
    types of, 228, 230
Procedure audits, 110–111
Processors, 228
Protocols
    address resolution, 214
    AppleTalk, 214
    definition, 226
    Ethernet, 221
    fiber distributed data interface, 221
    frame relay, 221
    hypertext transfer protocol, 223
    lower-level, 171–172
    Macintosh computers, 214
    Novell, 226
    upper-level, 172–173
Proxy servers, 230
Public access computers
    and academic libraries, 53–54
    appropriate use of, 55–57, **58i**
    and corporate libraries, 53–54
    and domain controllers, 153–155
    laptops, 118
    laws and regulations, 118
    log-in accounts, 198–199
    overview, 5–6
    patron privacy, 121–122
    patron rights, 54, **58i**
    and phishing, 119–121
    and public libraries, 53–54
    restrictions, 199i
    and school libraries, 53–54
    security checklists, 116i
    security of, 5–6, 115–116, 123–128,
        198–199
    thin client computers, 126
    use policies, 117–118
    user agreements, 54–55, **58i**
Public libraries and technology,
    53–57, **58i**

R
RAID array, 228
Record-keeping policies, 37–38, **45i**
Red Hat, 186, 228
Remote access, 39–40, 228–229
Remote procedure call (RPC),
    84, 229
Roaming profiles, 133–134
Rogue modems, 79
Routers
    definition, 229
    and dynamic host configuration
        protocol, 195–196
    and local area networks, 191–194
    network policies, 62, **68i**
    as security devices, 191–196
RPC (remote procedure call), 84, 229

S
Sanctions for policy violations, 56–57,
    58i
School libraries and technology,
    53–57, **58i**
Scripts, 229
Security audits
    checklists, 99i–103i, 116i, 130i
    definition, 104, 229
    implementation, 111–113
    procedure audits, 110–111
    purpose of, 99
    tool and techniques, 105–111
Security practices
    local area networks, 189–194
    patches, 43
    plans, 17–20, 229
    reasons for, 15–16
    software, 212
    software bypass, 55
    training, 129–131
    Web servers, 146–148
Sendmail and hackers, 85
Servers and server security. *See also*
    Firewalls
    access to, 35–37, **45i**
    administrator responsibilities, **45i**
    backups and restores, 40–43, **46i**
    backups for administrators,
        43–44, **47i**
    definition, 218, 229
    domain controllers, 41–42
    e-mail, 159–160

functions of, 143–145, 164–165
information classifications,
    32–34, **34i**
location of, 34–37, **45i**
passwords, 39, **46i**
patron updates, 44
personnel changes, 44, **47i**
record keeping, 37–38, **45i**
remote access, 39–40
security patches, 43, **47i**
software for, 214
switches, 63
terminal servers, 160–164
types of, 229–231
upgrades, 43, **47i**
Web servers, 41, 145–148
wireless access, 65
Service packs, 231
Shared drives, 231
Simple mail transfer protocol (SMTP),
    87, 105, 148, 230
Simple network management protocol
    (SNMP), 82
SMS, 230
SMTP (simple mail transfer protocol),
    87, 105, 148, 230
SNA (systems network architecture),
    173i, 232
Sniffers and hackers, 82
SNMP (simple network management
    protocol), 82
Software changes policies, 55, **58i**
Software upgrades, 43, **47i**
Spam, 159–160, 231
Spoofing, 231
Spybot: Search and Destroy, 140
Spyware
    definition, 231
    examples of, 94–96
    overview, 93–94
    protection against, 138–141, 212
Spyware Doctor, 140–141
SQL server, 231
Storage management system (SMS),
    230
Subnet and subnet masks, 231–232
Switches, 63, **69i**, 232
Symantec Antivirus, 137
Systems Management Server (SMS),
    230
Systems network architecture (SNA),
    173i, 232

T

Tape backups, 215
TCP/IP (transmission control
    protocol/Internet protocol), 173i, 233
TechAtlas, 28–29
Technology inventory
    conducting, 28–29
    and firewalls, 176–179
    MAC addresses, 22–23
    overview, 16–17, 21, 29–30
    sample forms, 25i, 26i, 27i
Technology plans, 232
Technology security personnel,
    48–49, **52i**
Technology use policies, 53–57, **58i**.
    See also Public access computers
Telnet, 85, 232
Temporary Internet files, 232
Terminal servers, 160–164, 231
TFTP (trivial file transfer protocol),
    178, 231
Thin client computers, 126, 219
Token Ring, 232–233
Towers, computer, 219
Training, security, 129–131
Transmission control protocol/Internet
    protocol (TCP/IP), 173i, 233
Trees, Active Directory, 214
Trivial file transfer protocol (TFTP),
    178, 231
Tunnels, 173, 197–198, 233
Turnkey systems, 2

U

Ubango, 233
UDP (user datagram protocol), 233
Universal Serial Bus (USB), 233
Upgrades, software, 43, **47i**
USB (Universal Serial Bus), 233
User accounts, 233
User agreements, 55–57, **58i**
User datagram protocol (UDP), 233
User profiles, 233

V

Virtual private networks (VPN), 7, 225
Viruses
    definition, 88, 233
    examples of, 90–93
    history of, 89–90
    protection against, 89, 135–138, 211

Voice-over Internet protocol (VoIP), 79, 87, 234
VPN (virtual private networks), 7, 225
Vulnerability scanners and security audits, 108–109

W

WAN (wide area networks), 9, 234
WAPs (wireless access points), 57, 65, 235
War dialing and hackers, 83
Web application assessment proxy, 110
Web browsers and phishing, 120–122
Web servers
    definition, 231
    denial of service attacks, 147
    functions of, 145–146
    hacker attacks, 87–88
    policies, 41, **46i**
    security for, 146–148
Web site forgery, 119–120
WebWatcher, 132
WEP. *See* Wired equivalent privacy (WEP)
Wide area networks (WAN), 9, 234
Windows
    Disk Cleanup function, 8
    and domain controllers, 148–155
    and MAC addresses, 22i, 24i
    network management, 213–214
Windows Defender, 140
Windows Internet Naming System (WINS), 234

Windows Registry, 7, 234
Windows XP firewall, 180–186
WINS (Windows Internet Naming System), 234
Wired equivalent privacy (WEP)
    definition, 234–235
    functions of, 194–195
    policies for, 65
    for staff computers, 194–195
    WEP key, 234
Wireless access points (WAPs), 57, 65, 235
Wireless encryption protocol. *See* Wired equivalent privacy (WEP)
Wireless networks
    definition, 225
    hacker attacks on, 83–84
    network policies, 65
    security of, 194–198
    use restrictions, 56, **58i**
Workgroups, 149–155, 235
Workstations, 219
Worms
    definition, 235
    examples of, 90–93
    first release of, 76

X

XML (extensible markup language), 221

Z

Zombie computers, 147, 219

ABOUT THE AUTHORS

Paul W. Earp is currently the User Support Technician for Summit College at the University of Akron, Ohio, supporting fourteen technology classrooms and computer labs in addition to staff and faculty computers. Paul has recently returned to school part time to complete his degree in technology and obtain his MLS. Paul has been in computer technology since 1985, and most recently worked as Network Manager at Jernigan Library, Texas A&M University–Kingsville for six years before moving to Ohio. With several years of experience in law enforcement, Paul brings a unique view to security in libraries. Publications include lighthearted comic cartoons in the A&M Kingsville school paper, poetry in *Writers Bloc,* and a coauthored chapter on computer gaming in *Casebook on Gaming in Academic Libraries: An ACRL Monograph.*

Adam Wright is currently the Executive Director for the North Texas Regional Library System where he handles all technology consulting for its 74 member public libraries. Adam has been a librarian for 11 years after obtaining his master of library science from the University of North Texas in 1995. He has worked in the public and special library environment where he dealt extensively with computers and technology. Adam is an active member of the Texas Library Association's Automation and Technology Round Table. Adam is a regular contributor to the North Texas Regional Library System Web site and blog. His Gates Sustainability and Replacement Plan was well received around the state and published on www.webjunction.org.